Environmental Tax Reforms for a Just Energy Transition

CRITICAL ISSUES IN ENVIRONMENTAL TAXATION

Series Editors: Janet E. Milne, *Vermont Law School, USA*, Mikael Skou Andersen, *Aarhus University, Denmark* and Hope Ashiabor, *University of New South Wales, Australia*

The *Critical Issues in Environmental Taxation* series provides insights and analysis on environmental taxation issues on an international basis and explores detailed theories for achieving environmental goals through fiscal policy. Each book in the series contains pioneering and thought-provoking contributions by the world's leading environmental tax scholars who respond to the diverse challenges posed by environmental sustainability.

Previous volumes in the series:

Original book published by CCH Incorporated

Volumes I–IV published by Richmond Law Publishers

Volumes V–VIII published by Oxford University Press

Volume IX onwards published by Edward Elgar Publishing

For a full list of Edward Elgar published titles, including the titles in this series, visit our website at www.e-elgar.com.

Environmental Tax Reforms for a Just Energy Transition

Perspectives from the Global North and South

Edited by

Lee-Ann Steenkamp

Associate Professor in Taxation, Stellenbosch Business School, Stellenbosch University, South Africa

Janet E. Milne

Professor of Law and Director of the Environmental Tax Policy Institute, Vermont Law School, USA

Mikael Skou Andersen

Professor of Environmental Policy Analysis, Aarhus University, Denmark

Hope Ashiabor

Adjunct Lecturer, University of New South Wales Business School, Australia

CRITICAL ISSUES IN ENVIRONMENTAL TAXATION

Edward Elgar PUBLISHING

Cheltenham, UK • Northampton, MA, USA

Published by

Edward Elgar Publishing Limited
The Lypiatts
15 Lansdown Road
Cheltenham
Glos GL50 2JA
UK

Edward Elgar Publishing, Inc.
William Pratt House
9 Dewey Court
Northampton
Massachusetts 01060
USA

Authorised representative in the EU for GPSR queries only: Easy Access System Europe – Mustamäe tee 50, 10621 Tallinn, Estonia, gpsr.requests@easproject.com

A catalogue record for this book is available from the British Library

Library of Congress Control Number: 2025940167

This book is available electronically in the **Elgar**online
Law subject collection
https://doi.org/10.4337/9781035366088

MIX
Paper | Supporting responsible forestry
FSC® C013604

ISBN 978 1 0353 6607 1 (cased)
ISBN 978 1 0353 6608 8 (eBook)
ISBN 978 1 0353 7291 1 (ePub)

Printed and bound by CPI Group (UK) Ltd, Croydon, CR0 4YY

Contents

PART III ENVIRONMENTAL TAXES AND THE PURSUIT OF CLIMATE JUSTICE

PART IV ENVIRONMENTAL TAX REFORM CASE STUDIES

Contributors

Susanne Aakerfeldt, World Bank, USA

Paulina Schulz Antipa, World Bank, USA

Hope Ashiabor, University of New South Wales Business School, Australia

Alexandra Campmas, World Bank, USA

Denise Lucena Cavalcante, Federal University of Ceará, Brazil

Paloma García Córdoba, Universitat Oberta de Catalunya, Spain

Roney Sandro Freire Corrêa, Fluminense Federal University, Brazil

Steve Dwyer, University of Manchester, United Kingdom

Saliem Fakir, African Climate Foundation

Arthur Maria Ferreira Neto, Universidade Federal do Rio Grande do Sul, Brazil

Laure Gnassou, Experienced economist, France

Herwig Immervoll, Organisation for Economic Co-operation and Development (OECD), France

Peter Jarvis, Stellenbosch University, South Africa

Jules Linden, Luxembourg Institute of Socioeconomic Research, Luxembourg and University of Galway, Ireland

Seutame Maimele, Trade and Industrial Policy Strategies (TIPS), South Africa

Nadia Mans-Kemp, Stellenbosch University, South Africa

Malebusetsa Jessica Matela, Stellenbosch University, South Africa

Jane Ndlovu, University of the Witwatersrand, South Africa

Cathal O'Donoghue, University of Galway, Ireland

Roque Martínez Olmos, National University of Distance Education (UNED), Spain

Rodolfo Salassa Boix, Pompeu Fabra University, Spain

Denisa M. Sologon, Luxembourg Institute of Socioeconomic Research, Luxembourg

Stefan E. Weishaar, Groningen University, the Netherlands

Sébastien Wolff, Catholic University of Louvain, Belgium

Editorial review board

ACKNOWLEDGMENT

The editors would like to acknowledge and thank the assistance of their language editor Karishma Bhoolia.

Foreword

It is my great honour to be able to write this foreword for a collection of chapters which considers the application and utility of environmental taxes in the context of the just energy transition. South Africa can be considered the global heartland of just transition application and thinking in Africa, given that we embarked on this journey a decade ago and secured the first Just Energy Transition Partnership (JETP) initiative at COP 26, in Glasgow in 2021.

The JETP is a living laboratory for the implementation of transition processes and demonstrates that techno-economic shifts have to be carefully calibrated to ensure just socio-economic objectives.[1] The JETP is a work in progress. While I am not an expert on environmental taxes and incentives, I have enough exposure to appreciate the important work many scholars, economists, lawyers, experts, and practitioners are grappling with when evaluating environmental externalities globally.

My own work has focused extensively on just transition policy frameworks, particularly examining the goals required for reducing global Greenhouse Gas (GHG) emissions and identifying optimal economic and tax policy instruments to achieve these objectives.

Scientific reports and the work of scholars have already observed that the last decade has been the hottest the planet has experienced. More importantly, we are already exceeding the 1.5°C temperature increase limit. Decision-makers are under increasing pressure to speed up the reduction in GHG emissions to meet the commitments of the Paris Agreement.

Unfortunately, the current pace and scale of global decarbonisation do not inspire confidence. The review of global Nationally Determined Contributions (NDCs) – which require parties to the UNFCCC to submit updated NDCs in 2025 – suggests that signatories need to raise their ambitions considerably.[2] However, most of the signatory countries missed the United Nations deadline of February 2025 to do so. Moreover, under orders from President Donald Trump, the world's second-largest emitting country has pulled out of the Paris Agreement altogether. The recent Los Angeles fires and the scale and speed at which they ravaged neighbourhoods underscore the growing need to not only focus on mitigation but also on what I would call the need for radical adaptation measures.

We have to win the battle to keep environmental issues on the political agenda. It is critical that we mobilise new sources of revenue to strengthen the fiscus, invest in key economic sectors (such as AI and other information tools), and support local action to speed up mitigation efforts and ensure adaptation and resilience.

In Africa, the necessity of just transition processes is inescapable – energy and adaptation solutions cannot be decoupled. Extreme weather events are becoming increasingly commonplace in Africa. The African Climate Foundation, which I lead, is working with the Malawian government to find additional fiscal resources to deal with future cyclones. Cyclone Freddy (a severe tropical storm in 2023) wreaked havoc on the economies and people of Malawi and neighbouring states.

In Zambia, an extended drought has impacted the hydrological cycle of the country and flows down the Zambesi River, which is a major source of hydropower. The lower rainfall has had knock-on effects on the ability of the government to provide sufficient energy for a variety of consumers, notably the mining sector. This has impacted copper mining production rates and the value of exports. Zambia has significant debt and an impaired balance of payments as a result of lower mining productivity and high debt service costs. Despite this, Zambia is also the first country to volunteer to address its debt under the G20 Common Framework.[3]

It is critical that just transitions are placed front and centre when developing and deploying environmental tax instruments. The focus of fiscal instruments must be to strengthen societal capacities and trigger the behavioural changes necessary to deal with the imminent climate challenges we face. Fiscal instruments cannot afford to only focus on mitigation efforts but must also ensure resources and capacity for adaptation solutions.

Environmental tax policies must serve two key purposes: incentivising investment in emissions-reducing technologies while creating frameworks that help businesses, workers, and communities adapt to climate challenges. These policies should support both economic continuity and climate resilience across multiple levels, from the development of climate-resilient infrastructure and community organisations through to business productivity. The interplay of all these socio-economic spheres is imperative to mount effective responses during a crisis.

Environmental taxation presents complex socio-economic challenges that extend beyond purely technical considerations. Successful implementation requires careful alignment of scientific evidence, policy instruments, and development goals. This creates a trilemma for policymakers: balancing environmental effectiveness, economic efficiency, and social equity. Whether these objectives should be addressed simultaneously or sequentially remains a critical question, pushing environmental tax practitioners into uncharted territory.

Environmental taxation is often subject to negative public opinion. To win public support, environmental taxes must be reasonable and easy to apply. Despite the fact that carbon taxes and the application of Carbon Border Adjustment Mechanisms (CBAMs) are conceived as instruments to align global carbon emissions reductions with the need for rapid transition shifts, it is not surprising that they spark robust discussions and debates.

The impact of the EU CBAM on the African continent is a subject of major concern and vigorous pushback by countries that need time to adjust and ensure their economies are protected. As a result, the EU CBAM has yet to meet the tests of reasonableness and ease of application. Some African countries, for example, perceive the EU CBAM as punitive. They argue it serves as a guise whereby climate goals are used as trade protection measures to defend nascent European industries from competition. I believe that the EU CBAM reflects a broader and deep-seated tension in environmental policy: the challenge of designing contextually appropriate tax measures that harmonise climate objectives with socio-economic realities. Environmental policies must carefully consider their distributional impacts across consumers, producers, and households. This requires a nuanced approach that recognises varying economic contexts and ensures fairness in policy implementation.

The theoretical merits of environmental tax instruments do not guarantee their practical success in achieving desired environmental, economic, and social outcomes. Just transitions require both technical expertise and enlightened political leadership. Even well-designed policies can be undermined by campaigns that seek to polarise public opinion by portraying environmental measures as economically harmful.

Recent extreme weather events, such as the severe flooding in Valencia, Spain, demonstrate the pressing need for environmental tax measures that support climate adaptation alongside mitigation efforts. While mitigation serves as a global public good, its costs are often borne at the national level. This creates a fundamental tension: major greenhouse gas emitters contribute to global climate impacts, yet the resulting economic and social costs are disproportionately distributed across regions and income levels worldwide. This inequitable distribution of burdens and benefits can fuel political division and resistance to climate action.

The world has yet to establish an equitable framework for allocating both carbon budgets and their associated costs. While emerging proposals, such as global levies on maritime fuels, aim to generate revenue for climate mitigation and adaptation, these potential funding streams remain small relative to the scale of global climate finance needs.

A central challenge in environmental taxation is designing instruments that effectively balance global and local public goods. The EU CBAM exemplifies this complexity: while designed as a regional environmental policy for the

European Union, its implementation has far-reaching global implications. The mechanism's rollout demonstrates how geographically targeted environmental policies can generate unintended political and economic consequences both domestically and internationally, despite their well-intentioned environmental objectives.

The Draghi report[4] raises critical questions about the impact of environmental taxes, particularly the EU CBAM, on European economic competitiveness. The CBAM debate also highlights the need to better understand the distributional effects of environmental taxes – not only nationally but also regionally and globally. This analysis must extend to intergenerational impacts, considering how current environmental fiscal policies will affect future generations.

Our noble intents should not be blindsided by our obsession to succeed at all costs with environmental taxes and instruments. Sometimes what's really needed is patience, practical wisdom, and a realistic approach to just transitions. I believe the interesting papers presented in this book offer valuable perspectives that help bridge the gap between idealism and pragmatism, and will enhance climate change dialogue between the Global North and South.

Saliem Fakir

NOTES

1. Kramer, K. 2022. *Just Energy Transition Partnerships: An opportunity to leapfrog from coal to clean energy.* Available: https://www.iisd.org/articles/insight/just-energy-transition-partnerships [2025, February 21].
2. World Economic Forum. 2025. *Paris Agreement: What are NDCs and why do they matter?* Available: https://www.weforum.org/stories/2025/02/cop29-ndcs-and-why-they-matter/ [2025, February 21].
3. Paris Club. 2020. *Common Framework for Debt Treatments beyond the DSSI.* Available: https://cdn.gihub.org/umbraco/media/5288/annex_common_framework_for_debt_treatments_beyond_the_dssi.pdf [2025, February 23].
4. Draghi, M. 2024. *The Future of European Competitiveness.* Available: https://commission.europa.eu/topics/eu-competitiveness/draghi-report_en#paragraph_47059 [2025, January 15].

PART I

Towards a just energy transition in Africa

1. Tug-of-war: balancing a just energy transition with South Africa's fossil fuel footprint

Jane Ndlovu

1. INTRODUCTION

This chapter examines South Africa's reliance on coal and its consequent impact on the nation's carbon emissions. First, it explores how a South African listed company, Sasol Limited (Sasol), is an example of a company contributing to South Africa's economic development but at the expense of climate change. It then explores the measures South Africa has undertaken to transition towards a just energy system, with a particular focus on the implementation of the carbon tax. The chapter provides a brief analysis of the carbon tax's implementation process and concludes by addressing the associated challenges.

2. STRANGLING PROGRESS: A SNAPSHOT OF SOUTH AFRICA'S STRUGGLE FOR A JUST ENERGY TRANSITION AFTER 30 YEARS OF DEMOCRACY

It is five months before South Africa celebrates 30 years of democracy. The date is November 2023, and the location is Sandton, a bustling city in South Africa. A striking scene unfolds at Sasol Limited's annual general meeting (AGM) when activists bring the proceedings to an abrupt halt.[1] Shareholder activists at the AGM voice their doubts, questioning whether Sasol could realistically reduce its emissions by 30% by 2030 and achieve net-zero status by 2050.[2] At the heart of this challenge lies a petrochemical plant in Secunda (Mpumalanga province of South Africa), Sasol Limited's largest facility and the world's most prolific carbon emitter by volume.[3] The question is no longer just about corporate pledges but whether Sasol's Secunda complex can successfully decarbonise or face the existential threat of closure.[4]

Sasol Limited is not just another company in South Africa—it is a colossal entity. Operating in 38 countries, Sasol Limited is a household name across South Africa and the African continent. Officially established in 1950 to produce synthetic fuels from coal, Sasol's growth was significantly influenced by the political upheavals of the 1960s, which threatened South Africa's energy security.[5] This led to the establishment of the Natref refinery in Sasolburg in 1966, followed by additional refineries.[6]

For many, Sasol is seen as a product of South Africa's apartheid era, born from the government's determination to achieve self-sufficiency amidst international sanctions.[7] The coal-to-liquids technology employed by Sasol is largely based on the Fischer-Tropsch process, initially developed in Nazi Germany.[8] By converting coal to oil, successive apartheid governments aimed to prolong their rule.[9] The Sustainable Energy & Climate Change Project[10] published a report titled *Sasol: Profits from Poison*, which details how Sasol, under apartheid, thrived by relying on a large workforce of low-skilled black labourers to sustain its industrial operations. However, the focus of this chapter is not on apartheid but on the broader context of Sasol Limited's role in South Africa's fossil fuel reliance and climate change in a democratic South Africa.

While the Secunda complex has fuelled Sasol Limited's success, the environmental toll is staggering. If you were to visit today, long before the towering refinery comes into view on the South African highveld, the acrid scent of coal would hang in the air, signalling the presence of one of the world's largest polluters.[11] This refinery is a relic of South Africa's coal-based energy dominance. The 40-year-old Secunda complex emits more carbon dioxide than the entire nation of Portugal.[12] Flames from gas flares illuminate the night sky, while steam and smoke pour from towering chimneys, with a vast web of steel pipes crisscrossing around boilers, gasifiers, and cooling towers.[13] It is one of Africa's tallest structures; a 300-metre flue looms over the site, dispersing pollutants across the region.[14] For the residents of the nearby township, living under this industrial shadow has become a daily hazard, with many reporting severe health issues—ranging from skin rashes to respiratory diseases and even blindness caused by sulphur dioxide exposure.[15]

Yet, Sasol's central role in a democratic South African economy complicates the path to stricter environmental regulations. The company contributes nearly 5% of South Africa's gross domestic product (GDP), and its largest shareholder is the government employees' pension fund (GEPF), holding more than 13% of Sasol Limited's shares.[16] Add to that the 8% ownership by a state development body (Industrial Development Corporation of South Africa Limited), and the prospect of robust regulatory enforcement seems precarious.[17] For many, Sasol's economic importance outweighs its environmental liabilities.

Nonetheless, the shift to a greener future in South Africa is inevitable, and Sasol is preparing for it. The company plans to invest between R16 billion to R25 billion in emissions reduction projects by 2030.[18] This investment is essential. Achieving environmental sustainability is not just about corporate promises but ensuring the integrity of the biophysical systems and safeguarding basic human well-being.[19] As a result, this requires an early, decisive commitment to renewable energy alternatives to avoid falling back on carbon-intensive practices.[20]

In Sasol's Climate Change Reports for 2021 and 2023, the term "emissions" appears over 300 times.[21] Sasol Limited's financial statements highlight that the carbon tax is a significant area of judgement in their preparation. Furthermore, the shift towards a low-carbon economy is expected to influence future commodity prices, such as oil and natural gas, potentially affecting the recoverable amounts of the Group's property, plant, equipment, and other non-current assets.

The financial world is taking note. While the road ahead for Sasol and South Africa's other carbon-intensive industries is fraught with challenges, the transition to a low-carbon economy is essential for the country's sustainable economic development. Investors are increasingly shying away from carbon-intensive industries as financing costs for oil and gas exploration soar and some banks withdraw their support altogether.[22] In the global community, corporations are embracing environmental, social, and governance (ESG) goals, propelled by public and shareholder pressure.[23] Frameworks like the Task Force on Climate-related Financial Disclosures (now the IFRS S1 and S2 standards) to manage climate risks and responses are integral to corporate disclosures.[24] Similarly, governments are revising their fiscal policies and reviewing their Nationally Determined Contributions (NDCs) under the Paris Agreement to align with the global shift towards climate-conscious economic planning.

Ensuring that this transition is both economically viable and socially equitable may be key to mitigating the risks posed by climate change while safeguarding the country's economic growth.[25] A just energy transition for South Africa is imperative. This transition should not only mitigate climate risks but also address the country's historical economic inequalities. The critical question is whether South Africa can successfully decouple its economic growth from fossil fuel consumption while ensuring no one is left behind.

3. COAL DEPENDENCY: BALANCING ECONOMIC GROWTH AND CLIMATE RESPONSIBILITY ON THE PATH TO A JUST ENERGY TRANSITION

South Africa's role in global climate change should not be understated. Coal-fired electricity generation is the backbone of South Africa's energy supply. The country's heavy reliance on fossil fuels positions it as a significant contributor to global greenhouse gas (GHG) emissions. This dependency is not simply an environmental concern but a complex economic and social challenge, given that coal-fired electricity generation powers over 90% of the nation's energy needs.

In 2017 alone, South Africa's net emissions totalled 512 million tons of carbon dioxide equivalent (CO_2e), reflecting a 14% rise since 2000.[26] As one of the world's top 15 greenhouse gas emitters, South Africa's energy sector stands at a crossroads where the urgency of transitioning to cleaner energy must be balanced against the nation's economic realities.[27]

The root of this challenge lies in the country's vast coal reserves. Historically, coal has been the bedrock of South Africa's industrial growth, fuelling energy-intensive sectors such as mining and manufacturing.[28] These sectors, which demand reliable and affordable energy, have entrenched coal's dominance, accounting for 75% of fossil fuel consumption and 93% of electricity production.[29] Approximately 80% of the country's total emissions come from the energy sector, making it the single largest source of South Africa's carbon footprint.[30] In 2004, the country emitted 387 million metric tons of carbon dioxide equivalent ($MtCO_2e$)—half the total emissions for the entire African continent at the time and 1.6% of global emissions.[31] By 2010, South Africa's per capita emissions hovered around 10 tons of CO_2e further highlighting the extent of its carbon dependency.[32]

The long-term sustainability of this coal dependency is questionable both in terms of environmental impact and economic growth. South Africa's National Development Plan (NDP) 2030, alongside its Nationally Determined Contributions (NDCs), outlines the ambitious goal of reducing emissions to between 350 and 420 $MtCO_2e$ by 2030, with a broader objective of achieving carbon neutrality by 2050.[33] Yet, this vision conflicts with the country's ongoing reliance on coal, particularly in light of economic drivers such as the Sasol Secunda complex. As stated earlier in this chapter, this facility alone is one of the world's largest single-site emitters of GHGs, emphasising the central role carbon-intensive industries play in South Africa's energy system.

Since 1990, South Africa's emissions have surged by over 67%, reflecting not only its growing energy demands but also the critical role fossil fuels have played in supporting economic expansion.[34] The electricity sector, coupled with the metals and transportation industries, accounts for the lion's share of the nation's carbon footprint.[35] Yet, there is an emerging recognition that the country cannot maintain its current trajectory without severe environmental and socio-economic consequences. Rising temperatures—double the global average rate since 1990—are already threatening agricultural productivity, water security, and the well-being of rural communities.[36]

At the 26th Meeting of the Conference of Parties (COP26) under the United Nations Framework Convention on Climate Change (UNFCCC), global efforts to accelerate the transformation of energy systems were renewed. The Glasgow

Climate Pact emphasised the urgency of transitioning to low-emission energy sources, emphasising the rapid expansion of clean power generation and energy efficiency measures.[37] Importantly, the pact called for the phase-down of unabated coal power and the elimination of inefficient fossil fuel subsidies. However, it also recognised the need for a "just transition"—one that accounts for the economic and social realities of vulnerable populations and is tailored to national circumstances.

On 24 October 2023, a landmark moment for South Africa's environmental policy arrived when the National Assembly approved the Climate Change Bill.[38] This legislative milestone represented a firm commitment to reducing the country's carbon footprint. While the South African government is making strides to implement climate policies that balance emission reduction with economic development, achieving this delicate equilibrium is a formidable challenge.

Several studies have been conducted to investigate how South Africa could implement a just energy transition, with strategic solutions outlined including:[39]

1. Gradually phasing out subsidies, particularly in the energy sector, which could significantly enhance the carbon tax's effectiveness by levelling the playing field for renewable energy sources and incentivising decarbonisation efforts.[40]
2. Introducing mechanisms such as tax breaks, grants, or preferential tariffs for clean energy projects that could accelerate the transition to low-carbon technologies.[41]
3. Devising a comprehensive plan to transition Eskom from coal towards cleaner energy sources. This should involve investments in renewable energy infrastructure, support for research and development in energy storage technologies, and the decommissioning of outdated coal-fired power plants.[42]
4. Implementing measures to protect low-income households from disproportionate increases in living costs resulting from the carbon tax.[43]
5. Investing in research on low-carbon technologies, sustainable agricultural practices, and climate-resilient infrastructure.[44]
6. Enhancing monitoring, reporting, and verification processes, implementing penalties for non-compliance, and streamlining administrative procedures to improve efficiency and transparency.[45]
7. Engaging in partnerships to share best practices, technical expertise, and financial resources for climate mitigation to amplify the impact of carbon tax implementation.[46] Leveraging platforms such as the Paris Agreement to advance South Africa's climate goals globally is imperative.[47]

The South African government aims to achieve net-zero emissions by 2050. Taxation is a key mechanism in achieving this. Carbon taxation has faced significant corporate lobbying. In 2022, it was announced that the first phase of the new Carbon Tax regime, which involves establishing the necessary systems, would be extended by three years until the end of 2025. While it is anticipated that companies will continue to receive basic tax-free emission allowances, these will be gradually reduced over the four years leading up to 2030. Sasol's then Chief Financial Officer (CFO), Hanre Rossouw (Sasol's CFO at the time of writing is Walt Bruns), indicated that the company's financial models predict Sasol would become cash-flow negative if the carbon tax allowances are rapidly phased out by 2030. Rossouw argued that under such circumstances it would be more practical for Sasol to scale back its operations rather than fully decarbonise.

Sasol has significantly influenced South Africa's carbon tax rates. In its 2022 submission to the Standing Committee on Finance (SCOF) on the carbon tax rate proposals, Sasol expressed its commitment to reducing GHG emissions by 30% by 2030, in alignment with the Paris Agreement. The company detailed its short- to medium-term strategies, which include transitioning to low-carbon energy sources such as renewable energy, implementing additional energy and process efficiency improvements using existing technologies, and introducing lower-carbon feedstocks. However, Sasol warned that the proposed carbon tax structure—if implemented without allowances—would severely impact its operations, potentially rendering the company unviable by 2029. Sasol estimated that a carbon tax of $20–30 per ton would result in an additional tax liability of R20–30 billion, exceeding the Group's pre-tax profits in five of the last 10 years.

4. MECHANISMS OF THE CARBON TAX: A CATALYST FOR SUSTAINABLE TRANSFORMATION

The South African Revenue Service (SARS) administers the carbon tax, which applies to emissions from specified activities such as fuel combustion and industrial processes. The Act targets six greenhouse gases—carbon dioxide (CO_2), methane (CH_4), nitrous oxide (N_2O), hydrofluorocarbons (HFCs), perfluorocarbons (PFCs), and sulphur hexafluoride (SF_6)—each contributing to global warming at varying levels based on their Global Warming Potential (GWP).[48] Entities exceeding emission thresholds, as outlined in Schedule 2 of the Act, are liable for the tax and must declare their emissions through the SARS eFiling system.

However, the effectiveness of the carbon tax depends not only on the tax rate but also on the availability of alternative energy sources. The tax operates through two primary mechanisms: a demand effect, which reduces consumption by increasing energy prices, and a substitution effect, which encourages a shift towards less carbon-intensive energy sources.[49] A criticism of the South African Carbon Tax Act is the inclusion of emissions allowances, which allows businesses some flexibility in meeting their tax obligations, but it also risks perpetuating a "business-as-usual" approach. This compromises the broader goal of reducing carbon emissions and hinders South Africa's efforts to meet its climate targets.[50] Additionally, while international environmental commitments under agreements like the Paris Agreement emphasise compliance, enforcement mechanisms remain largely facilitative rather than adversarial.

Furthermore, the implementation of South Africa's carbon tax necessitates careful consideration of its potential economic ramifications, especially for businesses operating in carbon-intensive sectors. As the first of its kind on the African continent, this groundbreaking policy signifies the country's commitment to global climate change mitigation. However, it also presents significant challenges that could threaten national welfare. The carbon tax may constrain production levels without achieving proportional gains in efficiency, thereby exacerbating existing economic issues, such as job losses and rising living costs. These concerns are particularly acute given South Africa's high unemployment rates and the risk of further declining living standards if sectors are compelled to reduce operations under the added tax burden.[51]

5. FACILITATING THE TRANSITION TO A LOW-CARBON ECONOMY: OPPORTUNITIES AND CHALLENGES FOR ECONOMIC GROWTH AND ENVIRONMENTAL RESPONSIBILITY

While the Carbon Tax Act focuses on industries like food processing, agriculture, forestry, and fisheries, the indirect consequences extend to the health sector and water provision services. As costs rise in these critical industries, marginalised communities may face further inequalities in accessing basic needs. For instance, rising transportation and electricity costs exacerbate challenges in delivering health services and threaten food security.[52]

The economic impacts of the carbon tax are significant, particularly in terms of rising production costs and consumer price increases. For low-income households, these effects can be devastating, as higher costs for food, transportation, and electricity reduce their financial resilience.[53]

The burden on food security is particularly troubling, as key sectors like agriculture and food processing are disproportionately affected by carbon taxes. Rising food prices risk undermining accessibility for vulnerable populations, exposing a complex tension between environmental policy and social equity. These social equity challenges are particularly evident in metropolitan areas, where historical inequalities continue to shape socio-economic realities.

During apartheid, policies such as the brutal forced resettlement between the 1960s and early 1980s uprooted individuals to designated urban "group areas" and rural "homelands".[54] This deliberate spatial segregation resulted in low-cost housing and informal settlements being located far from industrial areas and other places of employment. Even in post-apartheid South Africa, these inequities persist. Many informal settlements remain disconnected from places of work due to a poorly integrated public transport system.[55] The cost of commuting—whether by traditional commuter rail, subsidised and unsubsidised buses, or 16-seater minibus taxis—often exceeds workers' wages, deterring employment and exacerbating poverty.[56] South Africa's transport challenges include low ridership, inadequate public transport access in rural areas, equity imbalances, and urban congestion.[57] These barriers frequently force individuals to opt for unemployment, increasing the state's social grant burden.[58] As government spending shifts towards social welfare to address these inequities, fewer resources are available for investment in renewable energy, complicating efforts to achieve environmental sustainability.

While carbon taxation aims to reduce emissions, the adverse social consequences raise questions about the overall fairness and efficacy of such policies in developing nations. The cascading effects of increased costs in the transportation, food, and energy sectors highlight the tension between environmental policy and human rights protection in developing countries.

South Africa's energy sector, particularly the state-owned utility Eskom, continues to receive substantial subsidies that offset its carbon tax liabilities, reducing the financial pressure to transition towards renewable energy. Eskom's heavy reliance on coal remains a major driver of the country's carbon emissions, complicating efforts to meet its climate commitments under the Paris Agreement. Meanwhile, energy poverty persists as a significant challenge, with approximately 2.5 million households, predominantly in rural areas and urban informal settlements, lacking electricity access.

The intersection of energy poverty and gender inequality is particularly evident in these communities. Women and girls, often burdened by cultural stereotypes, are responsible for sourcing unclean fuels such as firewood, paraffin, coal, and animal dung to meet their household energy needs.[59] Rising electricity prices exacerbate this issue, as many households revert to these cheaper but highly polluting alternatives. The widespread use of unclean energy fuels results in household air pollution, also known as indoor air pollution, caused by the incomplete combustion of these fuels. This pollution contributes to approximately four million deaths globally each year, with 0.4–0.6 million of these occurring in children under five, primarily in sub-Saharan Africa and South and Pacific Asia.[60] This creates a paradox: while reducing Eskom's pollution levels is critical to mitigating climate change, higher electricity costs could push low-income households to increase their reliance on unclean energy sources, exacerbating indoor air pollution and its associated health risks.

In addition, transitioning to a lower-carbon economy while maintaining energy security and affordability presents significant challenges. The government faces the task of balancing investments in cleaner energy technologies with continued exploration and production of oil and gas to avoid the economic repercussions of stranded assets. Natural gas, though a fossil fuel, emits about 50% less CO_2 than coal and is positioned as a "transition fuel" as the country gradually shifts towards renewable energy.[61] This approach aims to ensure a just and equitable transition, especially for those employed in fossil-fuel-dependent sectors.

Despite the promise of renewable energy, significant challenges persist. Clean energy technologies such as solar photovoltaic systems and wind power have become cost-competitive with traditional fossil fuels. However, scaling these solutions requires substantial investment, particularly in battery storage, to ensure reliability and grid integration. South Africa's ongoing load-shedding crisis has further accelerated the adoption of alternative energy sources among citizens and businesses. In the first half of 2023, South Africa's solar panel imports from China surged by 438%, setting a record.[62] The second quarter alone saw R8.4 billion worth of panels imported—more than double the amount recorded in the first quarter.[63] By the end of 2022, South Africa's imports of solar panels, lithium-ion batteries, and inverters had reached a staggering $3.8 billion (approximately R70 billion), while wind turbines worth $200 million were imported, predominantly in the fourth quarter as demand began to recover after a two-year slump.[64] Although the customs duty on these imports is zero or minimal due to their classification as low-priced modules and panels, the value-added tax (VAT) imposed significantly increases their cost. According to Section 13(2)(a) of the VAT Act, the VAT is calculated based on an adjusted value known as the added tax value (ATV), determined as follows: [(Customs Value + 10% thereof) + (any non-rebated duties)] = ATV. The VAT payable is then calculated as 15% of the ATV. In addition to VAT, the International Trade Administration Commission of South Africa (ITAC) has imposed a 10% import tariff on solar panels to protect local manufacturers, attract investment, and deepen the value chain.[65] These combined costs, including VAT and import tariffs, make renewable energy technologies more expensive, posing a financial barrier to widespread adoption.

South Africa's climate commitments are not new. During the 2009 Copenhagen climate change negotiations, the country voluntarily pledged to reduce domestic GHG emissions by 34% by 2020 and 42% by 2025 from business-as-usual levels, contingent upon receiving adequate financial and technological support.[66] As global energy demand continues to rise, the challenge is how to meet this demand while minimising the environmental impacts associated with fossil fuel consumption.

The future of South Africa's energy sector—and by extension, its economy—is contingent on how it navigates these challenges. Increasingly, policymakers are required to not only raise awareness of the risks posed by continued reliance on fossil fuels but also to actively pursue the opportunities presented by a global shift towards low-carbon technologies. The task at hand is complex: reducing emissions, fostering economic growth, and ensuring a just transition for the people most affected by the transition to a greener future.

6. THE PATH FORWARD: BRIDGING THE GAP BETWEEN FOSSIL FUELS AND FUTURE SUSTAINABILITY

As aforementioned, the decarbonisation of Sasol's Secunda complex is no longer just an issue of corporate pledges but a question of survival, as its potential closure would threaten 28,000 direct jobs.[67] Compounding this risk, the delayed expansion of South Africa's liquefied natural gas pipeline network could result in the loss of over 60,000 manufacturing jobs when Sasol's access to natural gas ends in June 2026.[68] According to a study by Francois Steenkamp,[69] the impact would be dire as South Africa's coal value chain, centred in Mpumalanga province, underpins a significant portion of the economy, with 83% of the country's coal mines and 11 of Eskom's 14 coal-fired plants located there. While coal mining directly employs only 0.5% of the national workforce, the broader coal value chain supports industries like chemicals, petrochemicals, and metal production, all reliant on domestic coal.

According to Steenkamp, the coal workforce is predominantly semi-skilled (75%), with key roles including machine operators and miners. However, only 29% of workers, primarily those with post-secondary qualifications, are well-positioned to transition to new jobs. The majority (63%) of coal workers, who have only secondary education, will require skills development, while 8% in low-skill roles are unlikely to find alternative employment without income support. Early retirement packages may benefit 9.5% of the workforce nearing retirement. Lessons from Poland, Germany, and the UK emphasise the social and economic devastation caused by unplanned coal mine closures. South Africa must prioritise diverse, targeted policy interventions to ensure a just transition, mitigating job losses and supporting workers and their families in a sustainable shift from coal dependence.

A just energy transition for South Africa is essential—one that not only mitigates climate risks but also addresses the country's historical economic inequalities. The question remains: can South Africa successfully decouple its economic growth from fossil fuel consumption while ensuring that no one is left behind in the process?

Examining South Africa's energy situation reveals the prominent role of Sasol as a major player in the fossil fuel sector. While Sasol has long been a cornerstone of the country's economy, its heavy reliance on coal and other carbon-intensive resources poses significant challenges in the quest for a just energy transition. The implementation of carbon tax presents an opportunity to recalibrate the country's approach to emissions reduction and sustainable practices, but the pathway forward remains fraught with complexities.

Transitioning away from fossil fuels cannot happen overnight; it requires a concerted effort from government, industry, and civil society to collaborate on innovative solutions that mitigate the socio-economic impacts of decarbonisation. While carbon taxes aim to encourage cleaner practices, they risk exacerbating inequalities and hindering economic growth without accompanying support mechanisms.

Reflecting on Sasol's pivotal role, South Africa should consider how to transform this dependency into an opportunity for sustainable development. By embracing renewable energy investments, fostering technological advancements, and prioritising social equity, South Africa could pave the way towards a greener, more resilient future.

Moreover, this transition demands a re-evaluation of existing subsidies and a shift towards a more equitable distribution of resources that empowers low-income households and marginalised communities. For South Africa to embark on this journey, it must engage in robust dialogues that address the environmental and social dimensions of energy policy.

Developing countries like South Africa face heightened challenges in implementing carbon taxes compared to their developed counterparts. South Africa's carbon tax rate, set at R190 per tonne, remains significantly lower in practice, with an effective rate of just R7 per tonne. This discrepancy stems from tax offsets and delays in implementing the second phase of the tax.[70] These inefficiencies undermine the tax's capacity to influence behaviour and reduce emissions.

According to the IMF-World Bank Climate Policy Assessment Tool (CPAT), increasing the carbon tax rate alone will be insufficient for South Africa to meet its emission reduction targets; rather, enhancing the effective rate of the carbon tax is essential.[71] Complementary policies and measures are necessary to support the transition to a low-carbon economy and address the socio-economic impacts of the carbon tax. This includes investing in renewable energy infrastructure, promoting energy efficiency programmes, and providing financial assistance to affected communities to mitigate the higher costs of living.[72]

Since its introduction on 1 June 2019, the effectiveness of South Africa's carbon tax in reducing GHG emissions remains uncertain.[73] A key challenge lies in the lack of accurate methodologies for determining emissions, compounded by administrative difficulties in measuring and verifying them. These issues undermine the reliability of any evaluation of the carbon tax's impact. Moreover, other significant factors, such as persistent load-shedding, have independently accelerated the transition to alternative energy sources like solar power. South Africa has experienced an exponential rise in the installation of solar photovoltaic systems by homeowners, businesses, government entities, and industries. This surge is largely driven by supportive local government policies, rising electricity prices outpacing inflation, and declining technology costs.[74] Climate change concerns, recurring power outages, and the financial strain of escalating electricity prices have further motivated many South Africans to adopt solar power solutions.[75] However, it is difficult to isolate the role of the carbon tax or the solar incentive in driving this shift, as other external factors play equally significant roles. Additionally, the carbon tax on electricity is accompanied by an electricity generation levy introduced in 2009. This levy, applied to power generated from fossil-fuel and nuclear sources, was designed to mitigate electricity shortages, manage demand, and fund energy-efficiency tax incentives.[76] As a result, Eskom benefits from these offsets and continues to pay the electricity levy on power produced from non-renewable sources. However, the subsidies it receives—calculated on a per-ton CO_2e basis—exceed both the electricity levy and the official carbon tax rate. This creates a limited financial incentive for Eskom to transition away from coal-fired power generation, contributing to its lower effective carbon tax rate. To address these shortcomings, it is crucial for the National Treasury to explore supplementary tax measures, drawing from the experiences of countries like the United Kingdom and Sweden. Such measures could complement the carbon tax and enhance its effectiveness in reducing emissions while supporting South Africa's climate goals.

To enhance South Africa's energy transition, specific recommendations are critical. First, the Section 6C rooftop solar income tax incentive, which was limited to the 2023/2024 tax year, should be extended to encourage continued investment in solar energy by households. Additionally, instead of the costly expansion of the national grid to rural areas, a decentralised solution—installing rooftop solar systems—could provide electricity access at a comparable capital cost while reducing Eskom's burden. Solar financing mechanisms such as loans, leases, and Power Purchase Agreements (PPAs) can democratise energy access by empowering households and businesses to produce their own electricity.[77] Eskom, in turn, should adapt its business model and tariff structures to accommodate increased self-generation and support programmes like Small-Scale Embedded Generation (SSEG). This dual strategy of expanding solar adoption and modernising Eskom's infrastructure would alleviate pressure on the national grid, advance renewable energy goals, and contribute to long-term sustainability.

NOTES

1. Evans, Julia. "Sasol AGM cancelled after climate activists protest", *Daily Maverick*, 17 November 2023. Available at https://www.dailymaverick.co.za/article/2023-11-17-sasol-agm-cancelled-after-climate-activists-protest/
2. Erasmus, Denene. "Protesters halt Sasol AGM", *Business Day*, 19 November 2023. Available at https://www.businesslive.co.za/bt/business-and-economy/2023-11-19-protesters-halt-sasol-agm/#google_vignette
3. Baker, Lucy. "The political economy of South Africa's carbon tax", *The Institute of Development Studies and partner organisations*, 2022.
4. Pilling, David and Joseph Cotterill. "Inside the battle to decarbonise the world's dirtiest refinery", *Financial Times,* 10 December 2023. Available at: https://www.ft.com/content/f6385c6a-6ffe-488e-a28a-3a4474506648
5. Sparks, Stephen. "Between 'artificial economics' and the 'discipline of the market': Sasol from parastatal to privatisation", *Journal of Southern African Studies*, 42, no. 4 (2016): 711–724.
6. Sparks, Stephen. "Apartheid modern: South Africa's oil from coal project and the history of a company town", PhD dissertation (2012).
7. Verhoef, Grietjie. "Sasol: from state-owned enterprise to chemical leader management and strategy, 1952–1980", *Rivista di Politica Economica* (2015).
8. Stranges, Anthony. "Germany's synthetic fuel industry, 1927–1945", in *The German chemical industry in the twentieth century*, pp. 147–216. Dordrecht: Springer Netherlands, 2000.
9. Majozi, Thokozani and Patrick Veldhuizen. "The chemicals industry in South Africa", *American Institute of Chemical Engineers (AIChE)*, 46 (2015): 51.
10. Adam, Ferrial. *Sasol: profits from poison.* Johannesburg: Earthlife Africa, 2010.
11. Pilling, David and Joseph Cotterill. "Inside the battle to decarbonise the world's dirtiest refinery" *Financial Times*, 10 December 2023. Available at: https://www.ft.com/content/f6385c6a-6ffe-488e-a28a-3a4474506648
12. Pretorius, O.J. "The atmospheric impact of Sasol synfuels operations on adjacent residential development", *Clean Air Journal*, 16, no. 1 (2007): 18–24.
13. Pilling, David and Joseph Cotterill. "Inside the battle to decarbonise the world's dirtiest refinery" *Financial Times*, 10 December 2023. Available at: https://www.ft.com/content/f6385c6a-6ffe-488e-a28a-3a4474506648
14. Pilling, David and Joseph Cotterill. "Sasol on defensive over plans to cut emissions. South African group's Secunda complex is at centre of dispute with investors and campaigners about the pace of change", *The Financial Times* (2023): 7–7.
15. Pretorius, O.J. "The atmospheric impact of Sasol synfuels operations on adjacent residential development", *Clean Air Journal*, 16, no. 1, 2007: 18–24.
16. Mondliwa, Pamela and Simon Roberts. "From a developmental to a regulatory state? Sasol and the conundrum of continued state support", in *Ownership and governance of companies*, pp. 21–39. Routledge, 2021.

17. Kruger, Adriaan. "Disrupting Sasol's AGM while benefitting from its products", *Moneyweb*, 20 November 2024. Available at https://www.moneyweb.co.za/news/companies-and-deals/disrupting-sasols-agm-while-benefitting-from-its-products/
18. Evans, Julia. "Sasol AGM cancelled after climate activists protest", *Daily Maverick*, 17 November 2023. Available at https://www.dailymaverick.co.za/article/2023-11-17-sasol-agm-cancelled-after-climate-activists-protest/
19. National Treasury. "Reducing greenhouse gas emissions: the carbon tax option", *Discussion paper for public comment*, Pretoria, South Africa, 2010.
20. National Treasury. "Reducing greenhouse gas emissions: the carbon tax option", *Discussion paper for public comment*, Pretoria, South Africa, 2010.
21. Sasol Limited. Climate change reports. June 2021, June 2022, and June 2023. Available at https://www.sasol.com/esg/environment/climate-action
22. National Treasury. "Media statement: publication of the 2019 Carbon Tax Act", 2019.
23. Yeoh, Peter. *Environmental, social and governance (ESG) laws, regulations and practices in the digital era,* Wolters Kluwer, 2022.
24. Zenghelis, Dimitri and Nicholas Stern. "The importance of looking forward to manage risks: submission to the Task Force on Climate-Related Financial Disclosures", *Policy paper*, 2016.
25. National Treasury. "Reducing greenhouse gas emissions and facilitating the transition to a green economy", *Tax policy discussion paper for public comment*. Pretoria, South Africa, 2013.
26. Shikwambana, Lerato, Paidamwoyo Mhangara and Mahlatse Kganyago. "Assessing the relationship between economic growth and emissions levels in South Africa between 1994 and 2019", *Sustainability*, 13, no. 5 (2021): 2645.
27. National Treasury. 2010. "Reducing greenhouse gas emissions: the carbon tax option", *Discussion paper for public comment*, Pretoria, South Africa.
28. Alton, Theresa, Channing Arndt, Rob Davies, Faaiqa Hartley, Konstantin Makrelov, James Thurlow and Dumebi Ubogu. "Introducing carbon taxes in South Africa", *Applied Energy*, 116 (2014): 344–354.
29. Oladunni, Oluwole Joseph, Khumbulani Mpofu and Oludolapo Akanni Olanrewaju. "Greenhouse gas emissions and its driving forces in the transport sector of South Africa", *Energy Reports*, 8 (2022): 2052–2061.
30. Menyah, Kojo and Yemane Wolde-Rufael. "Energy consumption, pollutant emissions and economic growth in South Africa", *Energy Economics*, 32, no. 6 (2010): 1374–1382.
31. Devarajan, Shantayanan, Delfin S. Go, Sherman Robinson and Karen Thierfelder. "Tax policy to reduce carbon emissions in South Africa", *World Bank Policy Research Working Paper*, 4933 (2009).
32. National Treasury. "What is the most appropriate tax regime for the oil and gas industry", *Tax policy discussion paper for public comment*, Pretoria. South Africa, 2022.

33. International Monetary Fund. "South Africa carbon pricing and climate mitigation policy", 2023. Available at: https://www.elibrary.imf.org/downloadpdf/view/journals/002/2023/195/article-A003-en.pdf
34. International Monetary Fund. "South Africa carbon pricing and climate mitigation policy", 2023. Available at: https://www.elibrary.imf.org/downloadpdf/view/journals/002/2023/195/article-A003-en.pdf
35. National Treasury. 2010. "Reducing greenhouse gas emissions: the carbon tax option", *Discussion paper for public comment*, Pretoria, South Africa.
36. Brent, Alan C., Sibbele Hietkamp, Russell M. Wise and Kenney O'Kennedy. "Estimating the carbon emissions balance for South Africa", *South African Journal of Economic and Management Sciences*, 12, no. 3 (2009): 263–279.
37. Kuramochi, Takeshi, Andrew Deneault, Sander Chan, Sybrig Smit and Natalie Pelekh. "Supporting the Paris Agreement through international cooperation: potential contributions, institutional robustness, and progress of Glasgow climate initiatives", *npj Climate Action*, 3, no. 1 (2024): 31.
38. Murcott, Melanie Jean and Clive Vinti. "The judge-made 'duty' to consider climate change in South Africa", *Journal of Human Rights Practice*, 16, no. 1 (2024): 125–145.
39. Bohlmann, Heinrich R., Jessika A. Bohlmann, Margaret Chitiga-Mabugu, and Roula Inglesi-Lotz. "Just energy transition of South Africa in a post-COVID era", *Sustainability*, 15, no. 14 (2023): 10854.
40. Nyamusamba, Blessing. "The implementation and fulfilment of the Paris Agreement 2015 through South African climate change law", PhD dissertation, North-West University (South Africa), 2023.
41. Haegele, Ramona, Gabriela I. Iacobuţă and James Tops. "Addressing climate goals and the SDGs through a just energy transition? Empirical evidence from Germany and South Africa", *Journal of Integrative Environmental Sciences*, 19, no. 1 (2022): 85–120.
42. Winkler, H., E. Tyler, S. Keen and A. Marquard. "Just transition transaction in South Africa: an innovative way to finance accelerated phase out of coal and fund social justice", *Journal of Sustainable Finance & Investment*, 13, no 3 (2023): 1228–1251.
43. Nemavhidi, Muano and Ademola Oluborode Jegede. "Carbon tax as a climate intervention in South Africa: a potential aid or hindrance to human rights?", *Environmental Law Review*, 25, no. 1 (2023): 11–27.
44. Bryan, Elizabeth, Temesgen T. Deressa, Glwadys A. Gbetibouo and Claudia Ringler. "Adaptation to climate change in Ethiopia and South Africa: options and constraints", *Environmental Science & Policy*, 12, no. 4 (2009): 413–426.
45. Averchenkova, Alina, Kate Elizabeth Gannon and Patrick Curran. "Governance of climate change policy: a case study of South Africa", *Grantham Research Institute on Climate Change and the Environment Policy Report* (2019): 1–39.
46. Stoddard, Ed. "Weak carbon tax hinders South Africa's green energy transition, says IMF", *Daily Maverick*, 4 July 2023. Available at https://www

.dailymaverick.co.za/article/2023-07-04-weak-carbon-tax-hinders-south-africas-green-energy-transition-says-imf/

47. Steenkamp, Lee-Ann. "South Africa's carbon tax rate goes up but emitters get more time to clean up", *The Conversation*, 25 February 2022. Available at https://theconversation.com/south-africas-carbon-tax-rate-goes-up-but-emitters-get-more-time-to-clean-up-177834
48. Digitemic, Wags Numoipiri and Ifeanyi Onyedika Ekemezie. "Assessing the role of carbon pricing in global climate change mitigation strategies", *Magna Scientia Advanced Research and Reviews*, 10, no. 2 (2024): 022–031.
49. Ouyang, Tiancheng, Yinxuan Li, Shutao Xie, Chengchao Wang, and Chunlan Mo. "Low-carbon economic dispatch strategy for integrated power system based on the substitution effect of carbon tax and carbon trading", *Energy*, 294 (2024): 130960.
50. Iyke-Ofoedu, Maureen Ifeoma, Samuel Manyo Takon, David O. Ugwunta, Hillary Chijindu Ezeaku, Ebele Sabina Nsofor and Obiamaka P. Egbo. "Impact of CO2 emissions embodied in the agricultural sector on carbon sequestration in South Africa: the role of environmental taxes and technological innovation", *Journal of Cleaner Production*, 444 (2024): 141210.
51. Trollip, Hilton and Michael Boulle. "Challenges associated with implementing climate change mitigation policy in South Africa", *Energy Research Centre*, University of Cape Town (2017).
52. Udeagha, Maxwell Chukwudi, and Marthinus Christoffel Breitenbach. "The role of financial development in climate change mitigation: fresh policy insights from South Africa", *Biophysical Economics and Sustainability*, 8, no. 1 (2023): 1.
53. Bekun, Festus Victor. "Race to carbon neutrality in South Africa: what role does environmental technological innovation play?", *Applied Energy*, 354 (2024): 122212.
54. Turok, Ivan. *Urbanisation and development in South Africa: economic imperatives, spatial distortions and strategic responses.* London: Human Settlements Group, International Institute for Environment and Development, 2012.
55. Palmer, Ian, Nishendra Moodley and Susan Parnell. *Building a capable state: service delivery in post-apartheid South Africa.* Bloomsbury Publishing, 2017.
56. Walters, Jackie. "Public transport policy implementation in South Africa: Quo vadis?", *Journal of Transport and Supply Chain Management,* 8, no. 1 (2014): 1–10.
57. Jennings, Gail. "Public transport interventions and transport justice in South Africa: a literature and policy review", *Southern African Transport Conference* (2015).
58. Samson, Michael J. "The social, economic and fiscal impact of comprehensive social security reform for South Africa", *Social Dynamics*, 28, no. 2 (2002): 69–97.
59. Longe, Omowunmi Mary. "An assessment of the energy poverty and gender nexus towards clean energy adoption in rural South Africa", *Energies*, 14, no. 12 (2021): 3708.

60. Pachauri, Shonali, N.D. Rao, Yu Nagai and Keywan Riahi. *Access to modern energy: Assessment and outlook for developing and emerging regions*, IIASA, Laxenburg, Austria, 2012.
61. Sohail, Muhammad Tayyab, Sana Ullah and Muhammad Tariq Majeed. "Transportation taxes and CO2 emissions nexus in BCIST economies: implication for environmental sustainability", *Energy & Environment*, 35, no. 5 (2024): 2829–2845.
62. Nanyang Technology University. "South Africa records a four-fold spike in solar imports from China businesses and households are turning to off-grid solutions as power cuts roll on", *NTU-SBF Centre for African Studies* (CAS) (23 Oct 2023)
63. Daily Investor. "New solar record for South Africa", *Business Tech* (5 Aug. 2023).
64. Creamer, Terence. "Solar, battery, inverter imports surged to R70bn in 2023 as wind turbines recovered from two-year lull", *Creamer Media's Engineering News* (4 Mar. 2024).
65. Jowett, Patrick. "South Africa imposes 10% import tariff on solar panels", *PV Magazine* (4 July 2024).
66. Espoir, Delphin Kamanda, Regret Sunge, Biyase Mduduzi, Frank Bannor and Simion Matsvai. "Analysing the response of CO2 emissions to business cycle in a developing economy: evidence for South Africa post-apartheid era", *Frontiers in Environmental Science*, 11 (2024): 1321335.
67. Crompton, Rod and Bruce Douglas Young. "SA's massive Sasol petrochemical plant faces serious challenges – new report", *The Conversation* (11 Nov. 2024).
68. Nyathi, Mandisa. "Gas crisis endangers 60 000 jobs", *Mail & Guardian* (22 Mar. 2024).
69. Steenkamp, Francois. "End of coal in South Africa: what 100,000 workers will need when their jobs go", *The Conversation* (22 Oct. 2024).
70. Yiadom, Eric B., Lord Mensah, Godfred A. Bokpin and John KM Mawutor. "Carbon tax adoption and foreign direct investment: evidence from Africa", *Cogent Economics & Finance*, 12, no. 1 (2024): 2312783.
71. Black, Simon, Ian Parry, Victor Mylonas, Nate Vernon and Karlygash Zhunussova, "The IMF-World Bank Climate Policy Assessment Tool (CPAT): a model to help countries mitigate climate change", International Monetary Fund Working Papers, 2023.
72. Kumba, Hagreaves, Joseph Akpan, Belinda Twite, and Oludolapo Olanrewaju. "Renewable energy adoption and integration in South Africa: an overview", *12th International Conference on Clean and Green Energy (ICCGE 2023)*, Xiamen, China, 2023, pp. 74–87.
73. Abel, Sanderson, Julius Mukarati, Leward Jeke and Pierre Le Roux. "Carbon tax and environmental quality in South Africa", *International Journal of Energy Economics and Policy*, 13, no. 2 (2023): 484–488.
74. Green Energy Solutions. "Factors determining the energy production of a solar power system" (2015).

75. Green Cape. "The business case for solar PV in South Africa", *Industry Brief* (2020).
76. Qu, Haonan, Suphachol Suphachalasai, Sneha D. Thube and Sébastien Walker. "South Africa carbon pricing and climate mitigation policy", IMF Selected Issues Paper (SIP/2023/040), International Monetary Fund, 2023.
77. The Rental Company. "Understanding Eskom's influence on solar asset finance in South Africa" (2024).

2. Emerging kaleidoscope of carbon pricing and side effects in Africa

Laure Gnassou

1. INTRODUCTION

Developing countries, including those facing conflict and fragility, have experienced significant development finance challenges, putting in jeopardy their national development strategies for inclusive green growth. Due to a scarcity of climate finance in the Global South, developing countries are seeking alternative sources of sustainable financing. In this context, the development of carbon markets has revealed rising interest among African countries, particularly those holding Nature-based Solutions (NbS) such as forests, peatlands, and mangroves, constituting the main global climate mitigation tools. The chapter examines factors leading to the development of diverse carbon pricing mechanisms in Africa, with a focus on SSA (Sub-Saharan Africa), a region where the challenge of improving the management of forestry sectors is critical. It also highlights the side effects generated by carbon pricing mechanisms, not shying away from the adverse impacts on local stakeholders.

First, the chapter delves into competing development priorities of African resource-rich countries, notably forested countries experiencing challenges in leveraging sustainable carbon finance. Although the forest-rich countries are engaged in efforts to preserve and restore NbS, they have struggled to monetise their natural assets through carbon markets. In addition, they are exposed to the 'carbon credit curse' due to large-scale carbon offset deals in which the critical role played by local stakeholders has not been recognised, bringing the risk of greater social fragmentation.

Second, the chapter provides insights into various carbon pricing frameworks in SSA, which are mainly in the form of carbon taxes and carbon crediting. Most of these are nascent national frameworks responding to both climate and tax objectives. They outline challenges that African countries have encountered in increasing Domestic Revenue Mobilisation (DRM) to tackle poverty and inequality.

In conclusion, the chapter calls for African governments to seek support from development partners in designing and setting up fair carbon pricing schemes, strengthening forestry governance, and preserving the rights and livelihoods of local stakeholders.

2. DAUNTING DEVELOPMENT CHALLENGES OF AFRICAN RESOURCE-RICH COUNTRIES IN THE GLOBAL RACE TO NET-ZERO

African resource-rich countries are at a crossroads in fostering resilience to the effects of climate change. They have to proceed towards green structural transformation while unlocking the potential of carbon markets to bridge climate finance gaps and achieve their respective Nationally Determined Contributions (NDCs). As a result, they are exposed to challenges such as the protection and restoration of NbS and rising overseas investments in natural carbon sinks.

2.1 Leveraging African Natural Capital in the Pursuit of Economic Diversification

2.1.1 Towards green industrialisation

The world's demand for green technologies has increased, as developed countries are in a race for critical minerals to fuel their clean energy transition and to support their economic competitiveness and national security. In the Global South, African countries, including those struggling with political and security crises, are garnering more attention owing to the mineral intensity of the clean energy transition. Over 80% of these economies are commodity-dependent. Such economies can take advantage of the critical mineral commodity boom by pursuing economic diversification.[1] African resource-rich countries need to implement green industrial policies to participate in high-value-added segments of the global value chain.[2] For instance, since 29 April 2022, the Democratic Republic of the Congo (DR Congo) and Zambia have partnered to build a 'Made in Africa' electric vehicle battery supply to capitalise on

[1] UNCTAD, 'Economic Development in Africa Report – The Potential of Africa to Capture Technology-Intensive Global Supply Chains' (2023), 46–49, https://unctad.org/publication/economic-development-africa-report-2023.

[2] UNCTAD, 'The Least Developed Countries Report 2022 – The Low-Carbon Transition and Its Daunting Implications for Structural Transformation' (2022), 4–10, https://unctad.org/publication/least-developed-countries-report-2022.

the rising demand for electric vehicle batteries.[3] Overall, developing a green structural transformation programme is a key prerequisite for evolving from natural resource-based and agricultural economies into medium-high technology manufacturing-based economies in SSA.

2.1.2 SSA countries, burgeoning suppliers of nature-based carbon credits

Africa holds about one-sixth of the world's remaining forests and almost one-quarter of the world's biodiversity hotspots.[4] Some of the African commodity-dependent economies are also forest-rich countries. Beyond minerals, they have recorded a newfound focus on their green assets that include forests, peatlands, and mangroves. These assets represent untapped sources of carbon finance potential. Additionally, African countries rich in forests and minerals are exposed to an unprecedented conundrum, resulting in reconciling net-zero industrialisation development with a surge in demand for nature-based carbon credits. Countries facing this challenge include Zimbabwe, Zambia, Mozambique,[5] and the Congo Basin countries. The Congo Basin rainforest represents the world's second-largest tropical forest after the Amazon rainforest. As a major biodiversity hotspot, it comprises over 300 million hectares, corresponding to 70% of Africa's forests. It constitutes a primary source of livelihood for a population of over 75 million.[6] Furthermore, the Congo Basin is the world's second-largest carbon sink, often referred to as the 'lungs of Africa'. The Congo Basin countries consist of Cameroon, Central African Republic, Republic of the Congo, Equatorial Guinea, and Gabon, while the DR Congo forests constitute about 60% of the Congo Basin rainforest. Given their green wealth, these countries are carbon-negative emitters and provide carbon capture services.

---

[3] UNECA, 'Zambia and DRC Sign Cooperation Agreement to Manufacture Electric Batteries', Press release, April 29, 2022, https://www.uneca.org/stories/zambia-and-drc-sign-cooperation-agreement-to-manufacture-electric-batteries.

[4] Mo Ibrahim Foundation, 'The Road to COP27 – Making Africa's Case in the Climate Debate: Facts and Figures," May 2022, 52–53, https://mo.ibrahim.foundation/sites/default/files/2022-05/2022-Ibrahim-Forum_Facts-Figures.pdf.

[5] Along with Angola, Burundi, Southern DR Congo, Malawi, and Tanzania, these countries belong to the Miombo woodlands.

[6] Aquilas Nkwetta Ajong, Alfred Kechia Mukong, Jude Ndzifon Kimengsi, and Forbe Hodu Ngangnchi, 'Economic Activities and Deforestation in the Congo Basin: An Environmental Kuznets Curve Framework Analysis', *Environmental Challenges*, vol. 8, 2022. https://doi.org/10.1016/j.envc.2022.100553.

2.2 Addressing the Deforestation and Forest Degradation in SSA: A Matter of Forest Carbon Credits

2.2.1 The pivotal role of donor programmes in improving forest governance in SSA

According to the World Bank, from 1990 to 2021, forest lands decreased from 31.1% to 26.1% in SSA.[7] The deforestation and forest degradation led to biodiversity loss. The loss can be attributed to a series of factors, notably the development of agriculture and illegal logging activities. With donor support, African countries have engaged in reforestation and afforestation processes. In 2008, the UN-Reducing Emissions from Deforestation and Forest Degradation (UN-REDD) programme was set up. In 2024, the programme assisted nationally led REDD+ processes in 25 African countries to support the implementation of the Paris Agreement, especially Articles 5 and 6.[8] At the country level, the REDD+ processes cover these key activities: (i) the reduction of GHG emissions from deforestation and forest degradation; (ii) sustainable forest management; and (iii) conservation and reinforcement of forest carbon stocks. Forest carbon projects can also be integrated into these processes.[9]

Despite their commitment, forest-rich African countries still experience challenges in improving forest governance. In exchange for the full implementation of these activities, they have access to climate finance through the Results-Based Payments (RBPs) or the Voluntary Carbon Markets (VCMs).[10] In this context, a clear ownership identification of the Emissions Reductions (ERs) rights or nature-based carbon rights is critical to obtaining the said REDD+ incentives. In most African forested countries, the ERs or carbon rights belong to the state because lands and forests are state-owned. The REDD+ processes promote equity and inclusiveness. To build trust, African countries rich in natural carbon sinks establish benefit-sharing agreements

---

[7] World Bank, 'World Development Indicators', January 24, 2024, https://data.worldbank.org/indicator/AG.LND.FRST.ZS?locations=ZG.

[8] UN-REDD Programme, 'Forest Solutions to the Climate Emergency – A Case for Support for the UN-REDD Programme' (2022), 6, https://www.un-redd.org/sites/default/files/2022-10/UN-REDD%20Case%20for%20Support%20flyer%202022.pdf.

[9] Donna Lee, Pablo Llopis, Rob Waterworth, Geoff Roberts, and Tim Pearson, 'Approaches to REDD+ Nesting – Lessons Learned from Country Experiences'. World Bank, April 2018, 1–33, https://documents1.worldbank.org/curated/en/670171523647847532/pdf/Main-report.pdf.

[10] FAO, Carbon Rights in the Context of Jurisdictional REDD+: Tenure Links and Country-based Legal Solutions – Information Brief (2022), 1–5, https://doi.org/10.4060/cc2694en.

with key stakeholders, including smallholder farmers, the indigenous people, and local communities.[11] As ecosystem service beneficiaries, these vulnerable groups are critical to ecosystem restoration efforts.

2.2.2 The carbon credit projects under high scrutiny

According to the International Monetary Fund (IMF), from 2016 to 2021, carbon credits issued from SSA in the VCMs were estimated at 21% of the total traded credits on average. From 2010 to 2021, the forestry sector accounted for 61% of the carbon credits issued in SSA. Of these nature-based credits, 47.42% resulted specifically from REDD+ projects.[12] Over the same period, Kenya issued 39,000 carbon credits, while Zimbabwe, the DR Congo, Uganda, Zambia, Malawi, Ghana, and Ethiopia were among the key suppliers of nature-based carbon credits.

The pressing objective of achieving carbon neutrality by 2050 has driven a surge in demand for high-quality carbon credits stemming from the effective protection and enhancement of natural carbon sinks. This outlook has prompted African forest-rich countries to further monetise their natural assets, as stressed in the Nairobi Declaration of September 2023[13]. However, nature-based carbon projects are at the heart of the controversy affecting the legitimacy of carbon markets, especially the VCMs, valued at USD 1.9 billion in 2022.[14] The supply-side integrity of VCMs is severely questioned.[15, 16] Moreover, the carbon mar-

---

[11] FAO, Carbon Rights in the Context of Jurisdictional REDD+: Tenure Links and Country-based Legal Solutions, 9–10 and 12.

[12] Anna Belianska, Nathalie Bohme, Kai Cai, Youssouf Diallo, Sajal Jain, Grigory Melina, Prasenjit Mitra, Maria Poplawski Ribeiro, and Seydou Zerbo, 'Climate Change and Select Financial Instruments: An Overview of Opportunities and Challenges for Sub-Saharan Africa', IMF Staff Climate Note 2022/009 (IMF, 2022), 18, https://doi.org/10.5089/9798400225208.066.

[13] African Union, 'The African Leaders Nairobi Declaration on Climate Change and Call for Action', September 8, 2023, https://media.africaclimatesummit.org/Final+declaration+1709-English.pdf?request-content-type=%22application/force-download.

[14] Ecosystem Marketplace, '2023 State of the Voluntary Carbon Markets Report', November 28, 2023, 7, https://www.ecosystemmarketplace.com/publications/state-of-the-voluntary-carbon-market-report-2023/.

[15] Patrick Greenfield, 'Revealed: More than 90% of Rainforest Carbon Offsets by Biggest Certifier Are Worthless, Analysis Shows', *The Guardian*, January 18, 2023, https://www.theguardian.com/environment/2023/jan/18/revealed-forest-carbon-offsets-biggest-provider-worthless-verra-aoe.

[16] Heidi Blake, 'The Great Cash-for-Carbon Hustle', *The New Yorker*, October 16, 2023, https://www.newyorker.com/magazine/2023/10/23/the-great-cash-for-carbon-hustle.

kets are characterised by heterogeneous carbon credits and a restricted number of buyers. They are fragmented, unregulated, and opaque. There is no effective price discovery mechanism, and this causes underpriced carbon credits.[17] In 2023, the average price stood at USD 6.97 per tonne on the VCMs.[18] As in any other commodity markets, African countries are price-takers in the VCMs. The under-pricing of carbon credits has negatively impacted carbon finance flows in SSA. Altogether, African countries have faced difficulties navigating the VCM landscape. Greater market integrity and transparency are essential for carbon markets to function effectively.

2.3 Rising Carbon Offset Deals in SSA: The Emergence of the 'Carbon Credit Curse'

2.3.1 The case of Blue Carbon LLC: a foreign project developer taking over SSA

Demand for high-quality nature-based carbon credits arises from developed and emerging economies facing the challenge of transitioning away from fossil fuels. This perspective attracts project developers to leverage the potential in African countries rich in natural sinks. Among these developers, Blue Carbon LLC, a United Arab Emirates (UAE)-based company, drew attention in 2023 by upscaling its overseas investments in NbS across SSA through the operationalisation of Article 6.2 of the Paris Agreement. Its strategy has consisted of developing nature-based carbon projects to generate carbon credits in the form of Internationally Transferred Mitigation Outcomes (ITMOs). This led the Emirati firm to sign Memoranda of Understanding (MoU) and a Framework of Collaboration (FOC) with five African countries. Its portfolio of carbon offset deals of 24.5 million hectares encompasses: (i) 10% of land in Liberia[19]

17 Anna Belianska, Nathalie Bohme, Kai Cai, Youssouf Diallo, Sajal Jain, Grigory Melina, Prasenjit Mitra, Maria Poplawski Ribeiro, and Seydou Zerbo, 'Climate Change and Select Financial Instruments: An Overview of Opportunities and Challenges for Sub-Saharan Africa', 17.

18 Ecosystem Marketplace, 'Paying for Quality: State of the Voluntary Carbon Markets 2023', 7.

19 SourceMaterial, Scramble for Africa – Inside Carbon Offsetting's Megadeal, November 29, 2023, https://www.source-material.org/dubai-uae-cop28-blue-carbon-offsetting-forest-liberia/.

and Zambia;[20] (ii) 8% of land in Tanzania;[21] (iii) 20% of land in Zimbabwe;[22] and (iv) some millions of hectares in Kenya.[23] These deals included various carbon credit revenue-sharing agreements, notably the controversial agreement in Liberia. In this country, a 70/30% revenue-sharing agreement was set out between Blue Carbon and the government for a period of 30 years.[24] An undisclosed amount from government revenues will be allocated to local communities.[25] As a carbon credit supplier, the Emirati firm intends to sell carbon credits to governments to contribute to achieving their NDC targets, and to private sector operators to decrease their carbon footprints.

The aforementioned bilateral agreements raised some concerns due to a lack of transparency. First, Blue Carbon's large-scale carbon offset deals are often compared to greenwashing operations.[26] Second, African forested countries lost control over a significant fraction of carbon finance through unfavourable carbon credit revenue-sharing agreements. Beyond the Blue Carbon case, other private sector developers and more countries have pursued strategies relying on the ITMOs under Article 6.2 of the Paris Agreement to help reduce emissions. Nonetheless, countries rich in natural sinks, notably African countries,

---

[20] Gulf News Report, 'Blue Carbon and Government of Zambia Sign MoU to Unlock the Potential of Carbon Removal Projects', February 8, 2023, https://gulfnews.com/business/corporate-news/blue-carbon-and-government-of-zambia-sign-mou-to-unlock-the-potential-of-carbon-removal-projects-1.1675850886963.

[21] Gulf News Report, 'Blue Carbon and the Government of Tanzania Join Forces to Accelerate Transition to Low-Carbon Economy', February 7, 2023, https://gulfnews.com/business/corporate-news/blue-carbon-and-the-government-of-tanzania-join-forces-to-accelerate-transition-to-low-carbon-economy-1.1675752836855.

[22] Cyril Zenda, 'Doubts Grow Over Who'll Benefit from UAE Carbon Deal for Fifth of Zimbabwe', *African Arguments*, October 31, 2023, https://africanarguments.org/2023/10/doubts-rise-over-who-benefit-from-uae-firm-deal-for-a-fifth-of-zimbabwe/.

[23] Newsfile, 'Government of Kenya Accelerates Towards Compliance Market with UAE's Blue Carbon under Article 6', October 25, 2023, https://www.newsfilecorp.com/release/185173.

[24] SourceMaterial, Scramble for Africa – Inside Carbon Offsetting's Megadeal, November 29, 2023.

[25] Kenza Bryan, 'The Looming Land Grab in Africa for Carbon Credits', *Financial Times*, December 6, 2023, https://www.ft.com/content/f9bead69-7401-44fe-8db9-1c4063ae958c.

[26] SourceMaterial, Scramble for Africa – Inside Carbon Offsetting's Megadeal, November 29, 2023.

need to strike a balance to avoid issuing too many ITMOs and ensuring they can reach their own NDCs.[27]

Overall, green Foreign Direct Investment (FDI) centred on NbS could lead to a race to the bottom. Forest-rich countries with limited fiscal space might opt for carbon offset deals integrating unfair carbon credit revenue-sharing agreements. The 'carbon credit curse' has emerged at the expense of African forested countries. In response, some of these countries have initiated national carbon pricing legislations to address existing loopholes.[28]

2.3.2 Silencing the pivotal role of the small stakeholders in the carbon offset deals in SSA

The Blue Carbon offset deals, involving the temporary transfer of carbon credit ownership from host countries to a private firm, raise concerns owing to a lack of accountability. These deals occurred without prior consultation with national stakeholders, particularly smallholder farmers, the indigenous people, and local communities.[29] With such large-scale Blue Carbon deals across several African countries, land tenure and customary rights of these national stakeholders are potentially jeopardised.[30] One wonders if grievance mechanisms and remedies could be applied to protect vulnerable groups. The Blue Carbon deals could lead to social tensions and pose a risk of displacement for local communities and indigenous people. They could also exacerbate distrust between governments and local stakeholders and compromise cooperation on climate solutions. In SSA, the current rush on carbon offset deals highlights a potential new form of inequity. It could further marginalise vulnerable populations, already disproportionately affected by the impacts of climate change.

3. THE MOSAIC OF CARBON PRICING SCHEMES ON THE RISE IN SSA

The climate crisis has exacerbated pre-existing crises in African economies confronted with development challenges. They urgently require development

---

27 World Bank, 'State and Trends of Carbon Pricing 2023', May 2023, 48, http://hdl.handle.net/10986/39796.

28 See section 3 below.

29 FERN, 'International Statement on the Carbon Deal between Blue Carbon and the Liberian Government', July 20, 2023, https://www.fern.org/fileadmin/uploads/fern/Documents/2023/International_Statement_on_the_Carbon_Deal_-_Carbon_Blue_and_Liberia.pdf.

30 Esau E. Farr, 'Six Laws Blue Carbon Deal Would Violate Explained', *The DayLight*, July 30, 2023, https://thedaylight.org/2023/07/30/six-ways-blue-carbon-deal-would-be-illegal-explained/.

finance, notably climate finance. From this perspective, carbon pricing offers the potential to achieve key objectives: curbing GHG emissions, raising public revenue, and expanding fiscal space. Putting a price on carbon emissions is tailored to the African context, which is characterised by the emergence of a dual carbon pricing scheme. Some African countries have also shown interest in combining both schemes. The first accounts for the environmental externality of carbon-intensive activities. The second applies to valuing the carbon sequestration services of forests and natural ecosystems. As African forest-rich countries forge their own paths, they have expressed concerns on two major issues to prevent the 'carbon credit curse': the benefit-sharing agreement and the pricing of nature-based carbon credits.

3.1 A Nascent African Carbon Taxation Landscape and the Impact of the European Union (EU) Carbon Border Adjustment Mechanism (CBAM) in SSA

3.1.1 South Africa, the most advanced African country in terms of carbon taxation

According to the World Bank, as of 1 April 2024, 75 carbon pricing frameworks, comprising 39 carbon taxes and 36 Emission Trading Systems (ETSs), cover only 24% of global GHG emissions.[31] In SSA, South Africa is one of the most industrialised African countries, and it set out a carbon tax through the Carbon Tax Act in 2019.[32] The tax applies to emissions from the construction, industrial, power, and transport sectors. It covers about 80% of the country's GHG emissions. South Africa has paved the way for other African countries to establish national carbon taxation. Meanwhile, most African countries are in the early stages of establishing carbon pricing schemes. For instance, Côte d'Ivoire, Senegal, and Botswana are considering adopting carbon taxes, while Gabon and Nigeria have been working on adopting a hybrid carbon pricing framework, combining an ETS with the development of a national nature-based carbon credit market.[33] It is worth mentioning that several African countries have undertaken or announced reforms aimed at removing fuel subsidies

31 World Bank, 'State and Trends of Carbon Pricing 2024', May 21, 2024, 18–22, https://hdl.handle.net/10986/41544.

32 World Bank, 'State and Trends of Carbon Pricing 2018', May 2018, 49, https://documents1.worldbank.org/curated/en/480621554812881664/pdf/State-and-Trends-of-Carbon-Pricing-2018.pdf.

33 World Bank, 'State and Trends of Carbon Pricing 2023', May 2023, 31, http://hdl.handle.net/10986/39796.

(negative carbon pricing).[34] Nonetheless, the elimination of these subsidies remains a complex challenge in countries marred by acute social crises.

3.1.2 The CBAM: a matter of ownership of carbon pricing revenue in SSA

Despite a timid introduction of carbon taxation in SSA, African countries could be compelled to establish carbon taxation under the pressure of the CBAM. On 13 December 2022, the EU adopted the CBAM, which started operating on 1 October 2023. It will become fully effective on 1 January 2026. Non-EU importers will have to pay a levy on the carbon emissions embedded in goods from key carbon-intensive sectors (cement, steel, iron, aluminium, fertilisers, electricity, and hydrogen). The levy will only apply if these goods have not already been subject to a direct carbon price in their country of origin.

By preventing carbon leakage,[35] the CBAM aims to incentivise emission reductions in the non-EU trading partners. Beyond the risk of higher trade tensions, it has unveiled an unprecedented dilemma: the issue is whether the revenues from carbon pricing will be allocated to the EU or to the non-EU trading partners.[36] For African countries, the full implementation of the CBAM is a matter of concern, given that the EU is a major trading partner. Hence, a European carbon import levy could prevent them from raising carbon finance.

3.2 Diversity of National Nature-based Carbon Pricing Frameworks for African Forest Countries

3.2.1 Focus on the revenue-sharing provisions of carbon pricing framework in Zimbabwe

In recent years, African countries rich in natural carbon sinks, such as Zimbabwe, Kenya, and Tanzania, have made significant progress in adopting legal and institutional frameworks for carbon pricing initiatives (Figure 2.1). They plan to generate high-quality sovereign carbon credits and mobilise carbon finance effectively.

These countries paid close attention to framing the revenue-sharing provisions and tracking the nature-based credits through registries. Specifically,

---

34 Marie de Vergès, 'In Africa, Governments Cut Back on Fuel Subsidies', *Le Monde*, October 18, 2023, https://www.lemonde.fr/en/le-monde-africa/article/2023/10/18/in-africa-governments-cut-back-on-fuel-subsidies_6183341_124.html.

35 UNCTAD, The Least Developed Countries Report 2022 – The Low-Carbon Transition and its Daunting Implications for Structural Transformation (2022), 69–70.

36 World Bank, 'State and Trends of Carbon Pricing 2023', May 2023, 31.

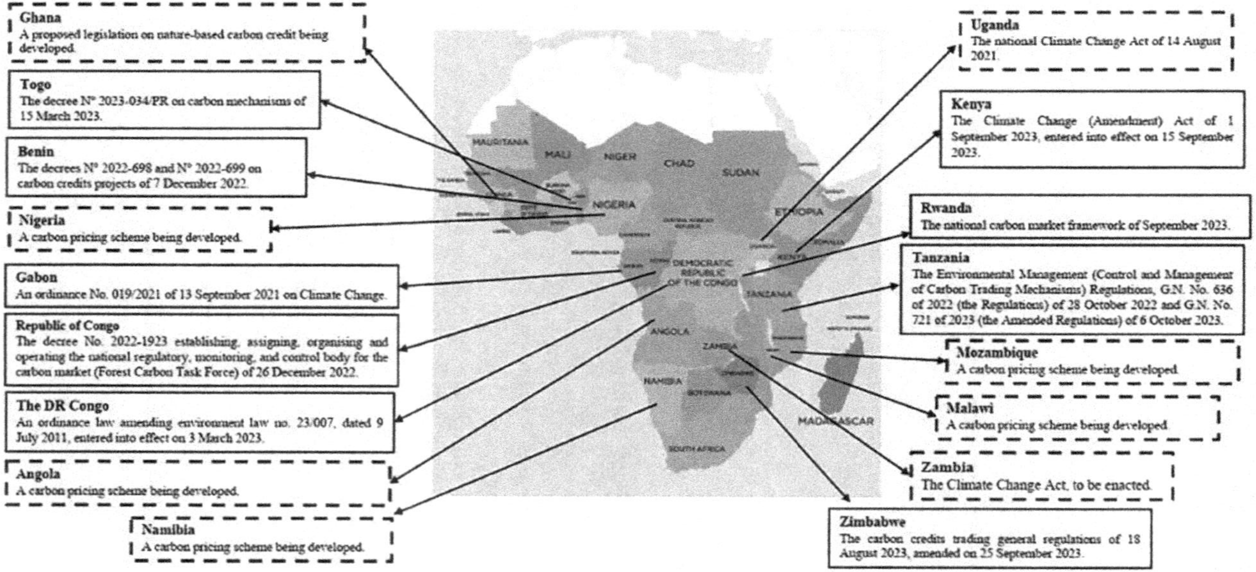

Source: Author, derived from a map from Jeanne Broad, Michigan Economic Development Corporation, 9 June 2016.

Figure 2.1 *A mosaic of nature-based carbon pricing schemes in SSA in 2024*

in Zimbabwe, in May 2023, the government initially announced a stringent revenue-sharing model for carbon credit projects. This model allocated 50% of the total revenue to the government, 30% to foreign investors, and 20% to small stakeholders. However, the carbon credits trading general regulations, released on 18 August 2023 and subsequently amended on 25 September 2023, set out more equitable revenue-sharing provisions.[37, 38] Non-sovereign project developers receive 70% of the revenue, with at least 25% assigned to local communities. The government receives 30% to be channelled into an environment fund. That revenue-sharing agreement showcases Zimbabwe's political will to become an attractive hotspot for trading carbon credits. In August 2023, this purpose was further emphasised by the launch of the Victoria Falls Carbon Registry (VFCR), a key component for establishing the Victoria Falls Stock Exchange (VFEX), which has a continental focus.[39]

In a nutshell, the African countries have attempted to provide a clear carbon credit trading roadmap to market participants through their legal and institutional frameworks. They have to keep improving their business climate to reassure non-sovereign developers and other market participants, while remaining committed to preserving and restoring NbS. In the meantime, they have to guarantee a fair distribution of carbon revenues to local communities and indigenous people to prevent exploitation. The precarious equilibrium is a prerequisite for expanding their tax bases to the nascent carbon credits industry in the race to net-zero.

3.2.2 The DR Congo pioneering a call for fair carbon pricing in the Global South

Amid growing challenges posed by carbon pricing, in 2021 the IMF proposed an international carbon price floor targeting large carbon-emitting countries and regions (the United States, the European Union, China, and India) to

---

[37] Zimbabwean Government Gazette Extraordinary, Statutory Instrument 150 of 2023 – Carbon Credits Trading (General) Regulations, August 18, 2023, 1021–1022, https://www.veritaszim.net/sites/veritas_d/files/SI%202023-150%20Carbon%20Credits%20Trading%20%28General%29%20Regulations%2C%202023.pdf.

[38] Zimbabwean Government Gazette Extraordinary, Statutory Instrument 150 of 2023 – The Carbon Credits Trading (General) (Amendment) Regulations, September 25, 2023, 1097–1098, https://archive.gazettes.africa/archive/zw/2023/zw-government-gazette-dated-2023-09-25-no-100.pdf.

[39] Vasil Velev, 'CTX Partners with Victoria Falls Carbon Registry and Exchange in Zimbabwe', *Carbon Herald*, July 14, 2023, https://carbonherald.com/ctx-partners-victoria-falls-carbon-registry-exchange-zimbabwe/.

limit global carbon emissions by 2030.[40] A price floor can be differentiated according to the development level, but it must rise to USD 75 per tonne by 2030. Price floor implementation also aims to avoid free-rider concerns and, as a result, carbon leakage. The IMF's proposal did not address the specific circumstances of developing and emerging countries that are rich in natural carbon storage solutions. Rather, it focused on carbon pricing as a global mitigation instrument. In 2021, Dalberg and the UN Economic Commission for Africa (UNECA) conducted a preliminary assessment using satellite data to outline the nature-based storage potential in African countries. It determined that the continent could meet up to 30% of the world's carbon sequestration needs by 2050.[41, 42]

Among the forested countries, the DR Congo has pioneered a singular position in the carbon credits sphere. On 3 March 2023, an ordinance law amending Environment Law No. 23/007, dated 9 July 2011, entered into effect. It aligned the Congolese legislation with the Paris Agreement. Among other issues, the law set up a national carbon credit framework comprising a carbon tax, a Carbon Market Regulatory Authority (ARMCA), and a national carbon credits registry.[43] Despite the ongoing development of its domestic carbon pricing framework, the DR Congo became the first Congo Basin country to advocate for fair carbon pricing for NbS at international fora, such as the Leaders' Summit on Climate held in April 2021. During the event, President Tshisekedi outlined that the price of nature-based carbon credits was estimated at only USD 5 per tonne for forest conservation. Hence, he called for increasing the carbon credits' price to at least USD 100 per tonne to ensure that ecosystem services delivered by NbS are taken into consideration. Referring to Dalberg and UNECA, African countries could raise significant carbon finance streams, ranging from USD 1 billion per year at a carbon price of USD 10 per tonne to

40 Ian Parry, Simon Black, and James Roaf, 'Proposal for an International Carbon Price Floor among Large Emitters', IMF Staff Climate Notes 2021/001 (IMF, 2021), 1–18, https://www.imf.org/en/Publications/staff-climate-notes/Issues/2021/06/15/Proposal-for-an-International-Carbon-Price-Floor-Among-Large-Emitters-460468.

41 Dalberg and UNECA, 'Climate Action Platform Africa', 2021, https://capa.earthrise.media/.

42 Independent High-Level Expert Group on Climate Finance, 'Finance for Climate Action – Scaling up Investment for Climate and Development', November 2022, 67, https://www.uncclearn.org/wp-content/uploads/library/b12021660.pdf.

43 Journal Officiel de la RDC, 'Ordonnance loi n° 23/007 du 3 mars 2023 modifiant et complétant la loi n° 11/009 du 9 juillet 2011 portant principes fondamentaux relatifs à la protection de l'environnement', 2023, https://medd.gouv.cd/wp-content/uploads/2023/05/Loi-sur-lenvironnement.pdf.

USD 82 billion per year at USD 120 per tonne.[44] Considering that a fair carbon price could be estimated at USD 50 per tonne, this implies that African countries could raise USD 15 billion per year, potentially generating over 30 million new jobs.[45] As a consequence, a fair price for nature-based carbon credits could incentivise environmental sustainability, thanks to critical investments in climate adaptation policies. It could also help increase DRM, which is a prerequisite for tackling poverty and inequality.

Finally, the DR Congo partnered with Brazil and Indonesia (G20 countries) to form a rainforest cartel, known as the 'OPEC of rainforests', at COP 27 in November 2022. The coalition concentrates the world's largest rainforests: the Congo Basin, the Amazon, and the forests of Borneo and Sumatra.[46] It could represent the world's largest suppliers of nature-based carbon credits.[47] This unique coalition constitutes a platform that could be extended to other forest-rich countries, as they have a similar agenda on the protection, restoration, and fair valuation of NbS. By presenting a united front, the Global South's forested countries might attempt to prevent the 'carbon credit curse' that has already emerged.

4. CONCLUSION AND POLICY RECOMMENDATIONS

The governments of African forested countries have an immense opportunity to generate sustainable carbon finance. However, given the scale of SSA, the production of nature-based carbon credits has entailed mounting concerns. To address the challenges ahead, African countries must invest in capacity building to fully capitalise on involvement in the carbon financing sphere and prevent the key side effects. Development partners, particularly the UN, might offer tailored support in three key areas:

---

[44] Vera Songwe and Jean-Paul Adam, Key to Climate Action – Chapter 9: 'Delivering Africa's Great Green Transformation', Brookings, working paper #180.9, February 2023, 6–7, https://www.brookings.edu/articles/delivering-africas-great-green-transformation/.

[45] Mo Ibrahim Foundation, 'The Road to COP27 – Making Africa's Case in the Climate Debate: Forum Report', July 2022, 84–85, https://mo.ibrahim.foundation/sites/default/files/2022-07/2022-forum-report.pdf.

[46] Patrick Greenfield, 'Brazil, Indonesia and DRC in Talks to Form OPEC of Rainforests', *The Guardian*, November 5, 2022, https://www.theguardian.com/environment/2022/nov/05/brazil-indonesia-drc-cop27-conservation-opec-rainforests-aoe.

[47] Henry Storey and Chuin Wei Yap, 'Shades of OPEC Loom over Global Carbon Market'. Hinrich Foundation, January 10, 2023, https://www.hinrichfoundation.com/research/article/sustainable/opec-global-carbon-market/.

- Designing effective and equitable carbon pricing schemes would involve helping countries take their first steps to establish legal and institutional environments, and even refining these environments for the countries already engaged in carbon pricing dynamics. The necessary legal and institutional frameworks would provide transparent and secure guidelines to all stakeholders, fostering conducive business climates in these countries. In 2021, the UN Tax Committee issued a practical guide on carbon taxation for governments and tax administrations,[48] while the United Nations Framework Convention on Climate Change (UNFCCC) set out the Collaborative Instruments for Ambitious Climate Action (Ci-ACA) initiative, launched at COP 22 in 2016. The initiative supported parties in developing carbon pricing instruments and operationalising Article 6, and was implemented in Ghana, Senegal, Cameroon, Nigeria, Guinea, and Guinea Bissau. It is set to expand to Benin, Gabon, and Togo. Better coordination within the UN System (UNS) would ensure more effective assistance to African countries participating or interested in carbon pricing activities, particularly in the context of the UN Tax Convention and the Fourth International Conference on Financing for Development.
- African forestry governance would be strengthened by extending the existing Illicit Financial Flows (IFFs) projects to the forestry sectors, for example the UN Development Account (DA) projects on measuring and curbing IFFs to ensure better DRM, jointly set up by the UNECA and other UN entities.[49] The IFFs resulting from environmental crimes, including illegal logging and timber trafficking, have entailed deforestation, forest degradation, and biodiversity loss, increasing GHG emissions. Implementing these projects would promote sustainable forest management and *de facto* help preserve African carbon sinks. This is of critical importance as carbon pricing must include environmental and biodiversity conservation efforts.
- Safeguarding the rights and livelihoods of local stakeholders should be prioritised while designing, implementing, and revising carbon pricing schemes. The social inclusivity of these schemes would acknowledge the critical role of local stakeholders in preserving African forestry sectors and their ecosystems, thereby preventing the detrimental risks of a 'carbon credit curse'. The use of NbS, a major climate change mitigation tool, should not entail climate injustice or exacerbate social tensions.

---

[48] UNDESA, 'UN Handbook on Carbon Taxation for Developing Countries', 2021, 1–244, https://financing.desa.un.org/document/un-handbook-carbon-taxation-developing-countries-2021.

[49] For further details on the IFFs projects funded by UN DA, a capacity development programme, please visit: https://da.desa.un.org/node/16216.

Ultimately, by opting for a variety of carbon pricing mechanisms, African forested countries can contribute to building climate-resilient and inclusive green African economies while mitigating any side effects.

REFERENCES

African Union. 'The African Leaders Nairobi Declaration on Climate Change and Call for Action', September 8, 2023. Available at: https://media.africaclimatesummit.org/Final+declaration+1709-English.pdf?request-content-type=%22application/force-download.

Belianska, Anna, Bohme, Nathalie, Cai, Kai, Diallo, Youssouf, Jain, Sajal, Melina, Grigory, Mitra, Prasenjit, Poplawski Ribeiro, Maria, and Zerbo, Seydou. 'Climate Change and Select Financial Instruments: An Overview of Opportunities and Challenges for Sub-Saharan Africa', *IMF Staff Climate Note* 2022/009. IMF. 2022. 1–41. Available at: https://doi.org/10.5089/9798400225208.066.

Blake, Heidi. 'The Great Cash-for-Carbon Hustle', *The New Yorker*, October 16, 2023. Available at: https://www.newyorker.com/magazine/2023/10/23/the-great-cash-for-carbon-hustle.

Bryan, Kenza. 'The Looming Land Grab in Africa for Carbon Credits', *Financial Times*, December 6, 2023. Available at: https://www.ft.com/content/f9bead69-7401-44fe-8db9-1c4063ae958c.

Dalberg and UNECA. 'Climate Action Platform Africa', 2021. https://capa.earthrise.media/.

de Vergès, Marie. 'In Africa, Governments Cut Back on Fuel Subsidies'. *Le Monde*, October 18, 2023. Available at: https://www.lemonde.fr/en/le-monde-africa/article/2023/10/18/in-africa-governments-cut-back-on-fuel-subsidies_6183341_124.html.

Ecosystem Marketplace. '2023 State of the Voluntary Carbon Markets Report', November 28, 2023. 1–28. Available at: https://www.ecosystemmarketplace.com/publications/state-of-the-voluntary-carbon-market-report-2023/.

FAO. Carbon Rights in the Context of Jurisdictional REDD+: Tenure Links and Country-based Legal Solutions – Information Brief. 2022. 1–18. Available at: https://doi.org/10.4060/cc2694en.

Farr, Esau E. 2023. 'Six Laws Blue Carbon Deal Would Violate Explained', *The DayLight*, July 30, 2023. Available at: https://thedaylight.org/2023/07/30/six-ways-blue-carbon-deal-would-be-illegal-explained/.

FERN. 'International Statement on the Carbon Deal between Blue Carbon and the Liberian Government', July 20, 2023. Available at: https://www.fern.org/fileadmin/uploads/fern/Documents/2023/International_Statement_on_the_Carbon_Deal_-_Carbon_Blue_and_Liberia.pdf.

Greenfield, Patrick. 'Brazil, Indonesia and DRC in Talks to Form OPEC of Rainforests', *The Guardian*, November 5, 2022. Available at: https://www.theguardian.com/environment/2022/nov/05/brazil-indonesia-drc-cop27-conservation-opec-rainforests-aoe.

Greenfield, Patrick. 'Revealed: More than 90% of Rainforest Carbon Offsets by Biggest Certifier Are Worthless, Analysis Shows', *The Guardian*, January 18, 2023. Available at: https://www.theguardian.com/environment/2023/jan/18/revealed-forest-carbon-offsets-biggest-provider-worthless-verra-aoe.

Gulf News Report. 'Blue Carbon and the Government of Tanzania Join Forces to Accelerate Transition to Low-Carbon Economy', February 7, 2023. Available at:

https://gulfnews.com/business/corporate-news/blue-carbon-and-the-government-of-tanzania-join-forces-to-accelerate-transition-to-low-carbon-economy-1.1675752836855.

Gulf News Report. 'Blue Carbon and Government of Zambia Sign MoU to Unlock the Potential of Carbon Removal Projects', February 8, 2023. Available at: https://gulfnews.com/business/corporate-news/blue-carbon-and-government-of-zambia-sign-mou-to-unlock-the-potential-of-carbon-removal-projects-1.1675850886963.

Independent High-Level Expert Group on Climate Finance. 'Finance for Climate Action – Scaling Up Investment for Climate and Development', November 2022, 1–98. Available at: https://www.uncclearn.org/wp-content/uploads/library/b12021660.pdf.

Journal Officiel de la RDC. 'Ordonnance loi n° 23/007 du 3 mars 2023 modifiant et complétant la loi n° 11/009 du 9 juillet 2011 portant principes fondamentaux relatifs à la protection de l'environnement', 2023. Available at: https://medd.gouv.cd/wp-content/uploads/2023/05/Loi-sur-lenvironnement.pdf.

Lee, Donna, Llopis, Pablo, Waterworth, Rob, Roberts, Geoff, and Pearson, Tim. 'Approaches to REDD+ Nesting – Lessons Learned from Country Experiences', World Bank, April 2018, 1–33. Available at: https://documents1.worldbank.org/curated/en/670171523647847532/pdf/Main-report.pdf.

Mo Ibrahim Foundation. 'The Road to COP27 – Making Africa's Case in the Climate Debate: Facts and Figures', May 2022, 1–64. Available at: https://mo.ibrahim.foundation/sites/default/files/2022-05/2022-Ibrahim-Forum_Facts-Figures.pdf.

Mo Ibrahim Foundation. 'The Road to COP27 – Making Africa's Case in the Climate Debate: Forum Report', July 2022, 1–140. Available at: https://mo.ibrahim.foundation/sites/default/files/2022-07/2022-forum-report.pdf.

Newsfile. 'Government of Kenya Accelerates Towards Compliance Market with UAE's Blue Carbon under Article 6', October 25, 2023. Available at: https://www.newsfilecorp.com/release/185173.

Nkwetta Ajong, Aquilas, Kechia Mukong, Alfred, Ndzifon Kimengsi, Jude, and Ngangnchi, Forbe Hodu. 'Economic Activities and Deforestation in the Congo Basin: An Environmental Kuznets Curve Framework Analysis', *Environmental Challenges*, vol. 8. 2022. Available at: https://doi.org/10.1016/j.envc.2022.100553.

SourceMaterial. Scramble for Africa – Inside Carbon Offsetting's Megadeal, November 29, 2023. Available at: https://www.source-material.org/dubai-uae-cop28-blue-carbon-offsetting-forest-liberia/.

Parry, Ian, Black, Simon, and Roaf, James. 'Proposal for an International Carbon Price Floor among Large Emitters', IMF Staff Climate Notes 2021/001, IMF, 2021, 1–18. Available at: https://www.imf.org/en/Publications/staff-climate-notes/Issues/2021/06/15/Proposal-for-an-International-Carbon-Price-Floor-Among-Large-Emitters-460468.

Songwe, Vera, and Adam, Jean-Paul. Key to Climate Action – Chapter 9: 'Delivering Africa's Great Green Transformation', Brookings, working paper #180.9, February 2023, 1–30. Available at: https://www.brookings.edu/articles/delivering-africas-great-green-transformation/.

Storey, Henry, and Wei Yap, Chuin. 'Shades of OPEC Loom over Global Carbon Market', Hinrich Foundation, January 10, 2023. Available at: https://www.hinrichfoundation.com/research/article/sustainable/opec-global-carbon-market/.

UNCTAD. 'Economic Development in Africa Report – The Potential of Africa to Capture Technology-Intensive Global Supply Chains', 2023, 1–217. Available at: https://unctad.org/publication/economic-development-africa-report-2023.

UNCTAD. 'The Least Developed Countries Report 2022 – The Low-Carbon Transition and Its Daunting Implications for Structural Transformation', 2022, 1–119. Available at: https://unctad.org/publication/least-developed-countries-report-2022.

UNDESA. 'UN Handbook on Carbon Taxation for Developing Countries', 2021, 1–244. Available at: https://financing.desa.un.org/document/un-handbook-carbon-taxation-developing-countries-2021.

UNECA. 'Zambia and DRC Sign Cooperation Agreement to Manufacture Electric Batteries', Press release, April 29, 2022. Available at: https://www.uneca.org/stories/zambia-and-drc-sign-cooperation-agreement-to-manufacture-electric-batteries.

UN-REDD Programme. 'Forest Solutions to the Climate Emergency – A Case for Support for the UN-REDD Programme', 2022, 1–10. Available at: https://www.un-redd.org/sites/default/files/2022-10/UN-REDD%20Case%20for%20Support%20flyer%202022.pdf.

Velev, Vasil. 'CTX Partners with Victoria Falls Carbon Registry and Exchange in Zimbabwe', *Carbon Herald*, July 14, 2023. Available at: https://carbonherald.com/ctx-partners-victoria-falls-carbon-registry-exchange-zimbabwe/.

World Bank. 'State and Trends of Carbon Pricing 2018', May 2018, 1–62. Available at: https://documents1.worldbank.org/curated/en/480621554812881664/pdf/State-and-Trends-of-Carbon-Pricing-2018.pdf.

World Bank. 'State and Trends of Carbon Pricing 2023', May 2023, 1–78. Available at: http://hdl.handle.net/10986/39796.

World Bank. 'State and Trends of Carbon Pricing 2024', May 21, 2024, 1–76. Available at: https://hdl.handle.net/10986/41544.

World Bank. 'World Development Indicators', January 24, 2024. Available at: https://data.worldbank.org/indicator/AG.LND.FRST.ZS?locations=ZG.

Zenda, Cyril. 'Doubts Grow over Who'll Benefit from UAE Carbon Deal for Fifth of Zimbabwe', *African Arguments*, October 31, 2023. Available at: https://africanarguments.org/2023/10/doubts-rise-over-who-benefit-from-uae-firm-deal-for-a-fifth-of-zimbabwe/.

Zimbabwean Government Gazette Extraordinary. Statutory Instrument 150 of 2023 – Carbon Credits Trading (General) Regulations, August 18, 2023, 1021–1022. Available at: https://www.veritaszim.net/sites/veritas_d/files/SI%202023-150%20Carbon%20Credits%20Trading%20%28General%29%20Regulations%2C%202023.pdf.

Zimbabwean Government Gazette Extraordinary. Statutory Instrument 150 of 2023 – The Carbon Credits Trading (General) (Amendment) Regulations, September 25, 2023. 1097–1098. Available at: https://archive.gazettes.africa/archive/zw/2023/zw-government-gazette-dated-2023-09-25-no-100.pdf.

3. Accounting for the views of corporate stakeholders on climate risk governance in South Africa

Malebusetsa Jessica Matela, Peter Jarvis and Nadia Mans-Kemp

1. INTRODUCTION

Climate change is attracting considerable interest as stakeholders' awareness of this phenomenon grows. Communities around the world are experiencing the detrimental effects of global warming. The United Nations (UN) has consequently recognised climate change as the main human development challenge of the 21st century.[1]

Climate change is defined in the United Nations Framework Convention on Climate Change (UNFCCC) as "a change of climate which is attributed directly or indirectly to human activity that alters the composition of the global atmosphere and which is in addition to natural climate variability observed over comparable time periods".[2] Climate change thus relates to changes in land and ocean temperature due to human activity.

In 2015, the UN adopted the 2030 Agenda for Sustainable Development, which aims to reinforce peace and prosperity for humans and the planet. The 17 Sustainable Development Goals (SDGs) are at the core of this agenda. To combat climate change, the UN members agreed on SDG 13, which aims to "take urgent action to combat climate change and its impacts".[3] Combatting climate change could also reinforce several other SDGs, particularly those related to inequality.[4]

As climate change risks are ever-increasing, sustainable corporate practices are of the utmost importance. Weather-related problems, such as fires, droughts, and severe storms ultimately have negative implications for organisations operating in diverse industries.[5] Furthermore, as the environmental awareness of corporate leaders increases, green innovation can be enhanced.[6]

In turn, a growing number of stakeholders globally are pressuring corporate leaders to reflect on their climate-related policies and practices.[7]

Yet, climate change studies have largely been conducted in developed countries and centred on environmental policies, measurement, and reporting on climate action.[8] The UN's expectation that companies should commit to sustainable activities has furthermore highlighted the significance of sound climate governance. South Africa is a corporate governance frontrunner as guidance on risk management has been offered to companies since the 1990s, and, more recently, on climate change. In 2021, the Institute of Directors in South Africa (IoDSA) published a guidance paper to assist corporate leaders in responding to climate change by enhancing their understanding of its implications for a range of stakeholders.[9] The possible severe consequences of taking a no-action climate response are outlined, including high carbon taxes and legal action.[10] Carbon tax was introduced in a phased approach in the country in 2019 to facilitate the transition to net zero emissions.[11]

Strong internal governance is furthermore essential to ensure that companies adapt and respond to swiftly changing environmental conditions. In turn, engagements with corporate stakeholders can assist directors in formulating climate change mitigation and adaptation strategies. Mitigation entails reducing greenhouse gas (GHG) emissions through a variety of strategies, such as the promotion of renewable energy and sustainable transportation systems. Adaptation considers anticipating and responding to the effects of climate change. This involves the creation of early warning systems, promoting climate-resilient agriculture, and enhancing water resource management.[12] This approach is crucial to achieving a just energy transition in South Africa. Given the country's substantive environmental and socio-economic challenges, it is essential to create a fairer and more equitable low-carbon economy.

According to Haque and Islam, more research is required on how stakeholders can impact climate change practices and accountability.[13] The primary objective of this exploratory investigation was thus to gauge the views of various corporate stakeholders on climate risk governance in South Africa, including directors, board committee members, and legal and sustainability experts. Related challenges and opportunities were furthermore explored in this highly unequal country[14] that is also Africa's largest carbon dioxide (CO2) emitter.[15] South Africa relies heavily on coal and recently experienced a severe energy crisis.[16] The findings of this study contribute to ensuring a more sustainable and resilient future for corporate stakeholders operating in a highly unequal country. Potential avenues will be highlighted to pave the way for more effective climate action to ultimately enhance climate resilience.

2. ESCALATING NEED TO TAKE CLIMATE ACTION

Sustainability is a multifaceted concept that encompasses a range of environmental, social, and governance (ESG) considerations. In the context of environmental sustainability, focus is placed on the ability of society to use natural resources in a way that does not compromise the ability of future generations to meet their needs.[17] Considerations related to profit, people, and the planet should hence be optimally balanced to create a harmonious relationship between humans and the natural environment. Sustainable practices must thus be integrated into all aspects of society, including business, government, and individual behaviour.[18]

Over the past 50 years, climate change experts and scientists have warned humanity that the use of fossil fuels is causing the Earth's climate to change considerably. They have cautioned against the devastating consequences if humanity does not take action to combat climate change.[19] Despite this outcry, CO2 emissions continue to increase. The harmful outcomes include a disconcerting rise in the Earth's average surface temperature and extreme weather conditions.[20]

Global warming is consequently resulting in the melting of polar ice caps, reducing potable water, increasing food insecurity, and rising sea levels.[21] The World Economic Forum (WEF) aptly highlights that the lack of climate change adaptation, increasing levels of GHG emissions, and food and water insecurity are key climate risks that decision-makers should consider.[22] Global warming evidently requires urgent attention, including initiatives to limit the release of CO2 in the atmosphere and the increased use of clean energy.[23]

The negative impacts of climate change are typically more severe in poorer and hotter countries.[24] Huckelba and Van Lange also indicated that humans with the most limited economic and social resources are the most likely to be negatively impacted by climate change, as they often do not have access to disaster relief.[25] As such, it is essential to account for effective climate risk governance and the related implications for stakeholders, especially in countries with high inequality.

3. DELINEATING CLIMATE RISK GOVERNANCE

Climate risk governance refers to the processes and rules that a company puts in place to manage the risks and opportunities related to climate change. The WEF released eight principles to guide climate governance globally, including climate accountability on boards, material risk and opportunity assessment, reporting, and disclosure.[26]

In turn, climate risk management encompasses the activities of identifying, evaluating, and mitigating the risks that climate change presents.[27] This process involves understanding the potential impacts of climate change on a company's assets, operations, and supply chain and developing strategies to mitigate these risks.[28] Therefore, corporate governance policies must be adapted to address climate change and related risks while considering the interests of key stakeholders and utilising related opportunities.

Corporate leaders can take several steps to address climate change, including setting emissions reduction targets, investing in renewable energy, and reporting on sustainability outcomes.[29] By taking these steps, directors can ensure that their organisations are committed to addressing climate change and contributing to a more sustainable future.[30] A key consideration of climate risk assessment is to identify the physical risks that climate change poses to a company. The financial implications of transitioning to a low-carbon economy, changes in consumer behaviour, and changes in government policies should also be considered.[31]

Ben-Amar and McIlkenny reported a link between a board's effectiveness and voluntary disclosure of climate change information.[32] Liao, Luo, and Tang furthermore noted that companies with environmentally-focused board committee members and more independent non-executive directors are more likely to disclose information on their GHG emissions.[33] Aguilera, Aragón-Correa, Marano, and Tashman confirmed that management scholars increasingly focus on how directors drive environmental initiatives.[34] Furthermore, stakeholders demand disclosure of measurable climate change outcomes to enable them to understand the impacts thereof.[35]

Following the release of the WEF's eight guiding principles,[36] the IoDSA published a guidance paper on climate change for directors operating in South Africa.[37] This guidance paper assists local governing bodies in conceptualising the impacts of climate change by accounting for their unique contexts. Boards should accordingly prioritise climate change as a strategic issue and integrate it into their risk management frameworks. This process involves identifying and assessing material climate risks, as well as developing strategies to mitigate such risks. Climate-related disclosures should furthermore be accurate, transparent, and in line with international reporting standards.[38] Standard 2 of the International Financial Reporting Standards (IFRS) centres on climate-related risks and opportunities.[39] IFRS S2 thus requires detailed reporting on GHG emissions, related targets, and the use of carbon credits.

The King IV Report on corporate governance emphasises that corporate leaders should consider diverse stakeholders' interests when reflecting on financial and sustainability issues.[40] Stakeholders include groups and individuals who are interested in and/or affected by a company, including investors, customers, suppliers, employees, and communities.[41]

Corporate stakeholders have a particular interest in a company's success. The stakeholder theory was hence applied in this study, as it implies that business leaders should consider corporate stakeholders' divergent interests when making decisions related to climate change, including setting emissions reduction targets and investing in renewable energy. Stakeholders thus have the potential to shape corporate approaches to embrace more environmentally conscious practices and technologies.

4. OUTLINING THE METHODOLOGY

Given the potential impact of diverse stakeholders on shaping environmental policies and corporate behaviour, it is crucial to comprehend the insights of corporate stakeholders on climate risk governance in South Africa, Africa's largest CO2 emitter.[42] Semi-structured interviews were conducted with directors and board committee members, as well as legal and sustainability experts serving selected local organisations.

The interview guide included background questions related to the interviewees in Section 1. Climate risk governance considerations were covered in Section 2, including initiatives to mitigate climate risks and identify related opportunities. The interview questions were based on relevant literature and the practical climate governance guidelines provided by the UN to achieve SDG 13, the IoDSA,[43] and the WEF.[44] The questions related to key climate change considerations based on the interviewees' lived experiences and their perceptions of the usefulness of the IoDSA's guidance paper on climate change, the prioritisation of the UN's proposed climate change actions, and the incorporation of the WEF's climate governance principles. Their views on opportunities to enhance climate risk governance in the future were also explored.

Following a discussion with a local climate change expert, the key role of financial services institutions in addressing climate issues was highlighted. This expert indicated that financial services institutions should pay closer attention to their readiness to account for the financial impact of climate change. As such, interviews were conducted with several directors and members of board committees of selected South African-based financial services companies.

Furthermore, a voluntary alliance that works towards promoting sustainable development and growth in South Africa, a local shareholder activism organisation, and representatives of several institutional investor organisations advised the researchers to also conduct interviews with legal and sustainability experts to gauge their views on climate risk governance in the country. They were described as key corporate stakeholders given their advisory roles on pressing sustainability matters, in particular climate governance in the case of this study. Snowball sampling was hence utilised to conduct interviews with 12 participants (see Table 3.1).

Table 3.1 Demographic overview of the participants

Participant	Job description	Qualification(s) declared by the interviewees	Experience
A	Senior stewardship professional	Masters in Finance; Honours in Economics and Environmental Science	11 years
B	Chief Investment Officer	Honours in Investment Management; Bachelor of Commerce degree	34 years
C	Director	Masters in Environmental Management; Honours degree in Biochemistry	15 years
D	Director	Post-graduate qualification in Environmental Economics; Engineering degree	19 years
E	Senior climate risk analyst	Doctorate degree in Geography	12 years
F	Founder of a sustainability consultancy firm	Masters degrees in Law and Sustainability Leadership	18 years
G	Candidate attorney; head of secretariat (focus on sustainability and risk management)	Masters in Finance	8 years
H	Certified renewable energy project developer	Engineering degrees	>10 years
I	Chief executive officer; corporate governance consultant	MSc in Quantitative Resource Ecology	>10 years
J	Sustainability consultant; Certified director	Bachelor of Laws and Arts degrees	21 years
K	ESG consultant	Masters degrees in Sustainable Development and Management Planning	7 years
L	Investment analyst (focus on the energy sector)	Chartered Financial Analyst; Bachelor of Science in Finance degree	10 years

Source: Compiled by the researchers based on the information provided by the interviewees.

Table 3.1 indicates that interviews were conducted with experienced individuals who had substantive knowledge of risk management, climate change, and other sustainability considerations. The diverse group of participants held a wide range of qualifications and fulfilled several corporate roles. We would like to thank them for sharing their unique perspectives on climate risk governance and the related challenges and opportunities in South Africa.

Thematic analysis was conducted on the transcribed interviews by following the six-step approach outlined by Braun and Clarke.[45] During Step 1, the transcriptions were read multiple times and notes were made, after which initial codes were generated (Step 2). Step 3 entailed searching for themes, at which point the potential themes were reviewed (Step 4). The themes were then finalised (Step 5), and the findings were reported (Step 6).

To enhance the study's transferability, close attention was paid to what was being said by each of the interviewees based on their lived experiences.[46] Direct quotations were included where applicable in the findings section to enhance confirmability. Informed consent was obtained before conducting the interviews. The identities of the individuals will be protected by using pseudonyms in the subsequent findings section.

5. FINDINGS AND DISCUSSION

Five main themes emerged from the thematic analysis, namely key concerns related to climate change, implications for divergent stakeholders, the need for enhanced climate governance and reporting, incentivising directors to achieve SDG 13, and utilising climate-related opportunities.

5.1 Key Concerns Related to Climate Change

Several interviewees believed that global warming is having a detrimental impact. Specific reference was made to the severe implications for the agricultural sector, which have ripple effects for logistics service providers and insurers. The country's vulnerability to severe weather events like droughts and floods thus makes climate adaptation crucial. Malhi, Kaur, and Kaushik confirmed the severe impact of climate change on agriculture.[47]

Food insecurity arising from climate change was also highlighted. Participant A cautioned that if this issue is not addressed in a timely fashion, the country will "become a non-investable destination". Onyutha likewise remarked that Africans experience very devastating impacts of climate change which exacerbate food insecurity and poverty.[48] As such, poverty alleviation should be prioritised when deriving adaptation strategies.

Interviewee D stated that "people do not go hungry in peace", thereby highlighting food security concerns. This participant explained that the negative impacts of climate change on food, water, and infrastructure are contributing to widening inequality in the country. Levy and Patz concurred that the environmental and health-related consequences of climate change pose a substantial threat to social rights, including access to safe food.[49]

The interviewees also commented on the potential corporate reputational risk related to climate change. Participant L mentioned that the risk profiles of companies that are heavy polluters are impacted due to backlash from the community, protests, and regulatory actions. In turn, operational challenges and related costs escalate. Yet, the participants mentioned that several local businesses seemed not to take this risk as seriously as their global counterparts. Interviewee C mentioned that "the risk that a company has on the climate versus the risk that the climate has on a company is not fully understood within [local] companies right now.

The Task Force on Climate-Related Financial Disclosures confirms that climate change is a potential source of reputational risk for companies arising from customers' perceptions of corporate attempts (or the lack thereof) to lower carbon emissions.[50] Researchers agree that failure to address risks related to climate change could lead to reputational damage and substantial difficulties in attracting customers and employees.[51]

Reference was also made to energy provision challenges in South Africa and the urgency of a just energy transition. Interviewee F stated that "people are absolutely fed up with load shedding. So even though people might not care too much about their carbon footprints, they care about having electricity". Load shedding entails the planned periodic interruption of electricity supply to avoid an excessive load on the energy provider. In light of the energy crisis, South Africa is making slow progress in adopting green energy.[52]

Several participants indicated that more focus should be placed on GHG reduction. Participant A cautioned that there is a very narrow window of opportunity to decrease emissions to avoid disastrous consequences for society at large. The Institute of Risk Management South Africa confirmed the urgency of mitigation and adaptation strategies given that the country is Africa's highest GHG emitter.[53] In light of these concerns, the interviewees emphasised the importance of efficient climate risk management. They urged companies to incorporate climate change considerations into their strategies to ultimately enhance climate resilience.

5.2 Accounting for the Implications of Climate Change for Divergent Stakeholders

The interviewees recognised that the implications of climate change vary considerably depending on the stakeholder groups and individuals under consideration. They agreed that the negative impacts fall disproportionately on certain stakeholders, especially the most vulnerable members of society. Interviewee A ascribed this tendency to the country's socio-economic context, including a high unemployment rate. Levy and Patz likewise noted that the consequences of climate change affect low-income countries disproportionately more, which has profound implications for human rights and social justice.[54]

Interviewee G explained that "those lower down the [societal] hierarchy will be most affected simply because they have fewer chances to reduce those risks. And especially in South Africa, this leads to significant vulnerabilities". Another participant added that "unfortunately, the impacts of climate change affect the poorest of the poor, riddled with unemployment".

Islam and Winkel confirmed that individuals with precarious employment and those who lack insurance or are dependent on government assistance are particularly susceptible to the adverse effects of climate change.[55] Marginalised population members are furthermore most vulnerable to the adverse effects of inadequate mitigation policies.[56] It was hence disconcerting to note that some participants deemed the government's efforts to address climate challenges to be ineffective.

Specific attention should consequently be given to the implications of climate change for the most vulnerable individuals and groups. In line with the stakeholder theory, corporate leaders who adopt a stakeholder-centric decision-making approach are likely to be more inclined to prioritise sustainability considerations and adopt a longer-term perspective.[57] Corporate stakeholders, including members of marginalised communities, should thus be consulted by governments and organisations when reflecting on climate risk governance endeavours and the potential outcomes.[58] Interviewee D indicated that if stakeholders obtain a better understanding of climate change, they can more effectively contribute to realising positive change.

5.3 Enhanced Climate Governance and Reporting

As corporate stakeholders are increasingly requesting more detailed information on climate strategies and the related outcomes, participant C believed that they are "driving companies into action". Other participants underscored the significance of public policy in driving change and fostering accountability for corporate sustainability. Participants C and D remarked that the government and the private sector should ideally closely collaborate to address climate change issues. They furthermore highlighted the importance of communication between the public and private spheres to enhance climate governance and encourage attempts to collectively mitigate climate risks.

Although several participants commended the climate change guidance provided by the IoDSA, the lack of enforcement thereof was deemed problematic.[59] Some interviewees were not even aware of this guidance paper, while others questioned whether it was actually used in practice. These participants were of the view that tax incentives rather encourage corporate leaders to place focus on SDG 13 and the related shift to clean energy. Participant H explained that environmental regulation entails both rewards (carrots) and consequences (sticks) to encourage companies to address climate challenges: "The carbon tax is a stick … and the tax incentives will be the carrot."

Yet, some participants raised concerns about unstandardised disclosures on carbon emissions and the potential manipulation of sustainability reporting. Interviewee B alluded to greenwashing, whereby companies could use communication and marketing to mislead shareholders on environmental practices.[60] The importance of reliable reporting and assurance mechanisms was hence highlighted to counteract potential greenwashing while concurrently fostering stakeholder trust.

The interviewees acknowledged that sustainability frameworks are complex, and that global frameworks might not curb reporting issues and the perceived lack of transparency at some local companies. Participant I thus highlighted the need for better alignment between global guidance and local actions.

The interviewees furthermore mentioned that it is challenging to quantify climate outcomes and ensure the accuracy of qualitative information. If stakeholders can obtain a more comprehensive understanding of the financial impacts of climate-related actions, their enhanced involvement in overseeing corporate climate efforts is likely to compel companies to be more transparent.[61]

The participants also expressed concerns about the transparency of measurements, inter alia, related to who regulates the measurements and whether these regulators are professionally verified. Interviewee A thus valued the recommendation of the IoDSA that assurance should be provided on organisations' responses to climate change.[62] Participant J added that "assurance is critical to encourage companies to report on substance".

5.4 Incentivising Directors to Achieve SDG 13

Companies that are operating in developed economies are increasingly linking their directors' incentives to climate metrics.[63] Yet, the participants disagreed on whether directors should be incentivised to prioritise sustainable practices in the local context. Interviewee C stated that "the only way forward" is to link climate change initiatives to executive incentives. This participant observed that when targets were put in place, they drove change, and the applicable companies more closely tracked the outcomes of their climate change objectives. Participant J agreed by stating that "certainly, when it comes to executive pay ... it should be connected to their compensation just like any corporate strategic goal".

However, Interviewee B cautioned that "if you use director remuneration for climate change, you get a bunch of stuff being bought that is already clean and green, that doesn't change any of the behaviour". This participant also warned against directors attempting to "tick the required boxes" to ensure that ESG metrics and climate change initiatives are perceived in a positive light merely to obtain the associated incentives.

Interviewee B hence emphasised that the word "change" is of the utmost importance when linking directors' incentives to ESG metrics and specific SDGs. Due attention should accordingly be given to timelines when reflecting on incentives. The following related example was provided by Participant D: If a company states that they want to reach net zero carbon emissions by 2050 (linked to SDG 13), but some of their directors would retire well before 2050, these directors might not be focused on the required long-term changes to achieve this SDG. As such, incentives must be carefully designed to encourage directors to reach measurable objectives over the short, medium, and long-term.

5.5 Utilising Climate-related Opportunities

The participants emphasised the importance of recognising and utilising the opportunities that climate change presents, particularly investments in renewable energy. In the context of a just energy transition, various references were made to mining and energy companies that embraced renewable energy sources to mitigate carbon emissions and abate climate-related vulnerabilities. Research confirms that by switching to renewable energy sources, companies could considerably reduce GHG emissions, enhance energy efficiency, and obtain independence from fluctuating fossil fuel prices.[64]

Green financing is also gaining prominence. Participant K mentioned that the potential is "absolutely endless … left, right and centre in the financial sector". Examples of green bonds and ESG-linked bonds were provided by some participants. Ngwenya and Simatele confirmed that South Africa has been actively engaging in the green bond market, with a focus on renewable energy projects.[65] Yet, Participant B was sceptical that companies might use renewable energy opportunities to seem sustainable by means of "the marketing angle of it, and not for the reality of it". This participant hence emphasised that the benefits should be measurable to hold companies accountable.

Some participants furthermore referred to the benefits of appointing sustainability and legal experts on governing bodies and sustainability committees to drive climate initiatives and contribute to securing a more sustainable and equitable future. Aguilera et al. confirmed that sustainability experts can play a key role in ensuring that corporate leaders place focus on environmental outcomes.[66]

6. CONCLUSION AND RECOMMENDATIONS

Climate change is a pressing issue that is substantiated by disconcerting evidence of the detrimental impact of human activities on the environment. South Africa is Africa's largest CO2 emitter. Advancing a just energy transition implies that the local government should curb its reliance on coal while tackling escalating income inequality. Semi-structured interviews were hence conducted with selected corporate stakeholders in South Africa to gauge their views on climate risk governance in the country and explore related risks and opportunities.

The interviewees highlighted several pressing climate change concerns, including food security and operational and supply chain disruptions due to extreme weather conditions. Companies could also be at risk of reputational damages related to climate change actions (or the lack thereof), which could impact their ability to attract customers and employees. Effective climate risk governance was hence deemed essential.

The participants explained that sectors that are heavily reliant on natural resources are particularly susceptible to climate change. Adaptation and mitigation strategies should therefore be derived based on sector- and company-specific considerations. Mitigation efforts should focus on curbing GHG emissions and promoting the use of renewable energy.

Furthermore, climate change disproportionately affects stakeholders. The participants remarked that the most vulnerable stakeholders often have limited capacity to mitigate climate risks. Boards and governments are hence urged to actively involve stakeholders, including community members to account for their concerns and expectations when establishing and refining climate policies.

The thematic findings also underscored the pressing need for corporate strategies to align with established international frameworks and local standards to effectively manage climate risks and enhance green reporting. This integration is crucial for enhancing climate resilience. Yet, the interviewees disagreed on whether directors should be incentivised to achieve SDG 13. As executives are typically responsible for executing strategies and monitoring risks related to climate change, they might be encouraged to place more focus on SDG 13 if their incentives are linked to climate action initiatives over the short, medium, and long-term.

Directors are urged to stay abreast of global and local climate governance guidance and reporting standards. Shareholders are furthermore encouraged to engage with investee companies to enquire about their climate governance endeavours and encourage enhanced transparency. Institutional investors can play a pivotal role in promoting climate-conscious practices and renewable energy investments.

Based on the findings, audit and risk committee members should ideally be assisted by sustainability committee members to actively prioritise climate assessment, mitigation, and adaptation. Sustainability consultants can assist corporate leaders in deriving and refining policies in this regard. They can also provide advice to the remuneration committee on suitable incentives and applicable time frames to encourage directors to reach measurable climate objectives.

The reported findings were based on semi-structured interviews conducted with a limited number of corporate stakeholders in South Africa. Regarding suggestions for future research, quantitative data could be collected to complement the reported qualitative insights by distributing surveys to corporate stakeholders in several emerging markets. Survey questions could cover key aspects to quantify corporate climate change efforts, including emissions reduction targets, renewable energy adoption, resource efficiency improvements, and investments in clean technologies. In-depth case studies could furthermore be conducted to better understand context-specific climate-risk governance policies and practices.

Based on the discussed findings, corporate leaders are urged to acknowledge that climate change is not just an environmental concern but a fundamental risk. Climate change can substantially impact corporate reputation and the livelihoods of the most vulnerable society members. More should be done to achieve a just energy transition in South Africa, thereby concurrently addressing pressing inequality and climate change concerns.

NOTES

1. Davis-Reddy, C.L. & Vincent, K. 2017. *Climate Risk and Vulnerability: A Handbook for Southern* Africa. 2nd ed. Pretoria: Council for Scientific and Industrial Research.
2. United Nations (UN). 1992. *United Nations Framework Convention on Climate Change*. Available: https://unfccc.int/files/essential_background/background_publications_htmlpdf/application/pdf/conveng.pdf [2024, August 14].
3. United Nations (UN). 2024. *The Sustainable Development Agenda*. Available: https://www.un.org/sustainabledevelopment/development-agenda/ [2024, August 14].
4. Markkanen, S. & Anger-Kraavi, A. 2019. Social impacts of climate change mitigation policies and their implications for inequality. *Climate Policy*, 19(7): 827–844.
5. Sullivan, R. 2017. *Corporate Responses to Climate Change: Achieving Emissions Reductions Through Regulation, Self-regulation and Economic Incentives*. New York: Greenleaf Publishing.

6. Tan, Y. & Zhu, Z. 2022. The effect of ESG rating events on corporate green innovation in China: The mediating role of financial constraints and managers' environmental awareness. *Technology in Society*, 68. https://doi.org/10.1016/j.techsoc.2022.101906
7. Haque S. & Islam, M.A. 2015. Stakeholder pressures on corporate climate change-related accountability and disclosures: Australian evidence. *Business and Politics*, 17(2): 355–390.
8. Dahlmann, F., Branicki, L. & Brammer, S. 2019. Managing carbon aspirations: The influence of corporate climate change targets on environmental performance. *Journal of Business Ethics*, 158: 1–24. https://doi.org/10.1007/s10551-017-3731-z
9. Institute of Directors in South Africa (IoDSA). 2021. *Guidance Paper: Responsibilities of Governing Bodies in Responding to Climate Change.* Available: https://www.iodsa.co.za/page/king-iv-practice-and-guidance-notes [2023, February 8].
10. *Id.*
11. Loewald, C. 2024. *South African Reserve Bank Occasional Bulletin of Economic Notes*, April. Available: https://www.resbank.co.za/content/dam/sarb/publications/special-occasional-bulletins/2024/special-occasional-bulletin-of-economic-notes-2401-contents-february-2024-combined.pdf [2024, August 8].
12. United Nations Framework Convention on Climate Change (UNFCCC). 2015. *Adaptation and Resilience: The Big Picture. Introduction.* Available: https://unfccc.int/topics/adaptation-and-resilience/the-big-picture/introduction [2023, February 9].
13. Haque S. & Islam, M.A. 2015. Stakeholder pressures on corporate climate change-related accountability and disclosures: Australian evidence. *Business and Politics*, 17(2): 355–390.
14. The World Bank. 2022. New World Bank report assesses sources of inequality in five countries in Southern Africa. Available: https://www.worldbank.org/en/news/press-release/2022/03/09/new-world-bank-report-assesses-sources-of-inequality-in-five-countries-in-southern-africa [2024, August 14].
15. International Energy Agency. 2024. How much CO2 does South Africa emit? Available: https://www.iea.org/countries/south-africa/emissions [2024, August 14].
16. Hanto, J., Schroth, A., Krawielicki, L., Oei, P.Y. & Burton, J. 2022. South Africa's energy transition – unraveling its political economy. *Energy for Sustainable Development*, 69: 164–178.
17. United Nations (UN). 2023. *Climate Action.* Available: https://www.un.org/en/climatechange/paris-agreement [2023, February 9].
18. Purvis, B., Mao, Y. & Robinson, D. 2019. Three pillars of sustainability: In search of conceptual origins. *Sustainability Science*, 14(3): 681–695.
19. Hornsey, M.J. & Fielding, K.S. 2020. Understanding (and reducing) inaction on climate change. *Social Issues and Policy Review*, 14(1): 3–35.

20. National Aeronautics and Space Administration. 2023. *Global Temperature.* Available: https://climate.nasa.gov/vital-signs/global-temperature/?intent=121 [2024, August 14].
21. Jan, M., Kakakhel, S., Batool, S., Muazim, K. & Chatha, I. 2017. Global warming: Evidence, causes, consequences and mitigation. *Journal of Development Policy, Research & Practice*, 1: 61–81.
22. World Economic Forum (WEF). 2015. *Global Risks 2015.* Available: https://www3.weforum.org/docs/WEF_Global_Risks_2015_Report15.pdf
23. Jan, M., Kakakhel, S., Batool, S., Muazim, K. & Chatha, I. 2017. Global warming: Evidence, causes, consequences and mitigation. *Journal of Development Policy, Research & Practice*, 1: 61–81.
24. Tol, R.S.J. 2018. The economic impacts of climate change. *Review of Environmental Economics and Policy*, 12(1): 4–25.
25. Huckelba, A.L. & Van Lange, P.A.M. 2020. The silent killer: Consequences of climate change and how to survive past the year 2050. *Sustainability Science*, 12(9): 3746–3757.
26. World Economic Forum (WEF). 2019. *How to Set Up Effective Climate Governance on Corporate Boards:* Guiding Principles *and* Questions (in collaboration with PwC). Available: https://www3.weforum.org/docs/WEF_Creating_effective_climate_governance_on_corporate_boards.pdf [2022, March 03].
27. Adaptation Community. 2023. *Climate Risk Assessment and Management: A Comprehensive Framework to Avert, Minimize, and Address Loss and Damage.* Available: https://www.adaptationcommunity.net/climate-risk-assessment-management/ [2023, March 8].
28. Fawzy, S., Osman, A.I., Doran, J. & Rooney, D. 2020. Strategies for mitigation of climate change: A review. *Environmental Chemistry Letters*, 18(4): 2069–2094.
29. Kiesnere, A.L. & Baumgartner, R.J. 2020. Top management involvement and role in sustainable development of companies. In: Leal Filho, W., Azul, A.M., Brandli, L., Özuyar, P.G. & Wall, T. (eds) *Responsible Consumption and Production. Encyclopedia of the UN Sustainable Development Goals.* Cham: Springer.
30. Krauß, W. & Bremer, S. 2020. The role of place-based narratives of change in climate risk governance. *Climate Risk Management*, 2(28): 100–221.
31. Adaptation Community. 2023. *Climate Risk Assessment and Management: A Comprehensive Framework to Avert, Minimize, and Address Loss and Damage.* Available: https://www.adaptationcommunity.net/climate-risk-assessment-management/ [2023, March 8].
32. Ben-Amar, W. & McIlkenny, P. 2015. Board effectiveness and the voluntary disclosure of climate change information. *Business Strategy and the Environment*, 24(8): 704–719.
33. Liao, L., Luo, L. & Tang, Q. 2015. Gender diversity, board independence, environmental committee and greenhouse gas disclosure. *The British Accounting Review*, 47(4): 409–424.

34. Aguilera, R.V., Aragón-Correa, J.A., Marano, V. & Tashman, P.A. 2021. The corporate governance of environmental sustainability: A review and proposal for more integrated research. *Journal of Management*, 47(6): 1468–1497.
35. Business for Social Responsibility (BSR). 2023. Climate risk management. Available: https://www.bsr.org/en/focus/climate-change/climate-risk-management [2023, February 8].
36. World Economic Forum (WEF). 2019. *How to Set Up Effective Climate Governance on Corporate Boards: Guiding Principles and Questions* (in collaboration with PwC). Available: https://www3.weforum.org/docs/WEF_Creating_effective_climate_governance_on_corporate_boards.pdf [2022, March 03].
37. Institute of Directors in South Africa (IoDSA). 2021. *Guidance Paper: Responsibilities of Governing Bodies in Responding to Climate Change.* Available: https://www.iodsa.co.za/page/king-iv-practice-and-guidance-notes [2023, February 8].
38. *Id.*
39. International Financial Reporting Standards (IFRS) Foundation. 2024. Introduction to the ISSB and IFRS Sustainability Disclosure Standards. Available: https://www.ifrs.org/sustainability/knowledge-hub/introduction-to-issb-and-ifrs-sustainability-disclosure-standards/#:~:text=IFRS%20S1%20and%20IFRS%20S2%20prescribe%20how%20a%20company%20prepares,prescribed%20in%20the%20ISSB%20Standards [2024, August 14].
40. Institute of Directors in South Africa (IoDSA). 2016. *King IV Report* [Online]. Available: https://www.iodsa.co.za/page/king-iv [2023, April 10].
41. Bowie, N. 2012. Book review. *Stakeholder Theory: The State of the Art*, R. Edward Freeman, Jeffrey S. Harrison, Andrew C. Wicks, Bidhan L. Parmar, and Simone de Colle. *Business Ethics Quarterly*, 22(1): 179–185.
42. Kiesnere, A.L. & Baumgartner, R.J. 2020. Top management involvement and role in sustainable development of companies. In: Leal Filho, W., Azul, A.M., Brandli, L., Özuyar, P.G. & Wall, T. (eds) *Responsible Consumption and Production. Encyclopedia of the UN Sustainable Development Goals.* Cham: Springer,
43. Institute of Directors in South Africa (IoDSA). 2021. *Guidance Paper: Responsibilities of Governing Bodies in Responding to Climate Change.* Available: https://cdn.ymaws.com/www/iodsa.co.za/resources/collection/04630F89-33B7-43E7-82B3 [2023, February 8].
44. World Economic Forum (WEF). 2019. *How to Set Up Effective Climate Governance on Corporate Boards: Guiding Principles and Questions* (in collaboration with PwC). Available: https://www3.weforum.org/docs/WEF_Creating_effective_climate_governance_on_corporate_boards.pdf [2022, March 03].
45. Braun, V. & Clarke, V. 2012. *Thematic Analysis.* Washington: American Psychological Association.
46. Coghlan, D. & Brydon-Miller, M. 2014. *The SAGE Encyclopedia of Action Research.* London: SAGE Publications.

47. Malhi, G.S., Kaur, M. & Kaushik, P. 2021. Impact of climate change on agriculture and its mitigation strategies: A review. *Sustainability*, 13(3): 1318. https://doi.org/10.3390/su13031318
48. Onyutha, C. 2019. African food insecurity in a changing climate: The roles of science and policy. *Food and Energy Security*, 8(1). https://doi.org/10.1002/fes3.160
49. Levy, B.S. & Patz, J.A. 2015. Climate change, human rights, and social justice. *Annals of Global Health*, 81(3): 310–322.
50. Task Force on Climate-Related Financial Disclosures (TCFD). 2017. *Recommendations of the Task Force on Climate-Related Financial Disclosures: Final Report.* Available: https://apo.org.au/node/97651 [2022, September 13].
51. Esty, D.C. & Bell, M.L. 2018. Business leadership in global climate change responses. *American Journal of Public Health*, 108(2): 80–84.
52. Hanto, J., Schroth, A., Krawielicki, L., Oei, P.Y. & Burton, J. 2022. South Africa's energy transition – unraveling its political economy. *Energy for Sustainable Development*, 69: 164–178.
53. Institute of Risk Management South Africa (IRMSA). 2022. *IRMSA Risk Report.* Johannesburg: IRMSA.
54. Levy, B.S. & Patz, J.A. 2015. Climate change, human rights, and social justice. *Annals of Global Health*, 81(3): 310–322.
55. Islam, S.N. & Winkel, J. 2017. *Climate Change and Social Inequality.* Department of Economic & Social Affairs, Working Paper No. 152. Available: https://www.un.org/sites/un2.un.org/files/2020/08/1597341819.1157.pdf [2023, October 20].
56. Markkanen, S. & Anger-Kraavi, A. 2019. Social impacts of climate change mitigation policies and their implications for inequality. *Climate Policy*, 19(7): 827–844.
57. Lee, Y.C. 2020. Communicating sustainable development: Effects of stakeholder-centric perceived sustainability. *Corporate Social Responsibility and Environmental Management*, 27(4): 1540–1551.
58. Adaptation Community. 2023. *Climate Risk Assessment and Management: A Comprehensive Framework to Avert, Minimize, and Address Loss and Damage.* Available: https://www.adaptationcommunity.net/climate-risk assessment-management/ [2023, March 8].
59. Institute of Directors in South Africa (IoDSA). 2021. *Guidance Paper: Responsibilities of Governing Bodies in Responding to Climate Change.* Available: https://www.iodsa.co.za/page/king-iv-practice-and-guidance-notes [2023, February 8].
60. Seele, P. and Gatti, L., 2017. Greenwashing revisited: In search of a typology and accusation-based definition incorporating legitimacy strategies. *Business Strategy and the Environment*, 26(2): 239–252.
61. Fernandez-Feijoo, B., Romero, S. & Ruiz, S. 2014. Effect of stakeholders' pressure on transparency of sustainability reports within the GRI framework. *Journal of Business Ethics*, 122(2): 53–63.

62. Institute of Directors in South Africa (IoDSA). 2021. *Guidance Paper: Responsibilities of Governing Bodies in Responding to Climate Change.* Available: https://www.iodsa.co.za/page/king-iv-practice-and-guidance-notes [2023, February 8].
63. Ritz, R.A. 2022. Linking executive compensation to climate performance. *California Management Review*, 64(3): 124–140.
64. Gielen, D., Boshell, F., Saygin, D., Bazilian, M.D., Wagner, N. & Gorini, R. 2019. The role of renewable energy in the global energy transformation. *Energy Strategy Reviews*, 24: 38–50.
65. Ngwenya, N. & Simatele, M.D. 2020. The emergence of green bonds as an integral component of climate finance in South Africa. *South African Journal of Science*, 116(2): 1–3.
66. Aguilera, R.V., Aragón-Correa, J.A., Marano, V. & Tashman, P.A. 2021. The corporate governance of environmental sustainability: A review and proposal for more integrated research. *Journal of Management*, 47(6): 1468–1497.

4. Revisiting the case for environmental tax reform in the African region

Hope Ashiabor

1. INTRODUCTION

Most African countries find themselves in a rather invidious situation in dealing with the negative externalities that environmental degradation presents. At one level, the externalities from the extraction of resources to support their economies are imposing substantial costs on human health, livelihoods, and the environment. While at the other level, these countries also find themselves highly vulnerable to the devastating impacts of climate change.[1] With respect to the latter, their dilemma is that their overall contribution to global greenhouse gas emissions, both generally and on a *per capita* basis, is quite insignificant. Being cognisant of the fact that the costs of inaction greatly outweigh the costs of action, they have put in place policy levers to address these challenges.

Environmental taxes and carbon pricing instruments are generally considered effective, low-cost instruments for internalising negative environmental externalities. However, of the 54 countries on the continent, South Africa is the only country that has implemented a carbon tax – while six others have either a carbon tax or an Emissions Trading Scheme (ETS) under consideration.[2]

Most countries in the developing South, for understandable reasons, have been hesitant to embrace environmental taxes and have opted for carbon markets as well as disbursements from UN agencies to enable them to transition to zero-carbon economies and adapt to the effects of climate change.

This chapter examines the role of traditional carbon pricing mechanisms with a view to ascertaining their adequacy in dealing with the environmental challenges that African countries face. Since the *per capita* emissions and overall contribution to global emissions of these countries (with a few exceptions) is at the lower end of the scale, the paper argues that environmental tax reform (hereafter referred to as ETR) could possibly be the most appropriate policy approach adapted to their experience. Such an approach, it is argued, aligns with the experience of most developing countries that have sought to implement "carbon taxes" and would be consistent with the UNFCCC's common but differentiated responsibilities principle.

The chapter starts off by setting the context, drawing upon examples of the experience of negative environmental externalities in developing countries in general, and Africa in particular. This is meant to highlight the impacts of these externalities as encountered during their pursuit of economic development.

Part 3 of the chapter examines the role of carbon markets as a policy tool in African countries' climate mitigation strategies. In the process, it highlights the potential traps and pitfalls associated with an over-reliance on voluntary carbon markets as the primary approach for addressing the challenges posed by the threat of climate change.

In part 4, the chapter starts off with an evaluation of the relative merits of different policy instruments for internalising negative environmental externalities (including climate change). It then makes the case for why African countries should consider ETR. Possible considerations that ought to be taken into account in pursuing this course of action are then discussed.

The chapter concludes with a cautionary note that pursuing ETR *per se* would not be a silver bullet solution to the negative environmental challenges these countries face. Possible suggestions are put forward for handling the outstanding issues.

2. THE NEGATIVE EXTERNALITIES CHALLENGE

Most African countries, in their pursuit of economic development, find themselves saddled with a legacy of negative environmental externalities. In other cases, such as the global greenhouse gas emissions challenge, though their contribution to the issue is dwarfed by that of the major emitting countries, they find themselves in an unenviable position whereby they end up being at the rough end of the stick. The costs imposed by these externalities on human health, livelihoods, and the environment are of such dimensions that, if left unaddressed, they can result in long-lasting and irreversible damage.

The challenge of human-induced environmental degradation and how to address it is not unique to the African experience and is one that countries all over the world are grappling with. Governments have implemented a range of policy levers to contain or remedy the ensuing damage, and a critical evaluation of these is the focus of the analysis in the rest of this chapter.

To demonstrate the scale of the devastating effects and insidious nature of some of the negative environmental externalities, and to underscore the fact that the challenges are not unique to the African experience, examples are drawn from other developing countries for the purposes of the discussion in this section.

Starting off with Shell's oil drilling operations in the Niger Delta, a UNDP report into the devastating environmental legacy and the fall-outs on human health and livelihoods concluded that while there were no consistent figures for the quantity of crude oil spilled "... it is widely believed that an estimated 13 million barrels (1.5 million tons) of crude oil have spilled since 1958 from over 7,000 oil spill incidents; a yearly average of about 240,000 barrels".[3] Contributing factors included *inter alia* "intentional company and government under-reporting; and inadequate government oversight".[4] The report concluded that if left unaddressed, this situation will not bode well for the future of Nigeria or an oil-hungry world.

Another example is drawn from the Papua New Guinea operations of the global mining giant Rio Tinto. Its decommissioned Panguna mine in the Bougainville Islands, which was its largest and most profitable gold-copper mine in the world, typifies the far-reaching devastation to the environment that can result from such large-scale mining. The mine's tailings dam, which had been operating since 1972, collapsed in 1984 and discharged more than a billion tonnes of mine waste into a major waterway. This left toxic waste and decaying infrastructure that posed catastrophic environmental damage and put lives and livelihoods at risk. The mine was forced to close abruptly in 1989 when conflict broke out, and since then formal decommissioning and rehabilitation have not been undertaken.[5]

Yet another example is the disaster caused by the 2015 collapse of a tailings dam owned and operated by the world's largest mining company, BHP, in Brazil. The dam released an avalanche of arsenic-laced iron ore waste, destroying an entire local village and killing 19 people in its wake. A $44bn (£33.6bn) compensation claim has been lodged by affected residents before the UK Courts.[6]

Apart from the risk of tailings dam collapses, direct carbon dioxide emissions associated with the extraction and use of fossil fuels and fugitive emissions linked to mining and industrial processes also contribute to the challenges posed by increasing atmospheric concentrations of global greenhouse gases.

Negative externalities in the form of scars on the landscape are not confined to the mining or drilling operations of the resource extraction sector. Land clearing and habitat destruction have also left a trail of environmental degradation of unimaginable dimensions in their wake. Land clearing erodes the sequestering role of forests, which play an invaluable role as nature's carbon sinks. Madagascar's experience is a case in point. Its indiscriminate felling of its endangered rosewood timber forests (despite a CITES ban and environmental outcries), which ended up being exported to markets in China where rosewood furniture is highly sought after, is illustrative of another dimension of these challenges.[7] This *inter alia* contributed to landslides and altered its microclimate, with far-reaching consequences. Illegal logging, however, it must be noted, is a much wider global problem and not a matter that is unique to Madagascar.[8]

3. CARBON MARKETS

Carbon markets are carbon pricing mechanisms that enable governments and non-state actors to trade greenhouse gas emission credits. The aim is to achieve climate targets and implement climate actions cost effectively.[9]

Two types of carbon markets exist: compliance and voluntary. These are used both domestically and internationally to reduce emissions. Compliance markets, such as national or regional ETSs, are regulated markets in which carbon offsets can be bought and sold. They are mandated by law, supported by common standards, and count towards national or sub-national targets. Voluntary carbon markets, on the other hand, are largely unregulated markets where carbon offsets are traded by individuals and organisations that are under no legal obligation to make emission cuts. However, participants seek to voluntarily offset their emissions, for example to achieve mitigation targets such as climate neutrality or net zero emissions.

Article 6 of the Paris Agreement establishes an international carbon market with multilateral governance under the UNFCCC, setting common global standards and guidance for development and trading in emission reductions and Internationally Transferred Mitigation Outcomes (ITMOs).[10]

Voluntary markets, on the other hand, have not been subject to the same regulatory strictures as the compliance markets. In the absence of a government regulator, voluntary registries emerged and assumed the role of the primary standard-setting bodies for voluntary carbon trade with a view to improving transparency in the voluntary markets.[11] In that capacity, they acted as "registries" for carbon offset projects in the voluntary market and oversaw standards for generating offsets.

The integrity of carbon offset projects is benchmarked against five criteria – credibility, accountability, permanence, additionality, and transparency. Offsets or credits that do not meet these criteria are generally considered worthless or described as "junk credits".

Governance failures, including failures in enforcing their stringent criteria to exclude substandard credits and promote best practices in the voluntary carbon markets at the level of these accrediting bodies, resulted in a lack of scrutiny of most projects. This led to a proliferation of offset projects of dubious value by carbon-intensive emitters and voluntary market participants, creating a pool of junk credits.[12]

The focus of the analysis in this section is on voluntary carbon markets. The utility of compliance-driven markets in the developing country context will be discussed in the next section of this chapter.

In establishing the emissions reduction framework under Article 6, the Paris Agreement envisaged *inter alia* that entities would reduce their carbon emissions through direct cuts (involving a systemic shift away from fossil fuels) as well as through various carbon credit mechanisms. Entities that were unable to achieve their emission reductions in-house have the option of purchasing credits either from another entity that made additional emissions cuts or from a scheme that invests in carbon sinks such as tree plantings. Cynically, high polluters (such as oil and gas companies) as well as industrialised countries have viewed the purchase of offsets as a strategy to reduce their net emissions.

In what amounts to a one-sided adherence to the spirit of the Paris Agreement, petrostates have been promoting green policies in the form of voluntary offset projects in countries of the South while still drilling for oil and gas. Instead of pricing carbon, they have single-mindedly focused on opening more oil and gas fields – while at the same time selling fossil fuels at subsidised prices in their domestic markets.

Most African countries, as well as developing countries in general, have opted for the voluntary carbon markets with a view to harnessing the benefits that offsetting provides in enabling them to adapt to the impacts of climate change and expedite their transition to a low-carbon economy. It has also been perceived as helping to achieve other sustainable development objectives, such as reducing poverty and restoring biodiversity. It was for this reason that the African Carbon Market Initiative was set up to shape and boost the potential for carbon markets in the region. Further to this was the culmination of the signing of the Brazzaville Declaration in June 2024, where several African leaders called on the UN to prioritise a decade of tree planting to combat climate change on the continent.[13]

At the United Nations COP28 held in 2023, the Qatar-backed international carbon credit and sustainable development programme – "the Global Carbon Council" (GCC) – entered into agreements with 16 West African countries (described as the "West African Alliance on Carbon Markets and Carbon Finance") to finance their green transition. Credits or offsets generated under the GCC projects focus on reafforestation, methane capture from landfill sites, renewable energy projects, and programmes intended to provide cleaner fuels in developing countries. Carbon Market Watch notes that as most of these GCC projects do not need carbon credits to exist, they are unlikely to be eligible under other standards owing to their failure to meet the key additionality criterion of environmental policy design.[14]

The operations of voluntary carbon markets in developing countries have come under sustained criticism on various grounds. These include:

- monies from the sale of carbon credits being soaked up by unscrupulous brokers and middlemen who have been exploiting carbon markets for their own ends while leaving communities and the projects with an unfair share of the proceeds;[15]

- unethical entrepreneurs peddling worthless credits in exchange for valuable resources at the expense of the environment.[16] A most egregious example of the scale of this level of fraud was published in a compelling investigative case study of Zimbabwe's experience in *The New Yorker*; and[17]
- complicity in human rights abuses of indigenous peoples.[18]

Criticisms about integrity issues in the operations of voluntary markets are not confined to the experience of developing countries. Similar concerns have been raised in developed countries such as Australia and elsewhere.[19] Though it must be mentioned that the Australian Government has since put measures in place to combat such abuses.

Despite their shortcomings, voluntary carbon offset projects and the attendant undermining of their credibility seem to be the preferred policy instrument of choice for most entities. Possible reasons for this preference by entities have many explanations. A Special Report in *The Economist* magazine sought to explain this as follows:

> … Offering a feel-good alternative to investors, financiers, big business, and regulators … may give an excuse to governments not to charge for carbon emissions. ... Carbon taxes would be the best way to direct investment to the most promising decarbonisation technologies. Yet, nobody should be fooled. The main reason the taxes are both low and insufficiently co-ordinated across the world … is because politicians are too timid to foist them on voters.
>
> Offsets could be worth doubling down on private sector and bureaucratic efforts to get companies to measure and reduce their carbon emissions. It may be the second-best solution, but with the right disclosure requirements and regulatory scrutiny, it could help direct capital where it is best needed.[20]

UNEP's *2021 Emissions Gap Report* assessed the significance of carbon markets and concluded that the full use of market mechanisms can enable cost savings in the order of 40 to 60 per cent in 2030. To attain its full potential of playing a valuable role in the decarbonisation process, integrity measures of transparency, credibility, accountability, permanence, and additionality would need to be addressed.[21]

Though the United Nations' COP29, held in Baku, Azerbaijan in 2024, was tasked with streamlining the carbon market rules, it made a clumsy head start by greenlighting the new rules that govern the trade in carbon credits on its very first day, without any deliberations.[22] The poor start to COP29 was further tainted by reports that (just like COP28), lobbyists from the coal and gas industry outnumbered delegates from all countries (with the exception of Azerbaijan, Brazil, and Turkey), and exceeded the number of delegates from the 10 nations most vulnerable to the climate crisis by almost 30 per cent.[23] These developments amounted to a missed opportunity in prioritising and bolstering the framework for reducing emissions.

Beyond the integrity issues flagged in this chapter about the carbon markets, disturbing questions are beginning to be raised about the inherent problems of deforestation, particularly the equivalence issues of replacing complex biodiverse forests with monoculture plantations. Questions are also being asked about the limits of nature-based sinks, as considerations such as the collapse of carbon sinks apparently were not factored into climate models.[24]

4. POLICY INSTRUMENT CHOICE CHALLENGE

The World Bank's *State and Trends of Carbon Pricing Report 2024* states that of the 54 African countries, South Africa is the only one that has implemented a carbon tax – while six others have either a carbon tax or an ETS under consideration.[25] This brings the issue of the appropriate policy instrument into focus. In its recognition of the challenges that developing countries would grapple with in dealing with the policy instrument choice issue in the climate change context, the UNFCCC came up with the common but differentiated responsibilities and respective capabilities principle. This indeed should be the guiding principle in such situations.

Starting with the compliance-driven carbon markets, much has been written about the relative merits of carbon taxes compared to ETSs. This chapter does not intend to revisit that debate. However, the World Bank, in comparing carbon taxes with ETSs, states:

> Overall, carbon taxes have significant practical advantages over ETSs (especially for developing countries) due to ease of administration, price certainty to promote investment, potential to raise significant revenues, and coverage of broader emission sources – but ETSs can have significant political economy advantages.[26]

It is also worth noting that no developing country to date has implemented a cap-and-trade ETS.

4.1 What About a Carbon Tax?

Carbon taxes are a subset of environmental taxes. The tax is levied on the carbon content of fossil fuels or greenhouse gas emissions. The tax rates are set by governments, and the liability falls upon companies for each tonne of emissions they emit.

Most countries in the developing South have, for understandable reasons, been hesitant to embrace environmental taxes and have opted for the voluntary carbon markets instead. Much of their hesitation in embracing environmental taxes stems from the experience that policies designed to increase domestic fuel prices have resulted in destabilising popular protests. Kenya's ill-fated attempt to introduce such taxes in June 2024 had to be scrapped as the tax measures fuelled deadly protests.[27] This experience is not unique to Africa, as the research of von Uexkull et al. has comprehensively demonstrated.[28]

The implementation of a carbon tax in these countries would not be without its challenges. Most resource-rich African countries are capital-importing countries whose primary source of revenue is the resource extraction sector and, to a lesser extent, primary production. Many countries in this group that are not endowed with natural resources depend on foreign aid or are ravaged by wars and political instability. Countries in this category are therefore not able to embrace either Environmental Tax Reform (ETR) or carbon pricing instruments. The resource-rich countries, on the other hand, have had to rely exclusively on foreign investment to exploit their resources. To attract foreign investment, these countries have concluded bilateral investment agreements that confer substantial tax holidays and generous concessions in return. Having divested themselves of their taxing powers in a bid to attract foreign investment, they sometimes find themselves hamstrung in attempts to reopen fiscal terms that they are contractually bound to. Attempts by host countries to impose new taxes in breach of these agreements can trigger a backlash from multinational corporations. The IMF cites the experience of Venezuela when it sought to re-balance existing fiscal arrangements by seeking to renegotiate the terms of one such contract with incumbents:

> When, for example, in 2007, the Government of Venezuela increased tax rates and lifted state participation to a controlling interest in the heavy oil projects of the Orinoco, Exxon Mobil and Conoco Phillips opted to withdraw from existing investments and filed legal claims for restitution and compensation.[29]

In other cases, some countries have resorted to unorthodox measures to resolve outstanding tax disputes.[30]

The experience of countries that have implemented carbon taxes has been that exemptions are often carved out for domestic industries in the emissions-intensive, trade-exposed sectors. Major fossil-fuel-exporting countries simply insulate this sector of their economies from carbon pricing. Expecting poor countries that expend huge outlays on energy imports to implement carbon taxes not only raises questions of equity but also begs the question as to whether this is consistent with the UNFCCC's guidelines on common but differentiated responsibilities.

The World Bank has consistently decried the fact that global carbon price levels in countries that have implemented carbon taxes are too low to meet the

Paris Agreement goals.[31] The expectation that carbon taxes imposed by poor countries would be higher than those in developed countries would simply be a travesty of unimaginable dimensions. By the same token, it is arguable that revenues raised by African countries that impose carbon taxes would be unlikely to raise any more revenues and could have rebound effects whereby impacted industries would simply pass on the additional costs of the tax to consumers. As the Trudeau Administration found out, the introduction of the Canadian federal carbon tax in 2019 set the Prime Minister's popularity on a steep decline in the wake of the post-COVID inflationary surge. This *inter alia* accelerated the demise of his government.[32]

A further challenge to the implementation of a carbon tax is that the primary sources of carbon emissions in most African countries are the transport and energy sectors. A large proportion of their transport fleet consists of used vehicles imported from developed countries, most of which are powered by inefficient fuels. A range of other taxes, such as differentiated fuel excises, motor vehicle ownership taxes, and road usage charges, already apply in these countries. From time to time these are complemented by fuel subsidy reforms. Electricity generation is mainly operated by State Owned Enterprises (SOEs), and constitutional provisions prohibit the imposition of tax on properties belonging to the state.

4.2 What are Environmental Taxes?

The OECD defines environmental taxes as a compulsory payment to the government that is levied on a tax base that is environmentally relevant.[33] Environmental taxes are generally grouped into four categories: energy, transport, pollution, and resources. The OECD goes on to state that this definition also includes carbon taxes. The design objective of environmental taxes is to balance the environment, economic activity, and collection. The design features of environmental taxes support the "polluter pays principle", which requires that the costs of pollution prevention and control should be reflected in the price and output of goods and services which cause pollution as a result of their production and/or consumption.[34]

There is a long line of literature about ETR. Simply put, ETR involves policy measures that shift revenue-raising instruments from labour and capital to resource use and pollution. ETR also extends to fossil fuel subsidy reforms in the policy instrument mix as well. For that reason, it is an important and integral part of a sustainable development strategy. Environmental taxes are an integral part of an ETR strategy. The World Bank, in acknowledging the contribution of environmental taxes to the UN's multiple Sustainable Development Goals, underscores its capacity for having multiple benefits beyond climate change.[35] It concludes by acknowledging the potential role of environmental taxes in helping developing countries cost-effectively achieve low-carbon transformation while supporting an inclusive and equitable growth pathway.

4.3 Why Should African Countries Consider Environmental Tax Reform (ETR)?

There are several reasons why African countries should give some consideration to revisiting ETR instead of just prioritising voluntary carbon markets.

Firstly, environmental taxes, as well as ETSs, are effective and low-cost instruments for internalising negative environmental externalities. These policy instruments offer the potential for revenue raised to be recycled to remediate the environmental damage caused by the negative environmental externalities. The ensuing reduction in pollution yields the first dividend of the double dividend theory.

The savings realised upon the reduction of negative environmental externalities can then be diverted towards funding other economic activities or to displace other distortionary taxes that slow economic growth – hence the second dividend.

The use of revenue to reduce the effect of more inefficient taxes in an economy is illustrated by the experience of the Province of British Columbia (BC). In the 2013–14 fiscal year, the Carbon Tax Act raised $1.2 billion, and the Province recycled the revenue to reduce corporate income taxes by $440 million and personal income taxes by $237 million and to offer $194 million worth of low-income tax credits.[36] Over the 2008–2013 period, the implementation of the carbon tax in BC reduced *per capita* use of fossil fuels in the Province by 16.1 per cent.[37] The benefits of the double dividend theory are not otherwise available under an offset scheme. Secondly, poor-quality offsetting projects have resulted in unintended negative impacts (e.g., loss of livelihood for farmers and local communities and declines in biodiversity resulting from monoculture planting). Thirdly, the carrot and stick features associated with taxes drive enduring behavioural change and foster innovation. Delivering a sustainable net zero economy requires societal change. Carbon offsetting can potentially give people the misleading impression that such goals can be achieved without this change. Fourthly, unlike taxes, offsetting fails to address the root of the problem and allows companies to pay to pollute – serving as a distraction from the real decarbonisation that is required. Lastly, substantial sums of money have been invested in carbon offsets where, in many cases, the intended emissions reductions have not been achieved due to poor quality offsetting programmes that do not conform to international benchmarks governing the issuance of offsets. This then leads to the question of what are some of the possible considerations that African countries should consider when implementing ETR?

4.4 Considerations for the Implementation of ETR

Kenya's ill-fated attempt to implement ETR highlights the missteps that policymakers inadvertently make in such cases. Briefly, the eco-levy measures in its 2024 Finance Bill applied to plastics and packaging, an increase in the fuel levy whose revenues were to be earmarked to repair damaged roads, and a road usage levy (the motor vehicle circulation tax).[38] To the extent that measures directed towards the phasing out of fossil fuel subsidies extended to necessities such as cooking fuels as well, there was left no room for doubt that the socio-economic impacts would fuel public discontent. In a developing country context where cost of living crises are exacerbated by poverty and underemployment, such measures if not handled with care can literally amount to lighting a match to a powder keg of pent-up frustrations.

Fuel subsidy reform is a widely acknowledged strategy that enables governments to have more space to boost their economies by redirecting fiscal spending towards infrastructure, human capital, and social programmes. Implementing such measures when global crude oil prices are falling presents much less of a challenge than when such prices are high. In the latter scenario, the socio-economic impacts have the potential to trigger public discontent. Indonesia's approach in managing the latter involved packaging the phase-out measures with compensation policies targeted towards protecting low-income groups.[39] When such approaches have been implemented, however, it cannot be a set-and-forget issue and would need to be reviewed and adjusted on a regular basis.

To bookend their strategies to embark on any meaningful path of ETR, two other considerations ought to be given primacy. First is a recognition of the fact that developing countries do not have the infrastructure to set up tax systems that work and are reliable. Addressing this would require support in capacity building, which can be readily accessed from the services international agencies can provide from their pool of expertise.

Second, the successful implementation of any ETR programme is dependent on community acceptance of any proposed changes. Instead of springing a surprise upon the public on budget night when the changes are announced, this should be preceded by an extensive period of public consultation and education. This approach assumes even greater relevance in a social-media-obsessed world that is full of misinformation, as it gives the public a sense of ownership of the proposed changes and makes them more resilient.

In other cases, African countries have concluded long-term commercial contracts whose terms are shrouded in secrecy. These contracts have been concluded with countries that have scant regard for transparency and the rule of law, whereby concessions for substantial chunks of valuable natural resources are granted in return for the construction of infrastructure projects, some of which are of marginal value. Transparency, like sunshine, it is said, is the best disinfectant. Revisiting some of these secret agreements with a view to renegotiating their terms, however, has turned out to be an insurmountable task. Disputes such as the one between the government of the Democratic Republic of Congo and the state-backed China Molybdenum stem from allegations that it had been under-reporting its exports, robbing the country of over $10 billion in royalties, and that the infrastructure promised in return was not delivered. Attempts at resolution at the highest levels of government in both countries yielded no results.[40]

5. CONCLUSION

Not all countries in the region have the same capacity and level of responsibility in managing the challenges of environmental degradation. With 54 different countries having diverging experiences and economic circumstances, it is not possible to prescribe a universally applicable set of suggestions. Each country's response will depend on its circumstances. When it comes to developing their respective courses of action for tackling the challenges of climate change, African countries ought to be guided by the differentiated responsibilities and respective capacity principle.

The complex nature of the challenges posed by negative environmental externalities is not confined to climate change. The optimal approach should involve implementing ETR in the context of a policy package by combining it with voluntary offsets, so long as they meet stringent integrity requirements governing the issuance of offsets.

Policy instruments in themselves, no matter how well they've been crafted, will not serve as a magic wand that will overcome the enormous challenges that environmental degradation poses to the continent. Despite the IMF's encouraging observation that most resource-rich developing countries have beefed up their mineral resource rent tax regimes and increased their equity stakes,[41] those savings in themselves would not be sufficient to cover the substantial costs required in restoring or stalling the degradation stemming from the mining operations, or the devastating impacts of climate change.

Revenue leakage is a major issue that these countries need to tackle head-on. The act of divesting their taxing rights in a desperate bid to attract foreign investments or coming to the negotiating table from a weak position needs to be reassessed. Many African countries are endowed with an abundance of natural resources, including critical minerals that are central to the clean energy transition. This should give them enough confidence to drive hard bargains when dealing with prospective foreign investors.

The issues raised and the suggestions put forward merely reflect the tip of the iceberg, as not all countries in the region have the capacity to implement either ETRs or carbon pricing instruments. These issues are therefore intended to prompt the start of a long and complex conversation that researchers and others with an interest in these matters would like to pursue and build upon.

NOTES

1. United Nations, *Global Issues: Africa*. Available at: https://www.un.org/en/global-issues/africa accessed on 1 November 2024.
2. The six countries are: Botswana, Ivory Coast, Senegal, Mauritania, Morocco, and Kenya. World Bank (2024), *State and Trends of Carbon Pricing 2024*. Available at: https://openknowledge.worldbank.org/server/api/core/bitstreams/253e6cdd-9631-4db2-8cc5-1d013956de15/content accessed on 20 August 2024.
3. UNDP (2006), *Niger Delta Human Development Report*. New York. Available at: https://hdr.undp.org/content/human-development-report accessed on 4 November 2024; see also Ordinioha, B. & Brisibe, S. (2013), The human health implications of crude oil spills in the Niger Delta, Nigeria: An interpretation of published studies. *Niger Med J.*, 54(1): 10–16. https://pubmed.ncbi.nlm.nih.gov/23661893/
4. UNDP (2006), above, note 3.
5. Faa, M. (2024), Landmark report uncovers human rights abuses at Rio Tinto gold mine in Bougainville, 35 years after closure. *ABC News*, 13 Oct 2024. Available at: https://www.abc.net.au/news/2024-10-13/human-rights-abuses-found-at-rio-tinto/104463224?utm_campaign=abc_news_web&utm_content=link&utm_medium=content_shared&utm_source=abc_news_web accessed on 30 October 2024.
6. House of Commons Library (2023), *Mariana Dam Disaster*, 20 June 2023. Available at: https://commonslibrary.parliament.uk/research-briefings/cdp-2023-0133/, Accessed on 2024 November 11; Boffey, D. (2024), BHP to face 620,000 claimants in Mariana dam collapse trial in London. *The Guardian*, 13 October 2024. Available at: https://www.theguardian.com/world/2024/oct/13/bhp-to-face-620000-claimants-in-mariana-dam-collapse-trial-in-london accessed on 11 November 2024.
7. Caramel, L. (2015), China's rosewood craving cuts deep into Madagascar's rainforests. *The Guardian*, 16 February 2015. Available at: https://www.theguardian.com/environment/2015/feb/16/rosewood-madagascar-china-illegal-rainforest accessed on 11 November 2024; Juma, J. (2023), Bringing mis-certified timber out of the woodwork: a Malagasy Rosewood court case review. *TRAFFIC – The Wildlife Trade Monitoring Network*, 28 September 2023. Available at: https://www.traffic.org/views/bringing-mis-certified-timber-out-of-the-woodwork-a-malagasy-rosewood-court-case-review/#:~:text=National%20Regulations-,Bringing%20mis%2Dcertified%20timber%20out%20of%20the%20woodwork%3A%20a%20Malagasy,of%20contentious%20legal%20battle%20ensued accessed on 15 July 2024; Ong, S. & Carver, E. (2019), The rosewood trade: an illicit trail from forest to furniture.

Yale Environment 360, 29 January 2019. Available at: https://e360.yale.edu/features/the-rosewood-trade-the-illicit-trail-from-forest-to-furniture accessed on 15 July 2024.

8. Greenfield, P. (2022), "Relentless" destruction of rainforest continuing despite COP26 pledge. *The Guardian*, 28 April 2022, Available at: https://www.theguardian.com/environment/2022/apr/28/destruction-of-pristine-rainforest-globe-relentless-rate-aoe accessed on 11 November 2024; Vidal, J. (2017), Amazon rainforest's final frontier under threat from oil and soya. *The Guardian*, 16 February 2017. Available at: https://www.theguardian.com/global-development/2017/feb/16/amazon-rainforest-final-frontier-in-brazil-under-threat-from-oil-and-soya accessed on 11 November 2024.
9. United Nations Environment Programme (UNEP) (2021), *Emissions Gap Report 2021. The Heat is On: A World of Climate Policies Not Yet Delivered*, pp. 56–57.
10. ITMOs are credits that can be traded between Paris Agreement parties to meet the climate goals under the Article 6.2 mechanism. Article 6.2 of the Paris Agreement enables countries to directly trade carbon credits and other units, such as gigawatts (GW) of renewable power, with each other, dubbed Internationally Transferred Mitigation Outcomes.
11. The four largest accrediting bodies are Verra, Gold Standard, American Carbon Registry, and Climate Action Registry.
12. Greenfield, P. (2023), Revealed: more than 90% of rainforest carbon offsets by biggest certifier are worthless, analysis shows. *The Guardian*, 19 January 2023. Available at: https://www.theguardian.com/environment/2023/jan/18/revealed-forest-carbon-offsets-biggest-provider-worthless-verra-aoe accessed on 11 November 2024; Greenfield, P. (2023), Carbon credit speculators could lose billions as offsets deemed "worthless". *The Guardian*, 25 August 2023.
13. Moyo, A. (2024), Brazzaville Declaration prioritises decade of tree planting. *The Herald*, 8 July 2024. Available at: https://www.herald.co.zw/brazzaville-declaration-prioritises-decade-of-tree-planting/ accessed on 15 July 2024.
14. Carbon Market Watch (2024), *Hidden in Plain Sight: Flawed Renewable Energy Projects in the Voluntary Carbon Market*, June 2024. Available at: https://carbonmarketwatch.org/wp-content/uploads/2024/06/2024-06_Short-Report_-Renewable-Energy-Projects-in-the-VCM-1.pdf, accessed on 4 September 2024; Carbon Market Watch (2024), *Policy Briefing. False Friends: Why UN REDD+ and Article 6 Carbon Markets Are Incompatible*, June 2024. Available at: https://carbonmarketwatch.org/wp-content/uploads/2024/06/2024_06_False-friends-Why-UN-REDD-and-Article-6-carbon-markets-are-incompatible-1.pdf accessed on 5 January 2025.
15. Dufrasne, G., (2023) *Climate Profiteering: Are Intermediaries Exploiting Carbon Markets for their Own Ends?* Carbon Market Watch, 2 February 2023. Available at: https://carbonmarketwatch.org/2023/02/02/climate-profiteering-are-intermediaries-exploiting-carbon-markets-for-their-own-ends/ accessed on 5 January 2025; Barrat, L. & Clarke, J.S. (2022), How middlemen carbon brokers take a cut from money meant to help offset emissions. *Unearthed*, 2

May 2022. Available at: https://unearthed.greenpeace.org/2022/05/02/carbon-offsetting-market-climate/ accessed on 28 September 2024; Cabello, J. & Hartlief, I. (2024), Carbon offsets often disenfranchise communities, *SOMO, The Centre for Research on Multinational Corporations*, 24 October 2024. Available at: https://www.somo.nl/carbon-offsets-often-disenfranchise-communities/ accessed on 5 January 2025.

16. Fernanda Wenzel, Verra suspends carbon credit projects following police raid in Brazil. *Mongabay*, 11 June 2024. Available at: https://news.mongabay.com/2024/06/verra-suspends-carbon-credit-projects-following-police-raid-in-brazil/ accessed on 5 November 2024; The Australia Institute, (2024), Here are 23 times carbon offsets were found to be dodgy. Available at: https://australiainstitute.org.au/post/here-are-23-times-carbon-offsets-were-found-to-be-dodgy-2/ accessed on 5 November 2024.
17. Blake, H. (2023), Hot air. *The New Yorker*, 23 October 2023.
18. Dell'Amico, A. (2024), Human rights abuses from carbon credits – a critique of "greenwashing" lawsuits and additional litigation techniques. *Environmental Law Journal*. Available at: https://nyuelj.org/2024/01/human-rights-abuses-from-carbon-credits-a-critique-of-greenwashing-lawsuits-and-additional-litigation-techniques/ accessed on 11 November 2024; Greenfield, P. (2023), "Nowhere else to go": forest communities of Alto Mayo, Peru, at centre of offsetting row. *The Guardian*, 19 January 2023. Available at: https://www.theguardian.com/environment/2023/jan/18/forest-communities-alto-mayo-peru-carbon-offsetting-aoe accessed on 2 October 2024; Human Rights Watch (2024), *Carbon Offsetting's Casualties*, 28 February 2024. Available at: https://www.hrw.org/report/2024/02/29/carbon-offsettings-casualties/violations-chong-indigenous-peoples-rights accessed on 10 November 2024.
19. McIntosh, A. (2022), Australia's carbon market a "fraud on the environment". *Australian National University*, 24 March 2022. Available at: https://law.anu.edu.au/news-and-events/news/australias-carbon-market-fraud-environment accessed on 18 December 2024; Morton, A. (2022), Australia's carbon credit scheme "largely a sham", says whistleblower who tried to rein it in. *The Guardian*, 23 March 2022. Available at: https://www.theguardian.com/environment/2022/mar/23/australias-carbon-credit-scheme-largely-a-sham-says-whistleblower-who-tried-to-rein-it-in accessed on 18 December 2024.
20. Tricks, H. (2022), In need of a clean-up. *The Economist: Special Report ESG Investing*, 23 July 2022.
21. UNEP (2021), above note 9, at 62.
22. Niranjan, A. (2024), Critics say approval of "climate credits" rules on day one of Cop29 was rushed. *The Guardian*, 12 November 2024. Available at: https://www.theguardian.com/environment/2024/nov/11/critics-say-approval-of-climate-credits-rules-on-day-one-of-cop29-was-rushed accessed on 12 November 2024.
23. Harvey, F., Noor, D., Carrington, D., & Niranjan, A. (2024), Cop summits "no longer fit for purpose", say leading climate policy experts. *The Guardian*, 15 November 2024. Available at: https://www.theguardian.com/environment

/2024/nov/15/cop-summits-no-longer-fit-for-purpose-say-leading-climate-policy-experts accessed on 16 November 2024.

24. Greenfield, P. (2024), What happens to the world if forests stop absorbing carbon? Ask Finland. *The Guardian*, 15 October 2024. Available at: https://www.theguardian.com/environment/2024/oct/15/finland-emissions-target-forests-peatlands-sinks-absorbing-carbon-aoe accessed on 22 October 2024; Greenfield, P. (2024), Trees and land absorbed almost no CO_2 last year. Is nature's carbon sink failing? *The Guardian*, 14 October 2024. Available at: https://www.theguardian.com/environment/2024/oct/14/nature-carbon-sink-collapse-global-heating-models-emissions-targets-evidence-aoe accessed on 22 October 2024; Huxham, M. (2019), I've seen mass tree-planting projects go awry around the world – UK politicians should take note. *The Conversation*, 5 December 2019, accessed on 1 July 2024; Waring, B. (2021), There aren't enough trees in the world to offset society's carbon emissions – and there never will be. *The Conversation*, 23 April 2021. Available at: https://theconversation.com/there-arent-enough-trees-in-the-world-to-offset-societys-carbon-emissions-and-there-never-will-be-158181 accessed on 2 October 2024.
25. World Bank (2024), above note 2.
26. Parry, I.W.H., Black, S., & Zhunnussova, K. (2022), *Carbon Taxes or Emissions Trading Systems? Instrument Choice and Design*, IMF Staff Climate Note 2022/006, International Monetary Fund, Washington DC.
27. Westfall, S., & Ombuor, R. (2024), After protests, Kenya's president backs down on controversial tax bill. *The Washington Post*, 26 June 2024. Available at: https://www.washingtonpost.com/world/2024/06/26/kenya-protest-finance-tax-bill-william-ruto/ accessed on 11 November 2024.
28. Von Uexkull, N., Rϕd, E.G., & Svensson, I. (2024), Fuelling protest? Climate change mitigation, fuel prices and protest onset. *World Development*, 177 (2024)106536.
29. IMF eLibrary (2010), *The Taxation of Petroleum and Minerals*: Chapter 8 – Resource Rent Taxes, https://www.elibrary.imf.org/display/book/9780415781381/ch008.xml accessed 11 November 2024.
30. ABC (2024), Mali releases Resolute Mining CEO and other executives after $US 160 million ransom paid. ABC, 21 November 2024. Available at: https://www.abc.net.au/news/2024-11-21/resolute-mining-ceo-released-by-mali-government/104629066 accessed on 18 December 2024; Savage, R. (2024), Australian goldminer to pay Mali $160m to free detained CEO and executives. *The Guardian*, 19 November 2024. Available at: https://www.theguardian.com/australia-news/2024/nov/18/resolute-mining-to-pay-247m-to-free-ceo-terence-holohan-and-executives-detained-in-mali accessed on 18 December 2024.
31. World Bank (2024), above note 2, Executive Summary.
32. Marsden, H. (2024), Under the radar: Canada's carbon tax in the crosshairs. *The Week*, 14 October 2024. Available at: https://theweek.com/environment/canadas-carbon-tax-in-the-crosshairs accessed on 18 December 2024; Al Mallees, N., (2024), 'The carbon tax has plagued the Liberals politically.

Research says that's not surprising. *Canadian Broadcasting Corporation*, 2 June 2024. Available at: https://www.cbc.ca/news/politics/carbon-tax-political-popularity-research-1.7221908 accessed on 18 December 2024; Fletcher, R. (2024), What the "inadvertent error" in the PBO's carbon tax analysis means, in as plain English as possible. *CBC News*, 31 May 2024. Available at: https://www.cbc.ca/news/canada/calgary/pbo-parliamentary-budget-office-carbon-tax-error-explained-1.7218520 accessed on 18 December 2024.

33. OECD (2001), *Environmentally Related Taxes in OECD Countries*, Paris: OECD.
34. *Id.* at 9.
35. World Bank (2024), The Global Tax Program: environmental taxes. Available at: https://www.worldbank.org/en/programs/the-global-tax-program/environmental-taxes.
36. Pembina Institute (2014), *The BC Carbon Tax*, Calgary: Pembina Institute for Appropriate Development, p. 1.
37. *Id.* at p. 2.
38. Magale, E., & Schmidt, M. (2024), Kenya protests show citizens don't trust government with their tax money: can Ruto make a meaningful new deal? *The Conversation*, 17 July 2024. Available at: https://theconversation.com/kenya-protests-show-citizens-dont-trust-government-with-their-tax-money-can-ruto-make-a-meaningful-new-deal-234008 accessed 30 July 2024; Malesi, T. (2024), Kenya's new Eco-Levy sparks debate: a waste management silver bullet or just another tax? *Down To Earth*, 18 June 2024. Available at: https://www.downtoearth.org.in/africa/kenyas-new-eco-levy-sparks-debate-a-waste-management-silver-bullet-or-just-another-tax-2 accessed on 11 November 2024.
39. Dartanto, T. (2017), Fuel subsidy reforms: lessons learned from Indonesia's experiences. *Asia-Pacific Social Science Review*, 17(1), 141–152.
40. Livingstone, E. (2024), Uncertainties remain with renegotiated Chinese mining deal in DRC. *VOA*, 26 January 2024. Available at: https://www.voanews.com/a/uncertainties-remain-with-renegotiated-chinese-mining-deal-in-drc-/7458908.html accessed on 20 December 2024; Bartlett, K. (2023), Whether DRC–China mining deal will be restructured remains uncertain. *VOA*, 1 June 2023. Available at: https://www.voanews.com/a/whether-drc-china-mining-deal-will-be-restructured-remains-uncertain-/7118892.html accessed on 20 December 2024; Byamungu, C.G.N. (2022), Who is behind China Molybdenum in the Democratic Republic of Congo? *The China-Global South Project*, 22 June 2022. Available at: https://chinaglobalsouth.com/2022/06/22/who-is-behind-china-molybdenum-in-the-democratic-republic-of-congo/ accessed on 31 October 2024.
41. IMF eLibrary (2010), above note 29.

PART II

Challenges with carbon border adjustment mechanisms

5. Learning from EU CBAM: major concerns for developing countries and responses to BCAs

Susanne Aakerfeldt, Alexandra Campmas and Paulina Schulz Antipa

1. INTRODUCTION TO CHALLENGES POSED BY BCAs IN DEVELOPING COUNTRIES

Under their current form, Border Carbon Adjustment Mechanisms (BCAs) could disproportionately impact developing countries. As many developing economies rely on carbon-intensive industries, their goods often have high emission intensities (see Figure 5.1), making them more vulnerable to BCA-related charges. Moreover, shifts to more labour-intensive production, which mitigation policies including BCAs are likely to encourage, especially affect developing countries. The absence of direct (or "explicit") carbon pricing instruments in these countries further compounds the issue when a BCA only recognises direct carbon pricing instruments. This is the way the European Union Carbon Border Adjustment Mechanism (EU CBAM or CBAM) is designed to mirror the major domestic direct carbon price applied in the EU, namely its Emission Trading Scheme (EU ETS). Only nine lower- and upper-middle countries have a direct carbon pricing instrument in place, and none has thus far been implemented in low-income countries (see Figure 5.1).

For developing countries that depend heavily on carbon-intensive exports, BCAs can introduce transition risks. These risks arise from the global shift to a low-carbon economy and are driven by factors such as regulatory changes, technological advancements, and evolving consumer preferences. As a regulatory change, a BCA bears key transition risks – e.g., competitiveness and employment impacts, trade deviations, or even disruptions – that heavily depend on several elements that need to be considered by exporting countries. These include: (i) the share of exports in BCA-covered goods, where the reliance on carbon-intensive goods and their contribution to overall exports

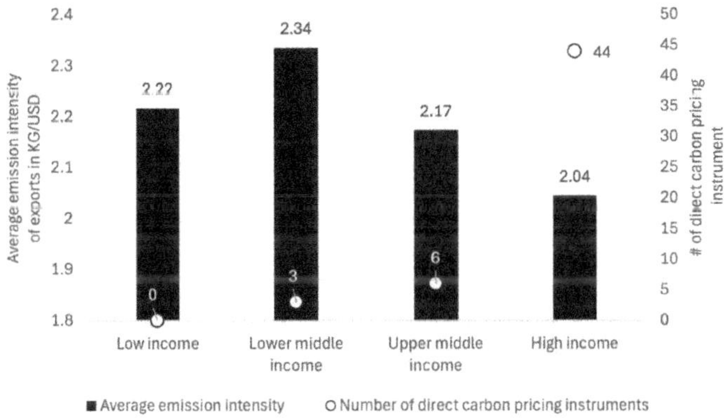

Note: Implemented direct carbon pricing instruments are reported and counted only once per country.
Source: Own calculations based on the World Bank Exposure Index (https://www.worldbank.org/en/data/interactive/2023/06/15/relative-cbam-exposure-index) and Carbon Pricing Dashboard (https://carbonpricingdashboard.worldbank.org/about#download-data).

Figure 5.1 *Average of carbon emission intensity and number of direct carbon pricing instruments across income group countries, 2019*

and gross domestic product (GDP) can significantly affect exposure; (ii) average embedded emissions across BCA goods, as countries with higher carbon intensity will face steeper BCA charges, diminishing the price competitiveness of their exports; (iii) the presence (or not) of a direct carbon pricing instrument, which could be deducted from the BCA obligations; and (iv) administrative and compliance costs arising from the calculation and reporting of embedded emissions at the product level.

Yet, BCAs are a fact of today's toolbox to fight climate change, and they are unlikely to just be a fleeting trend. BCAs aim to mitigate carbon leakage and promote fair competition by ensuring that the carbon price of imported goods is equivalent to the carbon price imposed on domestic production. Shapiro (2021) demonstrates that import tariffs and non-tariff barriers are significantly lower for polluting industries compared to cleaner ones, effectively incentivising the production and trade of dirtier goods. In this respect, BCAs help level the playing field by correcting the undue advantages previously granted to high-emission goods. Since all countries have committed to pricing carbon in endorsing the Polluter Pays Principle,[1] BCAs also remove first-mover disad-

1 United Nations General Assembly Decision A/CONF.151/26, Principle 16.

vantages in implementing a global agreement. Lastly, BCAs respond to a call that developing countries have long made for developed countries to recognise responsibility for emissions they cause in developing countries through their consumption – which also became an obligation through the Rio Declaration.[2] By charging their consumers for embodied emissions, BCA-implementing countries are acting on that responsibility.

At the moment, BCA initiatives are gaining momentum following the implementation of the EU CBAM, which is already operational. As of 1 October 2023, CBAM has entered its transitional phase, with the definitive period set for January 2026. Following the EU's lead, Australia began evaluating policy alternatives for establishing its own BCA, targeting sectors such as steel and cement.[3] Canada announced plans for a BCA regime in the 2021 National Budget and conducted public consultations,[4] though further action is still pending. The UK is similarly considering a BCA to align with its climate policies and maintain competitiveness.[5] In the US, several proposals have recently been tabled for consideration in the Senate, even in the absence of a national carbon pricing scheme, such as the polluter import fee[6] or the Foreign Pollution Fee Act.[7] Another proposal in the US, the Clean Competition Act,[8] considers the introduction of a domestic narrow-based carbon tax combined with import taxes and export rebates.

---

[2] United Nations General Assembly Decision A/CONF.151/26, Principle 8.

[3] Ernst & Young. (2023, August 21). Australia considers CBAM to address carbon leakage. https://www.ey.com/en_gl/technical/tax-alerts/australia-considers-cbam-to-address-carbon-leakage. In November 2024, the Australian government launched a second public consultation, seeking feedback on preliminary findings relating to carbon leakage risk for specific commodities and policy options to address the issue. https://www.dcceew.gov.au/climate-change/emissions-reduction/review-carbon-leakage.

[4] Government of Canada, Department of Finance. (2021). Consultation on border carbon adjustments. https://www.canada.ca/en/department-finance/programs/consultations/2021/border-carbon-adjustments.html.

[5] Government of the United Kingdom. (2023, December 28). Factsheet: UK carbon border adjustment mechanism. https://www.gov.uk/government/consultations/addressing-carbon-leakage-risk-to-support-decarbonisation/outcome/factsheet-uk-carbon-border-adjustment-mechanism.

[6] https://www.intereconomics.eu/contents/year/2021/number/6/article/carbon-border-adjustment-and-other-trade-policy-approaches-for-climate-protection.html.

[7] https://www.cassidy.senate.gov/wp-content/uploads/media/doc/foreign_pollution_fee_bill_text.pdf.

[8] https://www.whitehouse.senate.gov/wp-content/uploads/imo/media/doc/clean_competition_act.pdf.

Some of the risks posed by BCAs can be reduced through specific design choices of BCA-implementing countries ("BCA region"). Other risks can be managed by developing countries themselves. As many developing countries already impose indirect carbon prices, such as fuel taxes, they could modify these instruments to reflect carbon content and/or expand their coverage, making them eligible for CBAM credits. Beyond retaining revenues that would otherwise go to the BCA region, direct carbon pricing could be in countries' own interest as its benefits extend beyond climate goals, especially in developing countries.[9] Additionally, continuing to support climate policies along with carbon pricing policies to lower embedded emissions – such as adopting cleaner production technologies but also phasing out fossil fuel subsidies to disincentivise the use of carbon-intensive fuels – would help reduce the carbon intensity of exports. This, in turn, would lower BCA-related costs by minimising emissions and decreasing the financial obligations tied to carbon-intensive BCA goods. Importantly, BCAs could present an opportunity for developing countries with a comparative advantage in labour (i.e., countries which can produce certain goods or services more efficiently or at a lower cost due to factors like abundant labour or expertise) as mitigation policies like BCAs increase labour intensity (Artuc and Sommer, 2024). International cooperation, including harmonising measurement and reporting standards, is essential to mitigate administrative burdens and compliance costs associated with BCA mechanisms.

Against this background, this chapter aims to offer practical guidance for developing countries on how to adapt to BCA regulations. The focus will primarily be on the CBAM, as it is the only general BCA initiative[10] currently in force and provides a useful example of how such mechanisms might operate in practice. Section 2 outlines the scope and design of BCAs. Section 3 highlights key variables a developing country needs to consider when responding to BCA, focusing on the example of CBAM. Section 4 proposes policy options that developing countries can take to mitigate the impacts of BCA. Section 5 concludes by summarising the key variables to monitor and identifying gaps in the current CBAM legislation that require further attention to support developing countries.

9 Heine & Black (2019), Parry et al. (2015), Timilsina et al. (2024).

10 A BCA mechanism on electricity imports exists in California.

2. UNDERSTANDING THE BASICS OF BCAs, WITH A FOCUS ON CBAM

2.1 Rationale and General Features of BCAs

The most common rationales for introducing a BCA are to address risks of carbon leakage, where emissions shift to jurisdictions with lower environmental standards, undermining decarbonisation efforts; to preserve competitiveness for domestic industries resulting from increased climate ambition in the BCA region; and/or to promote carbon pricing worldwide (Pirlot, 2022).[11] While other forms of BCAs can exist, the prevailing design focuses on equalising the costs of embedded emissions, contributing to equalising abatement costs. Specifically, the carbon price paid in the exporting country incentivises firms to reduce emissions until the marginal abatement cost aligns with the carbon price. This reduction in emissions will be accounted for by deducting the carbon price paid in the exporting country from the BCA obligation, thus avoiding double pricing. However, other costs incurred by exporters – such as those arising from emissions-reducing regulations – cannot be deducted from the financial obligation under the BCA. Instead, these costs will be reflected in lower levels of embedded emissions. If this BCA mechanism uses embedded emissions to calculate the fiscal obligation on imports, either by applying globally defined default values or using observed emissions that fall below these defaults, it creates an incentive for exporters to lower and report emissions. This way, the reduced BCA fiscal obligation reduces the cost of mitigation action.

Each jurisdiction introducing such a BCA must determine the scope of the mechanism and fiscal obligations for the import of selected goods, aiming to align with the carbon price applied to domestic production of similar goods. While nothing legally prevents a jurisdiction from including a broad range of measures in the BCA design, the chosen system must remain administratively feasible and enable authorities to verify reported data. It is, therefore, reasonable to expect that BCA jurisdictions are likely to adopt a definition of a direct (explicit) carbon price. This is the case for the CBAM.

To equalise the cost of carbon in imported goods with that of domestically produced goods, the BCA fiscal obligation should not only mirror the applicable domestic direct carbon price, but also recognise any direct carbon price paid in the exporting country as a way to partially or fully fulfil the fiscal obligation. Any jurisdiction has a sovereign right to decide on its policies, but unless agreed with other jurisdictions, its legal ability to exercise authority

[11] See Pirlot (2022) for a broad assessment of BCAs' purposes and designs.

is restricted to its territory. As such, the legal obligations relating to goods imported into a BCA jurisdiction apply to importers, not to overseas exporters of the goods into that jurisdiction. However, most BCAs will likely require mechanisms for providing data on the embedded emissions or demonstrating emissions reductions of imported goods, which must be obtained from exporters in some form.

A jurisdiction introducing a BCA needs to decide on the methodology to be followed. The scope can cover direct emissions[12] and indirect emissions.[13] The impact of a BCA will vary according to several factors: the exposure to the market of the BCA jurisdiction for CBAM goods, emissions intensity of production, carbon price already paid in the exporting country, and administrative capacity to measure, report, and verify emissions.

2.2 Key Elements of the EU CBAM Design

The legal basis of CBAM is the CBAM Regulation (2023),[14] which also empowers the EU Commission to adopt complementary provisions by implementing or delegated acts.[15] After a transitional phase with a reporting obligation, the definitive period with a financial obligation will apply to specified goods imported into the EU from January 1, 2026. From that date, imports of CBAM goods can only be made by an authorised CBAM declarant, who will face a carbon price comparable to that paid by EU companies running installations covered by the EU ETS.

Any direct carbon price[16] already paid in the exporting country will be deducted from the CBAM fiscal obligation. The fiscal obligation will be gradually phased in during 2026 to 2034, reflecting the extent to which EU

---

[12] Direct emissions mean emissions from the production processes of goods, and in the CBAM also includes emissions from the production of heating and cooling used in the production processes, irrespective of the location of the production of the heating and cooling.

[13] Indirect emissions mean emissions from the production of electricity consumed during the production processes of goods, irrespective of the location of the production of the consumed electricity.

[14] For further information on CBAM: https://taxation-customs.ec.europa.eu/carbon-border-adjustment-mechanism_en#legislative-documents.

[15] Implementing acts ensure a uniform application of technical details in specific areas, being well-defined by the empowerments in the CBAM Regulation (2023). Delegated acts allow the EU Commission to, within certain specific areas, reflect developments unknown at the time the Regulation was adopted.

[16] 'Carbon price' means the monetary amount paid in a third country, under a carbon emissions reduction scheme, in the form of a tax, levy, or fee or in the form of emission allowances under a greenhouse gas emissions trading system,

ETS allowances are allocated free of charge in installations producing CBAM goods within the EU.

Each authorised CBAM declarant will, by 31 May of each year, report the embedded emissions in CBAM goods imported into the EU during the previous calendar year and surrender CBAM certificates covering those emissions, except for exporting countries already subject to a direct and effectively paid[17] carbon price. CBAM certificates must be purchased from a dedicated platform at the weekly average price for EU ETS allowances. These certificates cannot be traded between declarants or exchanged with EU ETS allowances. Declarants will store the certificates in a CBAM registry until they are surrendered for compliance, with only a portion of surplus certificates allowed to be carried over to the next year or resold to the EU Commission. Additionally, the declarant will have to hold and deposit in the registry certificates equal to 80 per cent of the embedded emissions in all goods that have been imported since the beginning of the year (CBAM Regulation, 2023, Article 22(2)).

While authorised CBAM declarants do not have to fill out their CBAM declarations for 2026 until 31 May 2027, they will still need detailed data on embedded emissions from exporters by then. This data transfer should ideally be part of the purchase agreement between the exporter and the importer, which is often negotiated well in advance.

During the definitive period, only direct emissions will be subject to CBAM for iron, steel, aluminium, and hydrogen, while both direct and indirect emissions will be accounted for in cement, electricity, and fertilisers. The emissions need to be verified by an independent verifier, accredited by an EU national accreditation body. This verifier can be from any country (inside or outside of the EU), but the specific conditions for accreditation will be established by the EU Commission through a delegated act. While verifiers accredited under the EU ETS can be used, ETS qualifications need to be for the relevant CBAM goods. Until these details are clarified through an implementing act, finding a qualified verifier to handle CBAM duties may be challenging. If actual embedded emissions cannot be adequately determined, set default values[18] should be used.

---

calculated on greenhouse gases covered by such a measure and released during the production of goods, CBAM Regulation (2023), Article 3 (29).

[17] 'Effectively paid carbon price' is defined in CBAM Regulation (2023), Article 9(1) to ensure that any rebate or compensation reducing the carbon price in the exporting country is considered when calculating the deduction from the CBAM obligation.

[18] Default values are to be determined in a forthcoming implementing act, CBAM Regulation (2023), point 4.1 of Annex IV.

Under the chosen BCA design, and in line with the EU's authority within its borders, CBAM obligations rest with importers. During the definitive period, importers must be pre-authorised as CBAM declarants before being allowed to import goods. These declarants will need to report detailed data on embedded emissions from exporters unless they choose to use the yet-to-be-defined default values.

The exporters may, however, face administrative challenges in tracking and reporting emissions. The use of default values with a high mark-up will not satisfactorily resolve these challenges, as this particular design of CBAM may require measuring, reporting, and verifying (MRV) systems, creating additional burdens and discriminating against countries with lower administrative capacities. Moreover, under the 80 per cent obligation rule described above, embedded emissions will be based on these high default values, with limits on how many certificates can be resold to the EU Commission or saved for the following year. This penalises producers with low embedded emissions and countries with a direct carbon price instrument, as the importers of these goods may still need to purchase certificates despite the existence of a direct carbon price.

3. ANTICIPATING IMPACTS: THE EXAMPLE OF CBAM

BCAs present risks for developing countries with large BCA exports and high emission intensities (often higher than in BCA regions), resulting in the transfer of revenues. This section uses the CBAM framework to assess these challenges for the 15 most exposed countries in terms of CBAM goods exported to the EU.

3.1 Exports of CBAM Goods

Relative metrics can be more insightful than simply looking at the total trade volume. For example, in absolute terms, China is the largest exporter of CBAM goods to the EU,[19] with exports in 2022 valued at USD 21 billion. However, these exports accounted for only 0.56 per cent of China's GDP, resulting in a relatively low exposure of China to the regulation. In contrast, Mozambique, while more modest in terms of total export volume (USD 1.7 billion in 2022), has 13.5 per cent of its exports destined for the EU. Figure 5.2 illustrates the countries most exposed to CBAM in terms of the share of total exports. If

[19] Based on CEPII-BACI trade data.

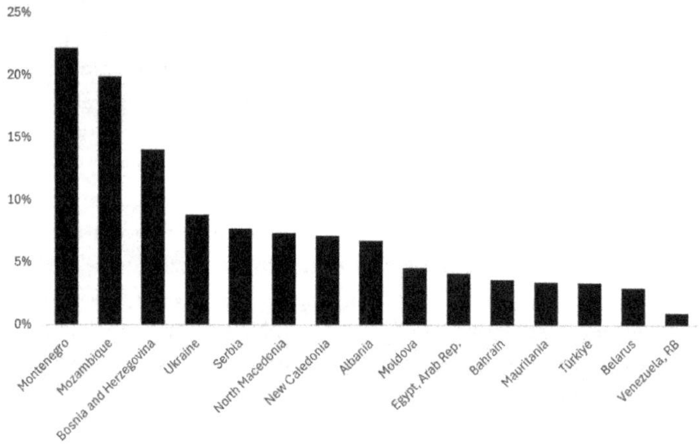

Note: Figures were created using the following approach: For each country-year pair, the Harmonised System (HS) version (e.g., HS 2022, HS 2017) with the highest total export value was selected, as it typically corresponds to the most comprehensive product codes for that country and year.
Source: Based on CEPII – BACI trade data. Gaulier, G., and Zignago, S. (2010). CEPII Working Paper, No. 2010–23. Available at: http://www.cepii.fr.

Figure 5.2 *Average share of CBAM exports to the EU-27 in total exports over the period 2012 to 2022, by country, for the top 15 countries*

Canada, China, Japan, the UK, and the US adopted similar regulations, countries' exposure would increase significantly.

3.2 Emission Intensities and Competitiveness

The carbon costs of CBAM increase according to the embedded emissions of goods. Thus, CBAM can provide a cost advantage for countries with low carbon footprints. Vidovic et al. (2023) find significant variability in the level of indirect emissions, particularly in the aluminium sector, across those investigated, which represents over 90 per cent of imports of goods regulated under CBAM. While the coverage of indirect emissions is still modest under CBAM, future reviews of the mechanism will likely expand the scope to also include indirect emissions, underscoring the importance for countries to monitor their emissions more holistically. This monitoring will help them anticipate and adapt to transition risks. Figures 5.3a–d illustrate emission intensities across the top 15 countries most exposed to CBAM.

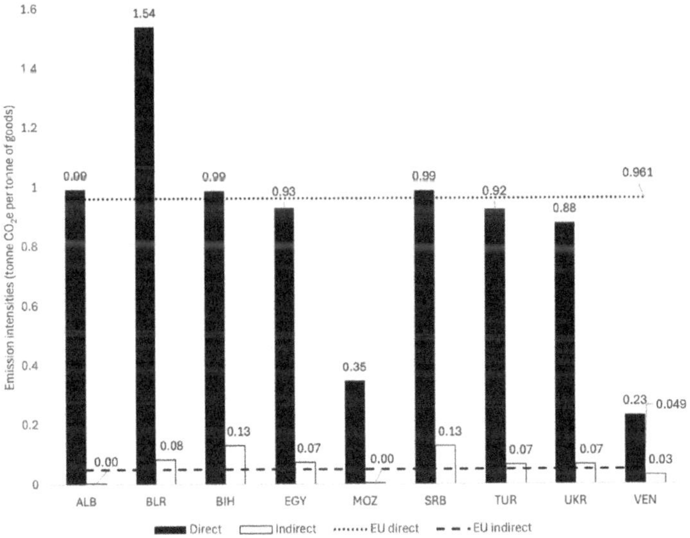

Figure 5.3a *Emission intensities (tonne CO_2e per tonne of goods), simple average per goods category: Cement*

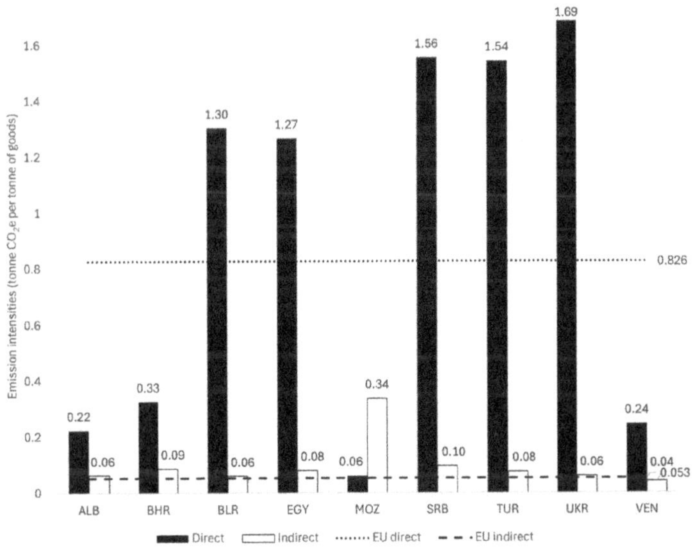

Figure 5.3b *Emission intensities (tonne CO_2e per tonne of goods), simple average per goods category: Fertilizers*

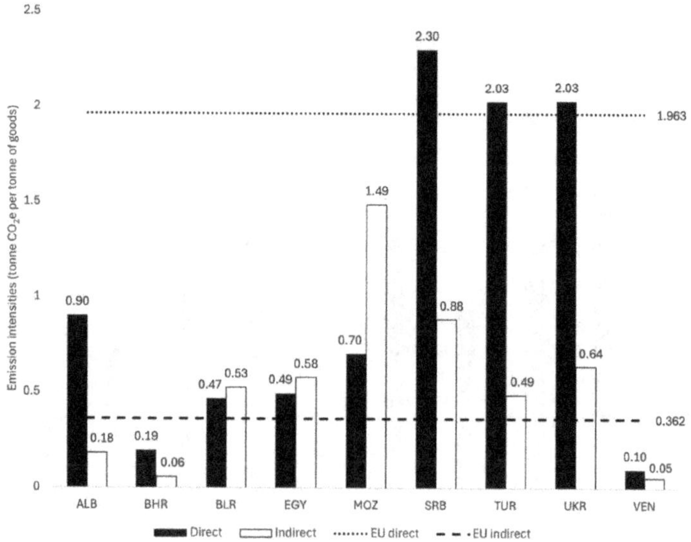

Figure 5.3c *Emission intensities (tonne CO_2e per tonne of goods), simple average per goods category: Iron and steel*

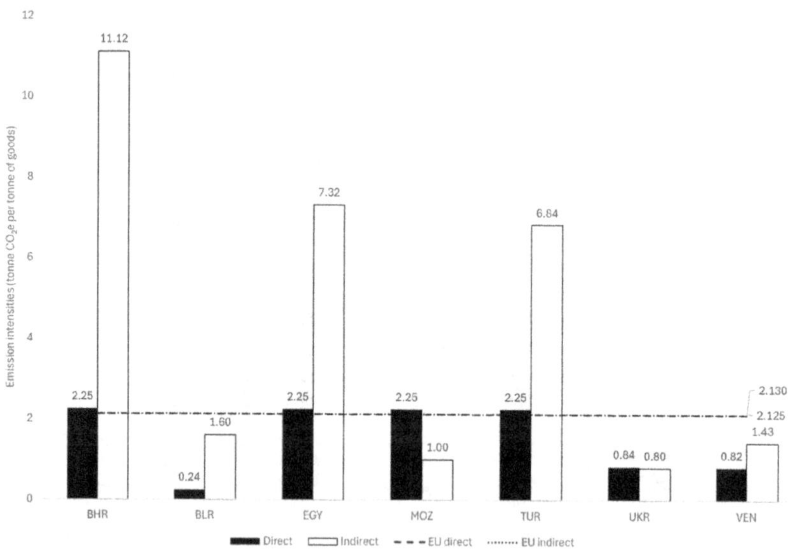

Source: Joint Research Centre of the EU Commission, detailed in Vidovic et al. (2023). Emission intensity values are displayed when available.

Figure 5.3d *Emission intensities (tonne CO_2e per tonne of goods), simple average per goods category: Aluminium*

3.3 Cost of the CBAM Certificates and Potential Transfer of Revenues

Based on the description of CBAM in Section 2.2, annual transferred revenues for each of the CBAM goods can be calculated as follows:

$$\begin{aligned} &Transferred\ Revenues = CBAM\ certificate\ costs \\ &= Max\{X * \left[CP_{EU} * \left(EE - EE_{Benchmark} * CBAM\ factor\right) - CP_c * EE\right], 0 \end{aligned} \quad (1)$$

Where:

X represents the quantity of goods (in tonnes)

CPc represents the carbon price in the exporting country (net of free allocation)

CP_{EU} represents the EU ETS price

EE represents the embedded emissions of the goods

$EE_{Benchmark}$ is the CBAM benchmark for embedded emissions (for each of the goods)

$CBAMfactor$ represents the free allocation share for CBAM goods over time[20]

Once free allocations are fully phased out in the EU, and assuming the EU ETS price (CP_{EU}) is equal to or higher than the domestic carbon price in the exporting jurisdiction (CP_c), the formula above simplifies, for each CBAM good under a specified CN code[21], as follows:

$$Maximum\ Transferred\ Revenue = X * EE * \left(CP_{EU} - CP_c\right) \quad (2)$$

Assuming a fully phased-in CBAM financial obligation by 2034 and a differential carbon price of USD 80 per tonne of CO_{2e} for each country, Figure 5.4 illustrates the total costs of CBAM certificates and revenue transfers to the EU across countries most exposed to CBAM by summing up the transferred revenue for each CBAM good. Using historical data to forecast the total cost of CBAM certificates in 2034 shows that it could range from less than 1 per

[20] CBAM will be gradually phased in, with a decreasing factor from 2026 until 2033, after which it will no longer apply.

[21] Goods covered by CBAM are identified by codes in the Combined Nomenclature (CN). Those CN codes come under the CN Code Regulation (1987).

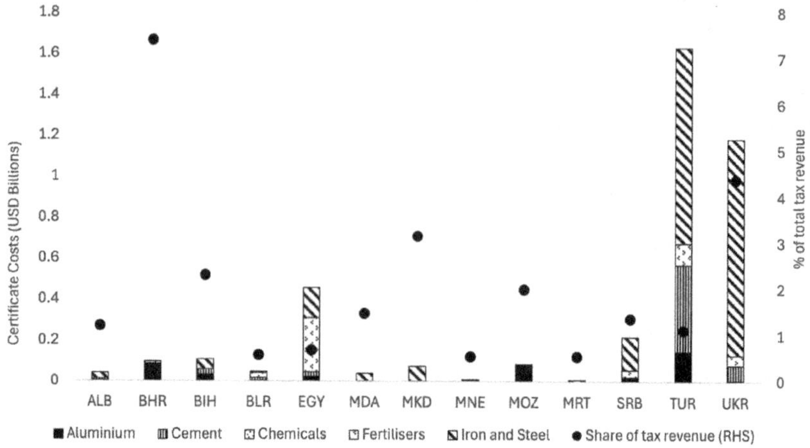

Source: Own elaboration based on CEPII – BACI trade data for the year 2022 (https://www.cepii.fr/CEPII/en/bdd_modele/bdd_modele_item.asp?id=37), emission intensities from Vidovic et al. (2023), and latest available data point on total tax revenues from WB prosperity data (https://databank.worldbank.org/metadataglossary/world-development-indicators/series/GC.TAX.TOTL.GD.ZS).

Figure 5.4 *Transferred revenue for most exposed countries to CBAM, assuming* $CP_{BCA} - CP_c = USD80$ *per tonne of* CO_2e

cent to over 7 per cent of a country's total tax revenues. In monetary terms, the maximum potential transferred revenue could exceed USD 1.6 billion for Türkiye.

4. POLICY OPTIONS TO MITIGATE CBAM IMPACTS IN DEVELOPING COUNTRIES

Several policy options can be considered in response to CBAM, including adjustments to the volume of traded CBAM goods exported to the EU, reducing embedded emissions, and introducing a direct carbon pricing mechanism.

4.1 Taxing Carbon through Direct Instruments: From Existing Tax to New Instruments

A straightforward policy option for exporting countries, based on the carbon price definition of the CBAM Regulation (see Section 2.2, Footnote 16), is to introduce a carbon tax or an ETS covering the GHG emissions released during the production of the CBAM goods. The CBAM recognises the carbon price paid in the exporting country as a way of fulfilling, partly or fully, a CBAM fiscal obligation for the imported goods. Despite consensus from international organisations that carbon pricing goes beyond direct instruments through the use of indirect (or implicit) and negative carbon prices (World Bank, 2025), it is not currently planned that indirect pricing, like energy taxes on fuels, qualifies for a reduction of the CBAM fiscal obligation.

Another adjacent issue is how the scope of a domestic carbon tax would affect its admissibility for such a reduction. In this context, the future interpretations by the EU Commission as well as WTO implications of different designs need to be carefully considered. A carbon tax only on emissions embedded in exported goods stands a better chance of being considered compatible than a tax only applied on goods exported to the EU.

Importantly, while carbon taxes and ETSs would qualify equally to receive credit, ETSs take several years before becoming fully operational. Carbon taxes are easier to administer, as they can be levied through existing tax collection systems. Many developing countries already tax carbon indirectly through fuel excises or price regulations (Figure 5.5), enabling them to reclassify these charges into a direct carbon tax. The exporting country could therefore convert its indirect pricing into a direct carbon tax by modifying fuel excise taxes to reflect the carbon content of the fuel, making it more likely to qualify for credits against the CBAM. For instance, Argentina and Uruguay introduced a carbon tax in March 2018 and January 2022, respectively, by converting their indirect carbon pricing to direct carbon pricing (Rabbia, 2023). As fuel excise taxes mostly apply to diesel and gasoline (Boesen, 2021), countries would need to ensure that the scope of the tax covers the fuels used in the production of the CBAM goods.

The CBAM thus encourages the adoption or increase of direct domestic carbon taxation. Beyond saving on the CBAM, there are additional reasons why that reform can be in the national interest. The benefits of carbon taxation extend beyond environmental goals, especially in developing countries. Upstream carbon taxation can have lower costs for economic growth than conventional taxes. Covering large informal sectors and using the revenues to substitute formal-sector taxes creates opportunities to boost output. A broad tax base allows carbon taxation to raise revenues more efficiently, with less negative impact on output compared to conventional taxes.[22] Employment outcomes are also likely better with upstream carbon taxes than with some

---

[22] See, for example, evidence for Cote d'Ivoire (Timilsina et al., 2024), Ghana (Elmaleh et al., 2021, p. 154f), Pakistan (Burns et al., 2021), China and India (Carson et al., 2021), Iran (Mirhosseini et al., 2017), Spain (Markandya et al., 2013), Eastern Europe (World Bank, 2022, p. 48f), the EU (Barrios et al., 2013), and globally (Bento et al., 2018, Schoder, 2023).

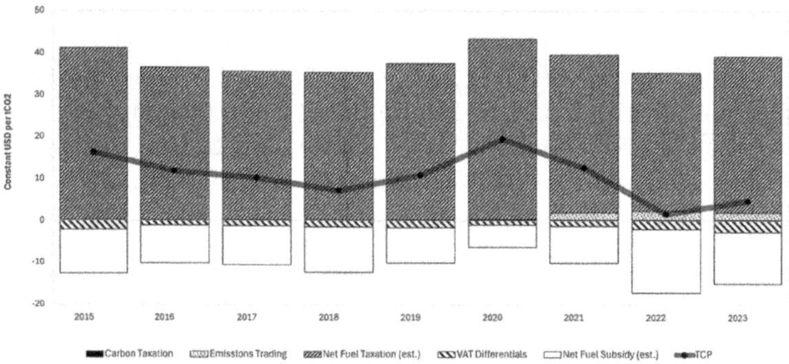

Note: TCP is initially calculated at the country level and then aggregated, weighted by emissions, across 137 developing countries
Source: Own estimations based on the methodology outlined in Agnolucci et al. (2024), with additional extensions described in World Bank TCP 2.0 (forthcoming).

Figure 5.5 Total Carbon Pricing (TCP) in developing countries

conventional taxes, especially those on labour[23] – for two reasons. Policy-driven decarbonisation shifts the economy towards more labour-intensive sectors and increases labour intensity within sectors by transforming production methods.[24] Furthermore, development co-benefits are particularly pronounced in developing countries. By discouraging pollution-intensive activities, carbon taxation can improve air quality, enhancing public health, and reduce social costs that come with road use, including congestion, accidents, and road damages. These effects are so large that many researchers have found them to exceed the economic cost of mitigation.[25] All this means that there are national economic interests for taxing carbon, independent from their contribution to climate objectives and reduced CBAM liabilities (Heine & Black, 2019).

[23] Schoder (2023), Elmaleh et al. (2021), Skrok et al. (2022), Metcalf and Stock (2023).
[24] Saget et al. (2020), Hille & Möbius (2019), Moszoro (2021), Malerba and Wiebe (2021).
[25] Vandyck et al. (2018); Markandya et al. (2013); Scovronick et al. (2019); Weitzel et al. (2019); Rauner et al. (2020).

4.2 Continuing to Support Climate Policies to Lower Embedded Emissions

While direct carbon pricing is a cost-effective instrument, it does not prevent countries from adopting other climate policies to ultimately lower embedded emissions. Positive carbon pricing, through energy taxes and carbon taxation, is the only instrument able to internalise the cost of emissions and reflect the Polluters Pay Principle, which all countries have committed to implementing in the Rio Declaration of 1992. At the same time, phasing out existing negative carbon pricing instruments, such as fossil fuel subsidies, is crucial to avoid weakening the overall carbon pricing signal and to level the playing field with renewable energy. Other non-pricing, complementary policies – such as renewable energy incentives, energy efficiency standards, and sectoral regulations – are equally crucial to address other existing market failures. Efforts towards supporting policy mixes will help reduce the carbon intensity of production (see, for example, Alt et al., 2024), which in turn lowers the embedded emissions in exported goods, decreasing CBAM financial obligations.

Therefore, complementary strategies reside in leveraging cleaner production technologies. If CBAM goods are produced in exporting countries with lower embedded emissions compared to goods produced in the EU, the fiscal obligation will be lower than the corresponding price paid by the producer in the EU, giving the exporter a cost advantage. An exporter lowering direct and/or indirect embedded emissions will also see this advantage versus other exporters to the EU market that have not reduced their emissions as much. Reducing actual embedded emissions can involve a range of strategies, including adopting energy-efficient technologies, switching to renewable energy sources, and implementing cleaner processes, such as using low-emission fuels or upgrading equipment to reduce emissions from combustion. Curbing indirect emissions involves switching from coal or natural gas to cleaner electricity or heat sources, such as solar, wind, or hydroelectric power.

Furthermore, international cooperation plays a pivotal role in facilitating the transfer of clean production. As developing countries may already benefit from low-cost and low-carbon technology, opportunities may arise to coordinate policies with advanced economies and large middle-income countries to help overcome initial barriers, such as high capital costs. For example, initiatives such as the Trade-Related Aspects of Intellectual Property Rights Agreement (TRIPS, 2017) could help developing countries utilise compulsory licensing for environmentally sound technologies, enabling them to access crucial innovations without prohibitive costs.

4.3 Reducing the Volume of Traded CBAM Goods

With high embedded emissions and no direct carbon pricing instrument, exporting countries might attempt to redirect exports affected by CBAM to non-CBAM countries. Nonetheless, this strategy might be costly or limited due to the availability of alternative markets, costs of switching, and the potential for new markets to also adopt BCAs in the future. With countries like Canada and the USA considering BCAs and the UK set to introduce one by 2027, the availability of alternative markets may decline over time. This strategy may also conflict with the decarbonisation goals outlined in NDCs.

4.4 Mitigating Administrative Burden Thanks to International Collaboration

Without international collaboration, the proliferation of BCA mechanisms is at risk of resulting in diverse methodologies for measuring, reporting, and verifying (MRV) emissions and recognising paid carbon prices, significantly raising compliance costs for developing countries. Different BCA regions may adopt similar administrative measures for BCAs, but inconsistent methodologies could increase the burden on exporters sending BCA goods to multiple BCA markets. Harmonising MRV standards across BCAs can simplify the complex requirements for calculating embedded emissions, which often differ from the general MRV for installations under domestic carbon pricing schemes like ETSs. For example, in CBAM, exporters need to provide specific emissions data for each consignment of goods, creating challenges in converting installation-level data into goods-specific values. Moreover, the uncertainty around future carbon price forecasts, due to the phase-in of CBAM, adds another layer of complexity. Increased technical assistance and cooperation between developing countries and advanced economies could streamline these processes, reduce costs, and ease integration into global carbon markets.

5. CONCLUSION: KEY INGREDIENTS FOR NAVIGATING BCAs AND STAYING ALERT TO THE FINALISATION OF CBAM

BCAs are not merely concerns for national Ministries of Environment and Trade but are equally important for Ministries of Finance. Governments in exporting countries need to consider implementing a direct carbon pricing instrument to retain fiscal revenues associated with the embedded emissions in goods subject to a BCA, such as CBAM. At the same time, with a broad tax base, carbon can generate significant revenues while minimising costs to output and employment, boosting local productivity, and generating co-benefits through reduced fuel use. Carbon pricing can thus serve a dual purpose: while it helps retain revenues that might otherwise be transferred to jurisdictions implementing BCAs, carbon pricing is uniquely capable of internalising the societal costs of local externalities caused by the burning of fossil fuels.

There is therefore a clear way forward for developing countries in responding to CBAM and other emerging BCAs – by pricing carbon, which is in their own interest. Yet, this national interest does not mean that BCAs will not raise important challenges, and governments considering responses to BCAs should design strategies that address these challenges effectively. Some of the challenges remain shrouded in uncertainty.

While the fundamental legal requirements of CBAM and detailed rules for the reporting methodology during the transitional period are established in the CBAM Regulation (2023) and the CBAM Implementing Regulation (2023) respectively, the EU Commission still needs to adopt additional implementing acts in several areas. These acts are crucial not only for ensuring that CBAM obligations can be effectively met from 2026 onwards but also for addressing the challenges faced by governments and exporters in developing countries and easing the implementation of CBAM.[26]

Some of these important challenges can be addressed to make CBAM more accessible and equitable for developing countries. First, setting default emission values equal to average emissions instead of applying punitive mark-ups would reduce compliance and administrative burdens, particularly for low-income countries and exporters with limited capacity, who often face difficulties navigating complex EU systems. Second, simplifying MRV requirements by providing alternatives for producers wishing to demonstrate advanced green practices, resulting in lower emissions, and considering allowing private certification bodies to manage compliance would alleviate pressures on exporters in countries with low administrative capacity. Permitting developing countries to rely on their existing upstream excise duty administration to levy direct carbon taxes on fuels will enable CBAM declarants to claim credits for such upstream payments when fulfilling financial obligations on imported CBAM goods produced by downstream firms in the exporting country. This will minimise disruptions to domestic systems and reduce the need for costly structural adjustments. Such adjustments would not only alleviate challenges for developing countries but also ensure CBAM's effectiveness in addressing global carbon leakage.

[26] The extent of empowerment for the EU Commission to adopt further implementing acts is found in CBAM Regulation (2023) Articles 2, 5, 6, 7, 8, 9, 14, 17, 18, 25, and 31. Further, the CBAM Regulation (2023) also includes empowerments for the EU Commission to adopt delegated acts in certain areas; see Articles 2, 18, 20, and 27.

REFERENCES

Agnolucci, P., Fischer, C., Heine, D., Montes de Oca Leon, M., Pryor, J., Patroni, K., & Hallegatte, S. (2024). Measuring Total Carbon Pricing. *The World Bank Research Observer, 39*(2), 227–258.

Alt, M., Bruns, H., DellaValle, N., & Murauskaite-Bull, I. (2024). Synergies of Interventions to Promote Pro-environmental Behaviors – A Meta-analysis of Experimental Studies. *Global Environmental Change*, 84, 102776.

Artuc, E., & Sommer, K. (2024). Trade, Outsourcing, and the Environment. World Bank Policy Research Working Paper, (10665).

Barrios, S., Pycroft, J., & Saveyn, B. (2013). The Marginal Cost of Public Funds in the EU: The Case of Labour Versus Green Taxes. European Commission, Taxation Paper, Working Paper N.35 – 2013.

Bento, A.M., Jacobsen, M.R., & Liu, A.A. (2018). Environmental Policy in the Presence of an Informal Sector. *Journal of Environmental Economics and Management, 90*, 61–77.

Boesen, U. (2021). Excise Tax Application and Trends. *Tax Foundation*, 753.

Burns, A., Jooste, C., & Schwerhoff, G. (2021). *Climate Modeling for Macroeconomic Policy: A Case Study for Pakistan.* The World Bank.

Carson, R.T., Jacobsen, M.R., & Liu, A.A. (2021). Are Carbon Taxes More Efficient in Industrialising Countries? Comparing China and India to the United States. *American Economic Association Conference.*

CN Code Regulation (1987). Council Regulation (EEC) No 2658/87 of 23 July 1987 on the tariff and statistical nomenclature and on the Common Customs Tariff.

CBAM Regulation (2023). Regulation (EU) 2023/956 of the European Parliament and of the Council of 10 May 2023 establishing a carbon border adjustment mechanism.

CBAM Implementing Regulation (2023). Commission Implementing Regulation (EU) 2023/1773 of 17 August 2023 laying down the rules for the application of Regulation (EU) 2023/956 of the European Parliament and of the Council as regards reporting obligations for the purposes of the carbon border adjustment mechanism during the transitional period.

Elmaleh, D.J., Stapleton, K.A., Dutz, M.A., Graham, E.G., Kruse, A., & Kwakye, K.G. (2021). *Ghana Rising: Accelerating Economic Transformation and Creating Jobs.* World Bank Group.

Ernst & Young. (2023, August 21). Australia considers CBAM to address carbon leakage. https://www.ey.com/en_gl/technical/tax-alerts/australia-considers-cbam-to-address-carbon-leakage

Gaulier, G. & Zignago, S. BACI: International Trade Database at the Product-level. The 1994-2007 Version. No 2010 – 23 October. CEPII. https://www.cepii.fr/PDF_PUB/wp/2010/wp2010-23.pdf

Government of Canada, Department of Finance. (2021). Consultation on border carbon adjustments. https://www.canada.ca/en/department-finance/programs/consultations/2021/border-carbon-adjustments.html

Government of the United Kingdom. (2023, December 28). Factsheet: UK carbon border adjustment mechanism. https://www.gov.uk/government/consultations/addressing-carbon-leakage-risk-to-support-decarbonisation/outcome/factsheet-uk-carbon-border-adjustment-mechanism.

Heine, D. & Black, S. (2019). Benefit Beyond Climate: Environmental Tax Reform. In Pigato, M.A. (ed.), *Fiscal Policies for Development and Climate Action*. Washington, DC: The World Bank.
Hille, E., & Möbius, P. (2019). Environmental Policy, Innovation, and Productivity Growth: Controlling the Effects of Regulation and Endogeneity. *Environmental and Resource Economics*, *73*, 1315–1355.
Malerba, D., & Wiebe, K.S. (2021). Analysing the Effect of Climate Policies on Poverty through Employment Channels. *Environmental Research Letters*, *16*(3), 035013.
Markandya, A., González-Eguino, M., & Escapa, M. (2013). From Shadow to Green: Linking Environmental Fiscal Reforms and the Informal Economy. *Energy Economics*, *40*, S108–S118.
Metcalf, G.E., & Stock, J.H. (2023). The Macroeconomic Impact of Europe's Carbon Taxes. *American Economic Journal: Macroeconomics*, *15*(3), 265–286.
Mirhosseini, S.S., Mahmoudi, N., & Pourali Valokolaie, S.N. (2017). Investigating the Relationship between Green Tax Reforms and Shadow Economy Using a CGE Model-A Case Study in Iran. *Iranian Economic Review*, *21*(1), 153–167.
Moszoro, M. W. (2024). The Direct Employment Impact of Public Investment. *International Journal of Management and Economics*, *60*(1), 59–74.
Parry, I., Veung, C., & Heine, D. (2015). How Much Carbon Pricing is in Countries' Own Interests? The Critical Role of Co-benefits. *Climate Economics*, *6*(4), 1–26.
Pirlot, A. 2022. Carbon Border Adjustment Measures: A Straightforward Multi-purpose Climate Change Instrument? *Journal of Environmental Law*, *34*(1), 25–52.
Rabbia, M. 2023. Why did Argentina and Uruguay Decide to Pursue a Carbon Tax? Fiscal reforms and Explicit Carbon Prices. *Review of Policy Research*, *40*(2), 230–259.
Rauner, S., Hilaire, J., Klein, D., Strefler, J., & Luderer, G. (2020). Air quality co-benefits of ratcheting up the NDCs. *Climatic Change*, *163*, 1481–1500.
Rio Declaration. (1992). Rio Declaration on Environment and Development.
Saget, C., Vogt-Schilb, A., & Luu, T. (2020). *Jobs in a Net-Zero Emissions Future in Latin America and the Caribbean*. Inter-American Development Bank and International Labour Organization, Washington D.C. and Geneva.
Schoder, C. (2023). Regime-dependent Environmental Tax Multipliers: Evidence from 75 Countries. *Journal of Environmental Economics and Policy*, *12*(2), 124–167.
Scovronick, N., Budolfson, M., Dennig, F., Errickson, F., Fleurbaey, M., Peng, W., ... & Wagner, F. (2019). The impact of human health co-benefits on evaluations of global climate policy. *Nature communications*, *10*(1), 2095.
Shapiro, J. S. (2021). The Environmental Bias of Trade Policy. *The Quarterly Journal of Economics*, *136*(2), 831–886.
Timilsina, G.R., Dissou, Y., Toman, M., & Heine, D. (2024). How Can a Carbon Tax Benefit Developing Economies with Informality? A CGE Analysis for Côte d'Ivoire. *Climate Policy*, *24*(1), 71–86.
TRIPS. Agreement on Trade-Related Aspects of Intellectual Property Rights (as amended on 23 January 2017) is Annex 1C of the *Marrakesh Agreement Establishing the World Trade Organization*, signed in Marrakesh, Morocco on 15 April 1994.
Vandyck, T., Keramidas, K., Kitous, A., Spadaro, J. V., Van Dingenen, R., Holland, M., & Saveyn, B. (2018). Air quality co-benefits for human health and agriculture counterbalance costs to meet Paris Agreement pledges. *Nature communications*, *9*(1), 4939.

Vidovic, D., Zore, L., Moya, J.A. & Marmier, A. (2023). *Greenhouse Gas Emission Intensities of the Steel, Fertilisers, Aluminium and Cement Industries in the EU and Its Main Trading Partners*. Publications Office of the European Union.

Weitzel, M., Vandyck, T., Keramidas, K., Amann, M., Capros, P., den Elzen, M., Frank, S., Tchung-Ming, S., Díaz Vázquez, A., & Saveyn, B. (2019). Model-based assessments for long-term climate strategies. *Nature Climate Change*, *9*(5), 345–347.

World Bank. (2022). *Green Fiscal Reforms: Part Two of Strengthening Inclusion and Facilitating the Green Transition*. EU Regular Economic Report; No. 7 Washington, D.C.: World Bank Group.

World Bank. (2025). *Carbon Pricing Metrics: Analyzing Existing Tools and Databases of Platform for Collaboration on Tax (PCT) Partners*. Washington, D.C.: World Bank Group.

6. Unpacking and responding to Border Carbon Adjustments (BCAs): a Global South perspective

Seutame Maimele

1. INTRODUCTION

A global transition to sustainable development is gaining momentum, representing a comprehensive effort that spans all levels of government and policy. This transition is not solely an environmental issue; it also poses significant socio-economic challenges that affect trade and industrial development. It impacts the structure and dynamics of entire value chains, influencing competitiveness, trade performance, and economic growth.

Climate change regulations, such as carbon pricing, shifts in trade patterns away from carbon-intensive products, and the promotion of green industrial policies in regions like the USA, EU, China, and Brazil, are becoming more prevalent than ever. Additionally, measures such as BCAs and other non-tariff barriers, like deforestation rules, are becoming increasingly common in countries such as the EU, USA, UK, Australia, Canada, and Japan.

This chapter delves deeper into BCAs and explores potential non-exhaustive responses from the Global South. It aims to identify collaborative opportunities among Global South countries to address these challenges. The chapter begins by outlining BCAs currently under development and those in transition, followed by an analysis of their impacts, particularly on BRICS+[1] and African nations. The fourth section examines the implications of BCAs for the Global South, while the fifth section outlines non-exhaustive strategies for how these countries can effectively respond to such measures.

2. BORDER CARBON ADJUSTMENTS (BCAs): UNDER DEVELOPMENT AND TRANSITIONING

In Global North countries, a key strategy has been the formation of carbon clubs (through the G7 countries) to align with carbon border taxes and decarbonisation policies.[2] The USA, Canada, and the UK have engaged in discussions regarding regulatory frameworks to adopt or support carbon border taxes in response to the EU's Carbon Border Adjustment Mechanism (EU CBAM). However, despite these governmental initiatives, industries and firms have raised significant concerns about the potential for dual carbon tax imposition, particularly in relation to the EU. They worry that this could create unfair competitive advantages for certain economic blocs.[3] The following discussion focuses on the development of BCAs and the responses from various jurisdictions. It begins by examining the actions taken by Global North countries and then shifts to highlight the position of the Global South.

The European Union (EU) was the first to introduce an ambitious climate change policy package under the European Green Deal (EGD). Since its launch in 2019, the EGD has sparked significant debates on climate policy, aiming to reduce the EU's net greenhouse gas (GHG) emissions by 55% by 2030 and achieve carbon neutrality by 2050.[4] Central to this initiative is the EU CBAM, which imposes carbon border taxes on high-emission imports to align prices with EU prices and prevent carbon leakage.[5] Initially covering direct emissions from electricity and 29 product categories in sectors like cement and steel, the CBAM's scope has expanded to include hydrogen and certain indirect emissions, now encompassing 42 product groups across cement, iron and steel, aluminium, hydrogen, fertilisers and electricity.[6] The implementation will occur in two phases: a transitional period starting in October 2023, focusing on administrative reporting, followed by operational status starting in 2026, when importers must declare GHG emissions and purchase CBAM certificates based on EU emissions trading system prices. The CBAM is designed to apply primarily to EU importers; the CBAM also allows for reduced certificate requirements for those with their own carbon pricing systems. The European Commission will oversee the governance and implementation, ensuring transparency and efficiency.[7] Non-compliance will lead to penalties, and any attempts to circumvent the rules could result in stricter regulations on imported goods.[8]

With the EU CBAM introduced, responses across the EU have varied, with middle-income countries and sectors like steel and electricity raising concerns about the implementation timeline and the legality of the EU CBAM. Despite overall support for the mechanism, various countries and industries have voiced apprehensions about its implementation. Industry representatives in Belgium and Germany generally support the EU CBAM; however, they have called for an extension of the December 2025 deadline and a reduction in the administrative costs associated with emissions reporting.[9]

The United Kingdom has also introduced a BCA, currently in the design phase, which allowed feedback from countries in early 2024. The latest version of the UK CBAM closely resembles the EU CBAM with different terminology, albeit with distinct proposed carbon pricing and GHG emissions accounting methodologies.[10] The latest UK CBAM, after the results of consultations have been incorporated, includes less sector coverage, specifically omitting electricity, with ceramics and glass also omitted, although previously included in the initial version.[11] Essentially, the UK CBAM imposes a charge on emissions embodied in relevant imports, which functions as a carbon border tax on high-emission imports to the UK, paralleling the EU CBAM.

The UK CBAM is set to operate with a one-year accounting period, interpreted as a transition phase, from January to December 2027. This period will allow firms exporting to the UK to develop the necessary infrastructure for monitoring, reporting, and verifying GHG emissions associated with goods covered by the UK CBAM. Governance of the UK CBAM will primarily involve two institutions: HM Revenue & Customs and HM Treasury.[12]

In other developed countries, there has been significant interest in the emergence of BCAs. In the United States, the country has played a pivotal role in forming carbon clubs, particularly through the G7. However, the USA has yet to implement a BCA, though several policies are in development that aim to align with BCA objectives.[13] Noteworthy proposals include the PROVE IT (Providing Reliable, Objective, Verifiable Emissions Intensity and Transparency) Act, which seeks to provide detailed GHG emissions data for various products in the USA, Group of Seven countries (G7), US free trade agreement (FTA) partners, and other countries of concern, and has bipartisan support as of January 2024. The act covers a range of products, such as industrial raw materials (e.g. aluminium, cement, glass, and iron and steel), energy products (natural gas, crude oil, lithium-ion batteries, and solar cells and panels), and critical minerals (copper, cobalt, graphite, and lithium). The Energy Innovation and Carbon Dividend Act is another policy proposal aiming to promote clean energy by discouraging fossil fuel use and penalising polluters, with a mechanism for monthly carbon dividends for citizens.

The Foreign Pollution Fee Act, Clean Competition Act, MARKET CHOICE Act, and FAIR Transition and Competition Act are other key proposed policies aligned with BCAs. The Foreign Pollution Fee Act proposes taxing foreign goods with higher emissions than domestic products, although it raises concerns about compliance with WTO rules. The Clean Competition Act, introduced in June 2022, aims to impose a carbon price of $55 per tonne on both domestic and imported goods, with revenues earmarked for decarbonisation initiatives in the USA and developing countries. The MARKET CHOICE Act seeks a similar approach, applying a carbon price to fossil fuels and linking to a trust fund for low-income households. Finally, the FAIR Transition and Competition Act proposes an implicit carbon tax targeting specific sectors, offering exemptions for least-developed countries, and using collected revenues for decarbonisation and community support. While these proposals mainly target carbon-intensive sectors like aluminium, cement, and steel, there is potential for future expansion to include agriculture and construction, as highlighted in the Inflation Reduction Act regarding GHG emissions accounting.[14]

After the 2024 USA elections, with Donald Trump as President of the USA, the administration's position on climate change remains to be determined. It is also yet to be revealed to what extent the proposed policies will be adopted and their position on climate clubs.

In addition to the USA, UK, and EU, other developed countries, including Japan, Canada, and Australia, are considering BCAs for climate mitigation. Japan is closely monitoring the EU CBAM, with its Ministry of Trade and Industry reviewing a potential Japanese version to combat carbon leakage.[15] While concerns have been raised by iron and steel and aluminium exporters regarding the EU CBAM, the Japanese government has stated that its transitional implementation does not violate WTO rules. In Canada, as of October 2024, there has been no progress on a proposed BCA after consultation closed in 2022, although the government expressed interest in carbon border taxes in 2020 as part of its Climate Actions plan.[16] The Department of Finance in Canada plans to increase carbon pricing by CAD 15 per tonne annually, reflecting concerns about its impact on trade relationships, especially with the EU.[17] In Australia, discussions about a domestic BCA began in August 2023, focusing on carbon taxation alongside reforms to emission limits for major facilities, initiated on July 1, 2023. The aim is to address carbon leakage while aligning with existing regulations in response to the EU CBAM.[18]

In the Global South, particularly among BRICS+ and African countries, there have been significant advances in responding to BCAs – specifically the EU CBAM. The responses from the founding BRICS member states have resonated throughout the African Union and other developing countries. BRICS nations have been vocal in their criticism of the EU CBAM, arguing that it undermines the principles of equitable trade and development as outlined in Article 6 of the 2015 Paris Climate Accord.[19] Their positions are rooted in the principles of Common But Differentiated Responsibilities and Respective Capabilities (CBDR-RC), as well as the Special and Differential Treatment (S&DT) provisions established in the General Agreement on Tariffs and Trade (GATT) and the United Nations Framework Convention on Climate Change (UNFCCC) – especially the historical responsibilities of industrialised nations to reduce carbon emissions, as articulated in the Paris Agreement.[20]

Additionally, BRICS countries contend that industrialised nations are leveraging carbon taxes to shield local industries and promote protectionism under the pretext of mitigating carbon emissions and preventing carbon leakage.[21] The CBAM's impact on high-carbon industries, crucial to the economies of BRICS nations, has prompted unified opposition. At the 6th BRICS summit, member states condemned any measures perceived as green protectionism or carbon taxes that would disproportionately burden developing countries. China, Brazil, and India specifically argued that CBAM acts as a form of protectionism that undermines the spirit of the Paris Agreement.[22]

Across Africa, regional responses have focused on addressing trade disparities. African countries and stakeholders have formed coalitions, advocating for more flexible EU CBAM policies at multilateral institutions to avoid hindering growth and development. The African Group at the WTO emphasises that implementing carbon taxes to "level the playing field" exacerbates inequalities between industrialised nations.[23] They argue that revenues generated from carbon certification should be redirected to support African states in their decarbonisation efforts.[24] This comes as African states have contributed less to historical GHG emissions. African coalitions accuse the EU and Western nations of undermining trust in multilateral institutions by forming carbon clubs, while the EU maintains that CBAM measures are intended to advance global decarbonisation efforts.[25]

Overall, BRICS and African responses to the BCAs reflect significant disagreement and uncertainty. While industry stakeholders show some optimism in engaging with the EU in the case of the EU CBAM, government actors remain highly critical and focused on addressing concerns through multilateral institutions like the WTO.[26] However, frustrations are mounting as the dispute settlement system has stagnated.[27] Despite limited success in convincing the EU to make global concessions, there is potential for key BRICS nations, such as South Africa, India, and China, to leverage their influence with newly joined member states to press the EU for concessions. This could pose further challenges for the European Commission, especially amid growing opposition from the Global South.

The next section focuses on the impact of BCAs on the Global South, specifically in relation to the EU CBAM.

3. IMPACT OF BCAs ON THE GLOBAL SOUTH: ANALYSING THE EU CBAM

This section examines the impact of BCAs, specifically the EU CBAM, on the Global South, with a particular focus on Africa and BRICS+ countries (although affected differently). Global South countries, particularly in Africa and within the BRICS+ group, face significant challenges from climate change, experiencing greater economic disruption and loss of life compared to their Global North counterparts.[28] These nations often lack the resources and fiscal capacity needed for effective climate change mitigation, which compounds their vulnerability.

The introduction of the EU CBAM is set to have profound implications for trade between the EU and these countries. Understanding these impacts requires an examination of their trading relationships with the EU and identifying which sectors will be most affected by the EU CBAM. This analysis is divided into two parts: first, the effects on BRICS+ countries, followed by a focus on Africa. Each sub-section explores the trade dynamics and highlights the vulnerabilities of sectors covered by the EU CBAM, underscoring the urgent need for targeted support to mitigate these risks.

3.1 CBAM in BRICS+

The BRICS+ countries play a significant role in global trade, with total exports reaching $5 trillion in 2022, accounting for about a quarter of global exports. However, the emergence of climate change policies, particularly BCAs, poses challenges for these nations, as many of their manufactured exports are carbon-intensive. While BCAs are often seen as necessary for combating climate change, they can also be perceived as protectionist measures (see Section 4.2).

Between 2011 and 2021, trade between BRICS+ countries and the EU remained consistent at around $640 billion on average, with an increase post-COVID-19. In 2021, BRICS+ exports to the EU totalled $853 billion, while imports were $571 billion, resulting in a positive trade balance of $281 billion.

The key exporters in this group are China, Russia, and India, with China alone accounting for $518 billion of exports to the EU in 2021. In terms of imports, the same dominant players are evident: China imported $309 billion from the EU in 2021, followed by Russia with $94 billion and India with $46 billion.

Despite this trade activity, the BRICS+ countries represent only 13% of the EU's total exports and 9% of its imports, indicating that their trade is insignificant within the EU market. Nonetheless, the EU remains a crucial market for BRICS+ exports.

Regarding the EU CBAM, approximately $52.4 billion of BRICS+ exports are at risk, based on the 2022 data. This represents about 6% of BRICS+ exports to the EU and about 0.2% of their GDP. This vulnerability is expected to increase as more products fall under the CBAM.

3.2 CBAM in Africa

In 2022, Africa's exports totalled $661 billion, representing just 2.7% of global exports, while imports reached $694 billion, accounting for 2.8% of global imports, resulting in a negative trade balance of $33 billion.[29] Trade dynamics between Africa and the EU reflect a similar trend observed in BRICS+

countries. While the EU is Africa's largest trading partner, African trade with the EU remains minor, comprising only 2.2% of total EU imports.[30]

From 2011 to 2022, Africa's trade with the EU showed consistent underperformance, with exports declining by 0.5% and imports by 0.2%. Since 2014, Africa has imported more from the EU than it has exported, although post-COVID-19 recovery began in 2021, resulting in a trade surplus.

The increase in African exports to the EU in 2022 was driven by global trade recovery and heightened demand for fossil fuels amid the Russia–Ukraine crisis. More than 65% of Africa's exports to the EU are primary goods, primarily energy products, while manufactured goods account for 34% in 2022. Due to limited industrialisation, over 67% of Africa's imports from the EU in 2022 were manufactured products.[31] This highlights a persistent trade imbalance.

Regarding the EU CBAM, approximately $7.3 billion of African exports are at risk, which is about 3.2% of African exports to the EU and around 0.4% of Africa's GDP (based on 2022 data). Key affected sectors include aluminium, iron and steel, and fertilisers, with North and Southern Africa being the most vulnerable.[32]

4. IMPLICATIONS FOR THE GLOBAL SOUTH: ANALYSING THE CHALLENGES ARISING FROM THE INTRODUCTION OF BCAs

This section addresses three interconnected but different issues arising from BCAs. While this list is non-exhaustive, these issues have direct implications for the Global South. They include green trade barriers, green protectionism, and the inadequacy of diversified carbon pricing in providing sufficient protection for the Global South.

4.1 Green Trade Barriers

The introduction of climate change policies worldwide has garnered significant challenges, particularly for the Global South. A key issue emerging from these policies is the intersection of environmental and trade regulations, exemplified by the EGD. The EGD has sparked intense debates in multilateral forums regarding whether its components constitute trade barriers or serve purely environmental purposes.

For decades, the relationship between trade and the environment has been a central focus at the WTO.[33] The notion that debates around environmental policies affecting trade are recent is misleading.[34] Issues related to environmental measures and trade have been discussed at the WTO since the 1970s, beginning with the Environmental Measures and International Trade group established in 1971. This evolved into the Committee on Trade and Environment under the Marrakesh Agreement in 1994, which continues to address trade-related environmental measures, albeit without achieving consensus on many issues.[35]

Climate and trade issues are not new phenomena; however, they have gained momentum recently with the introduction of the EGD. For instance, in the early 1990s, the USA imposed trade restrictions on tuna imports from Mexico to protect dolphins, due to concerns about dolphin bycatch in Mexican fishing practices, leading to a WTO ruling against using trade restrictions for environmental objectives in other countries.[36] While concerns about the environmental impacts of goods produced abroad have been raised repeatedly, they pose market access challenges by imposing restrictions on certain products.[37] Other authors assert that BCAs and environmental policies should serve solely environmental goals, rather than protect domestic industries.[38]

With the advent of BCAs like the EU CBAM, the debate has intensified, involving discussions at multilateral levels, including the UNFCCC, G20, and WTO. As the first flagship BCA, the EU CBAM has been scrutinised from legal, economic, and environmental perspectives. However, the mechanism is intended to promote national carbon pricing, level the playing field, and encourage international climate action amid rising global GHG emissions.[39] The EU CBAM functions as a carbon border tax on embedded greenhouse gases in GHG-intensive products imported into the EU, aiming to equalise carbon prices between EU products and imports and prevent carbon leakage.[40]

BCAs effectively act as barriers to market access, akin to tariffs on affected products.[41] Additionally, there is potential for "reshuffling", where jurisdictions capable of producing both green and carbon-intensive products divert cleaner goods where needed and dirty products to areas with no climate policies.[42] Looking at the EU CBAM, the mechanism violates WTO most-favoured nation rules by discriminating against other countries based on carbon pricing and differentiated treatment based on their link to the EU ETS. This also violates GATT Article XX, which highlights that any measure introduced must comply with the chapeau of Article XX, which prohibits arbitrary or unjustifiable discrimination between countries where the same conditions prevail, or a disguised restriction on international trade.[43]

4.2 Green Protectionism

Since the onset of debates surrounding environmental and trade-related issues, a clear divide has emerged between the Global North and the Global South. The Global North has prioritised the introduction of environmental measures that impact trade, such as BCAs – exemplified by the EU CBAM – and substantial green industrial policy initiatives like the USA Inflation Reduction Act. The rise of "climate-justified protectionism" is fuelled by competition for dominance in low-carbon products, technologies, and solutions.[44] Such measures are intended to protect citizens' well-being in the Global North, where there are growing concerns about the negative environmental consequences of intensified free trade.[45] In contrast, developing countries[46] perceive these policies as a form of green protectionism.[47]

The environmental policies introduced by the Global North have been unilateral, protectionist, and discriminatory, often disregarding their potential impact on developing countries.[48] This behaviour violates principles established by international rules.[49] Some measures violated by the introduction of these policies include national treatment under GATT Articles III:2 and/or III:4, tariff binding under GATT Article II, GATT Article XI, which sets out to prohibit quantitative import restriction, and most favoured nation provision under GATT Article I.[50] These policies also serve to shield domestic industries in the Global North, backed by green industrial policies aiming to develop domestic industries where these mechanisms are introduced.[51] For example, after the EU CBAM was criticised internally by member states noting that they receive less protection from the EU in the midst of EU CBAM, the EU in 2023 introduced a Green Deal Industrial Plan for the net-zero age. This incentive-based policy aims to protect EU industries by enhancing their competitiveness amid growing protection of industries worldwide.[52]

This protectionist behaviour is driven by citizens' concerns about climate change and its potential impacts, leading politicians to adopt these measures to maintain voter support.[53] A study by Bechtel[54] et al indicates that environmental concerns are positively correlated with protectionist attitudes, including opposition to globalisation, job-related protectionism, and product-related protection (e.g., environmentally-friendly production and consumer safety).

As the Global North continues to protect its industries, the Global South should also be protected amid the rising debate about climate and trade. This is done in some parts of the Global South, such as China, Brazil, and South Africa for example. The Global North countries introduce green policies that impact trade and, to some extent, violate key international rules as outlined above. These measures are predominantly unilateral and contribute to a greater sense of green protectionism.[55] In effect, the specific circumstances of developing countries must be considered, emphasising the need for mutual recognition in policy implementation.[56] Furthermore, environmental measures should be strictly aimed at ecological objectives and not at protecting domestic industries.[57]

Given the Global North's protectionist stance in implementing environmental policies affecting trade, there is a substantial disregard for the adverse effects these policies will have on the Global South, which stands to suffer from their introduction. While there has been some progress at the multilateral level, such as the establishment of a task force at the WTO focusing on creating an international carbon pricing system to address trade distortions,[58] much work remains to be done.[59] The Global South must collaborate to address the intertwined issues of climate change and trade.

4.3 Low Protection from Global Heterogeneous Carbon Pricing

The World Bank's 2024 carbon pricing data reveals that at least 110 carbon pricing schemes are currently active worldwide, spanning 53 national and 40 subnational jurisdictions.[60] Together, these cover 24% of global GHG emissions. The development of carbon pricing mechanisms is increasingly recognised as a global trend for environmental protection. However, countries in the Global South often view these mechanisms as revenue collection techniques aiming to enhance the competitiveness of the Global North countries by using funds collected from the Global South to support the decarbonisation efforts of the Global North – therefore defeating the idea of the historical responsibility of the Global North.[61]

The introduction of carbon pricing by individual jurisdictions, without a global carbon price, can diminish competitiveness for those jurisdictions.[62] This is primarily due to higher product prices, making their goods more expensive compared to those from regions without carbon pricing. Moreover, the Global South has limited protection from global carbon pricing, largely because of low or non-existent carbon pricing.

In Africa, for example, carbon pricing has only been implemented in South Africa, although several other countries – including Botswana, Senegal, Côte d'Ivoire, Morocco, Gabon, and Nigeria – are considering its introduction.

The Global South countries such as Colombia, Chile, China, and Indonesia have carbon pricing in place. Current carbon pricing mechanisms introduced there include carbon taxes and Emission Trading Schemes (ETS), with carbon prices ranging from \$0.61 to \$12 per tonne of CO_2e. In contrast, Global North countries mostly have established higher carbon prices, with a minimum of \$17 and a maximum of \$142 per tonne. Notable exceptions charging over \$100 per tonne of CO_2e include Norway, Sweden, Switzerland, Finland, and Liechtenstein, with Uruguay as a non-North country in this group. Most of these countries are exempt from the EU CBAM, likely due to their higher carbon prices compared to the EU ETS, which averages around \$60 per tonne based on World Bank data updated on April 1, 2024.

Countries in the Global South generally pay less for carbon emissions than those in the Global North. However, with the introduction of the EU and UK CBAMs, which adjust for carbon pricing in exporting jurisdictions that already have carbon pricing policies, the impact shifts. This adjustment leads to reduced carbon price adjustments for exports from the Global South, effectively increasing the carbon costs they bear outside their jurisdictions when exporting to regions with a BCA in place.

5. RESPONDING TO BCAs: A GLOBAL SOUTH PERSPECTIVE

This section examines how the Global South can respond to the development and implementation of BCAs. The list of possible responses is non-exhaustive. The section begins by outlining the necessity of establishing Monitoring, Reporting, and Verification (MRV) systems. Next, it focuses on advocating for reforming the multilateral system to promote equitable development and transition. The discussion then highlights the importance of green industrial policy and climate-resilient development. Following this, the section emphasises the need for capacity building and technology transfer. Finally, it advocates for differentiated treatment in carbon pricing, calling for a global carbon price.

5.1 Creating Monitoring, Reporting, and Verification Systems

Based on a survey of executives from 1,290 organisations across nine major industries globally, it was found that approximately 86% manually monitor and account for GHG emissions.[63] Despite the manual accounting of GHG emissions, the EU and UK CBAMs require MRV of GHG emissions at a product level on a quarterly basis, which the world fails to achieve – in particular the Global South lacks both the financial and human resources to deploy and adopt MRV systems. However, companies in the Global South can start adopting new technologies such as AI, automation, and digital platforms for more precise and real-time accounting of embedded emissions. Countries in the Global South can also learn from each other's experiences in developing GHG emissions accounting systems.

For example, South Africa is making significant progress in this area. The South African Council for Scientific and Industrial Research (CSIR)[64] is developing a GHG observatory designed to collect and manage real-time data. This platform aims to provide accurate GHG emissions data at the product level for exporters required to report emissions to certain jurisdictions. Utilising blockchain technology for secure data management and analysis, the platform is currently in its pilot phase.

The observatory's ecosystem supports the installation of hardware, such as energy meters and Raspberry Pi devices, which gather real-time energy consumption data. This information is used to calculate GHG emissions for each product throughout the production process. The data is then summarised using blockchain technology, enabling the platform to generate dashboards and detailed GHG emission reports. These reports can inform customers in the EU and other regions implementing BCAs about the embedded emissions in their products.

5.2 Reform of the Multilateral Systems (WTO and Global Financial Systems)

Over five decades ago, the Committee on Trade and Environment was established, and in 2023, during a Trade and Environment Week at the WTO, the EU CBAM faced its first major scrutiny as its transition period was set to begin. During this event, the European Commission asserted that the EU CBAM aligns with existing WTO frameworks, including GATT, and serves as a crucial tool for decarbonisation within EU member states and among key trading partners like China and India.[65]

In response to concerns from developing countries, the EU highlighted mechanisms like the Generalised System of Preferences to support trade development in these nations. It emphasised that trade facilitation efforts would accompany the implementation of the EU CBAM. EU representative David Boublil countered accusations that the EU CBAM "punishes" developing countries by implementing carbon taxes.[66] The EU argued that while carbon taxes generate internal revenue, they also mitigate the risk of shifting carbon-heavy responsibilities onto developing nations by certifying emissions on imports.

The European Commission has robustly defended the mechanism against criticism from developing countries at key multilateral institutions. However, despite expressing a willingness to support these nations, most EU responses have primarily focused on addressing concerns from major trading partners like China and India.[67]

While the EU defends the mechanism, the Global South, as a collective alliance, could initiate negotiations for WTO reform alongside its engagement with the EU. For example, during the COVID-19 pandemic, South Africa played a pivotal role in advocating for a waiver of certain Trade-Related Aspects of Intellectual Property Rights (TRIPS) provisions to enhance vaccine access for African nations.[68] In this case, prominent countries like India and South Africa could lead the Global South group at the WTO to address the inequities in the current multilateral system, particularly concerning trade and environmental issues. Key negotiation points could include promoting free transfers of green technologies, allowing flexibility in TRIPS, and harmonising WTO principles with those of the UNFCCC regarding S&DT and CBDR-RC.

Additionally, the Global South should advocate for comprehensive reform of the multilateral system, which has been undermined by the Global North's protectionist policies masquerading as green initiatives. The climate emergency presents a unique opportunity for Global South countries to push for a fairer, more inclusive multilateral framework.

Alongside the reform of the WTO, the global financial system must evolve to better address developmental needs and climate financing. The World Bank's mission should expand to encompass climate change, with the Bridgetown Initiative[69] led by Barbados advocating for essential reforms.

5.3 Green Industrial Policy and Climate Resilient Development

The USA's Inflation Reduction Act (IRA) and the EU's Green Industrial Policy Plan aim to lower the costs of the energy transition in the Global North by promoting green industrial policies, such as providing subsidies and tax rebates for green initiatives. Public investment in green initiatives is rising in these countries to support the production of competitive low-carbon products.[70] Transitioning local carbon-intensive value chains requires urgent attention, particularly in the Global South, given the EU CBAM transition period. Technological advancements in production processes are essential for decarbonisation, though they are costly in the short term.[71]

In the context of issues of trade and environment further fragmenting the global trade system, the need for Global South cooperation on issues of climate and trade must be acknowledged.[72] In this context, climate-resilient development should be pursued in a cooperative way that fosters mutually beneficial trade integration, advances industrial development, upgrades regional value chains across the Global South, enhances cross-border infrastructure, and promotes democracy, good governance, and peace across regions.[73]

5.4 Capacity Building and Technical Transfers

Countries in the Global South face significant financial and non-financial constraints that hinder their ability to develop low-carbon and climate-resilient economies. To address these challenges, it is essential to equip these nations with the necessary mechanisms and tools for climate mitigation, alongside increasing technical assistance to comply with BCAs.

Dedicated mechanisms must be increased to facilitate technology transfers and capacity building throughout the Global South. These initiatives should empower these nations not only to supply critical minerals for green industrialisation but also to actively engage in combating climate change. Within the context of the EU CBAM, increasing capacity building and technical assistance are urgently needed across the Global South.

Increasing this support is particularly crucial for developing effective MRV systems for GHG emissions, which will help offset compliance costs related to testing and setting standards in the short term. Developed nations, in fulfilling their climate responsibilities, must assist Global South countries in preparing to implement these global climate change policies. This assistance could at least partially contribute to restorative justice, among other issues.

5.5 Moving Towards an Equitable Global Carbon Price

The revenue generated from the EU CBAM is expected to aid economic recovery following the COVID-19 pandemic. Seventy-five per cent of CBAM revenue will contribute to the EU budget[74] while 25% will go to member states.[75] Projected revenue from CBAM charges stands at €9.1 billion, with administrative costs estimated between €9.8 million and €14.3 million for importers, plus an additional €15 million for customs and national authorities. While some jurisdictions benefit financially, others incur costs to support the decarbonisation efforts of these regions, which poses significant concerns for the Global South. The imposition of carbon pricing on Global South countries presents challenges for their financial stability and adjustment efforts.

In this context, the WTO has established a task force to develop a global carbon pricing system that considers the distributional impacts of carbon pricing, particularly accounting for the developmental status of emerging economies. In 2021, the International Monetary Fund proposed an International Carbon Price Floor (ICPF) for large emitters.[76] This proposal aims to tailor carbon pricing to the capacities of individual countries rather than impose a blanket approach that could negatively affect developing nations. The ICPF would be negotiated among large key emitters, focusing on establishing a minimum carbon price for CO_2 emissions.[77]

The ICPF emphasises flexibility for emerging economies, allowing them to industrialise at a lower carbon price compared to developed countries. Given that the Global South has contributed less to historical GHG emissions, their climate responsibilities should be aligned with their development status. The ICPF could alleviate pressures from unilateral measures like the EU CBAM, enhance competitiveness among developing countries, and support the objectives of the Paris Agreement.[78] Differentiated carbon pricing is essential for promoting international equity in climate action, considering each country's level of development. Where support is needed, financial and technical assistance should be prioritised. Current BCAs generally overlook this differentiation, except for potential aspects of the US CBAM, which focuses on benefits for local industries. Insufficient attention has been given to the most affected and vulnerable economies, raising significant concerns regarding the fairness of international climate efforts.

6. CONCLUSION

The global transition to sustainable development is gaining momentum, encompassing a broad array of governmental and policy efforts. This transition extends beyond environmental concerns, introducing significant socio-economic challenges that impact trade and industrial development while reshaping entire value chains. The increasing emergence of measures such as BCAs and non-tariff barriers is reshaping the global economic environment, particularly for countries in the Global South.

This chapter has explored the intricacies of BCAs and the potential responses (non-exhaustive) that the Global South can adopt to mitigate potential negative impacts in the short term. By identifying collaborative opportunities among Global South countries, this work aims to equip them with strategies to effectively navigate the evolving landscape of sustainable development. As the transition unfolds, it is essential for these nations to leverage their collective strengths and engage in innovative solutions that promote equitable development and sustainability.

NOTES

1. Stuenkel, Oliver and Margot Treadwell. 2024. "Why Is Saudi Arabia Hedging Its BRICS Invite?". Carnegie Endowment. Available at: https://carnegieendowment.org/emissary/2024/11/brics-saudi-arabia-hedging-why?lang=en, accessed in December 2024.
2. Climate Trade. 2022. "What the G7 Climate Club Means for Carbon Markets." Available at: https://climatetrade.com/what-the-g7-climate-club-means-for-carbon-markets/ accessed in December 2024.
3. Ramos, Dominic. 2023. "Global Perspectives on the European Union's Carbon Border Adjustment Mechanism (CBAM)." Trade & Industrial Policy Strategies (TIPS). Available at: https://www.tips.org.za/research-archive/sustainable-growth/green-economy-2/item/4701-global-perspectives-on-the-european-union-s-carbon-border-adjustment-mechanism-cbam, accessed in November 2024.
4. European Commission. 2019. "The European Green Deal." Available at: https://commission.europa.eu/strategy-and-policy/priorities-2019-2024/european-green-deal_en, accessed in December 2024.
5. European Commission. 2023. "Regulation (EU) 2023/956 of the European Parliament and of the Council of 10 May 2023 – establishing a carbon border adjustment mechanism." Available at: https://eur-lex.europa.eu/legal-content/EN/TXT/PDF/?uri=CELEX:32023R0956, accessed in December 2024.
6. Maimele, Seutame. 2023. "Responding to the European Union's Carbon Border Adjustment Mechanism (CBAM): South Africa's Vulnerability and Responses." Trade & Industrial Policy Strategies (TIPS). Available at: https://www.tips.org.za/research-archive/sustainable-growth/green-economy-2/

item/4590-responding-to-the-european-union-s-carbon-border-adjustment-mechanism-cbam-south-africa-s-vulnerability-and-responses, accessed in November 2024.
7. European Commission. 2023, supra note 5.
8. Ibid.
9. Ramos. 2023, supra note 3.
10. Maimele, Seutame. 2024. "Understanding the United Kingdom's Carbon Border Adjustment Mechanism (UK CBAM): Is it the European Union CBAM?" 2024. Available at: https://www.tips.org.za/policy-briefs/item/4758-understanding-the-united-kingdom-s-carbon-border-adjustment-mechanism-uk-cbam-is-it-the-european-union-cbam, accessed in November 2024.
11. United Kingdom Government. 2024. "Introduction of a UK Carbon Border Adjustment Mechanism from January 2027: Government Response to the Policy Design Consultation." Available at: https://assets.publishing.service.gov.uk/media/672a00dfabb279b2de1e8b8a/_Updated__4038_-_Introduction_of_a_UK_Carbon_Border_Adjustment_Mechanism_from_January_2027_-_Government_response_to_the_policy_design_consultation.pdf, accessed in December 2024.
12. Maimele. 2024, supra note 10.
13. Rasool, Sanam, William Reinsch A., and Thibault Denameil. 2024. "Crafting a Robust U.S. Carbon Border Adjustment Mechanism." CSIS Brief. Available at: https://www.csis.org/analysis/crafting-robust-us-carbon-border-adjustment-mechanism#:~:text=The%20bill%20aims%20to%20create,inflationary%20trends%20in%20subsequent%20years, accessed in November 2024.
14. Ibid.
15. Ramos. 2023, supra note 3.
16. Government of Canada. 2023. "Consultation on Border Carbon Adjustments." Available at: https://www.canada.ca/en/department-finance/programs/consultations/2021/border-carbon-adjustments.html, accessed in December 2024.
17. Ramos. 2023, supra note 3.
18. Ibid.
19. Ibid.
20. Kazan Declaration (Russia). 2024. "Strengthening Multilateralism for Just Global Development and Security." XVI BRICS Summit. Available at: https://cdn.brics-russia2024.ru/upload/docs/Kazan_Declaration_FINAL.pdf?1729693488349783, accessed in December 2024.
21. Ibid.
22. Ramos. 2023, supra note 3.
23. WTO African Group. 2023. "Policy Space for Industrial Development – A Case for Rebalancing Trade Rules to Promote Industrialisation and to Address Emerging Challenges Such as Climate Change, Concentration of Production and Digital Industrialisation." Communication from the African Group. World Trade Organization. Available at: https://docs.wto.org/dol2fe/Pages/

SS/directdoc.aspx?filename=q:/WT/GC/W868.pdf&Open=True, accessed in December 2024.
24. Ruto, W. 2022. Remarks by His Excellency Hon William Samoei Ruto, PhD., C.G.H., President of the Republic of Kenya and Commander-In-Chief of the Defence Forces, on behalf of the African Group and Kenya at the 27th Conference of Parties (COP 27) to the United Nations Framework Convention on Climate Change (UNFCCC). 7 November 2022. Available at: https://unfccc.int/sites/default/files/resource/KENYA_cop27cmp17cma4_HLS_ENG.pdf, accessed in December 2024.
25. Ramos. 2023, supra note 3.
26. Ibid.
27. Ismail, Faizel. 2020. "WTO Reform and the Crisis of Multilateralism: A Developing Country Perspective." South Centre, Switzerland. Available at: https://www.southcentre.int/wp-content/uploads/2020/09/Bk_2020_WTO-reform-and-the-crisis-of-multilateralism_EN.pdf, accessed in December 2024.
28. Clausing, Kimberly A., and Catherine Wolfram. 2023. "Carbon Border Adjustments, Climate Clubs, and Subsidy Races When Climate Policies Vary." *Journal of Economic Perspectives* 37(3): 137–62. https://doi.org/10.1257/jep.37.3.137.
29. Maimele, Seutame. 2023. "The European Green Deal (EGD) and Its Implications for African Trade - Working Paper." Trade & Industrial Policy Strategies (TIPS). Available at: https://www.tips.org.za/research-archive/sustainable-growth/green-economy-2/item/4722-the-european-green-deal-egd-and-its-implications-for-african-trade, accessed in November 2024.
30. MacLeod, Jamie, and David Luke. 2023. "Trade and Investment Flows and a Perspective for Analysing Trade Policy in Africa." In Luke, David (Ed) *How Africa Trades*, 1–21. London: LSE Press.
31. Maimele. 2023, supra note 29.
32. Ramos. 2023, supra note 3.
33. Lydgate, Emily, and L. Alan Winters. 2024. "The UK's Border Carbon Leakage Trilemma." *Energy Policy* 198 (March): 114393. https://doi.org/10.1016/j.enpol.2024.114393.
34. Persaud, B. 2003. "Environment and the WTO." *The Round Table* 92(372): 623–35. https://doi.org/10.1080/0035853032000150636.
35. Ismail. 2020, supra note 27.
36. Bechtel, Michael M., Thomas Bernauer, and Reto Meyer. 2012. "The Green Side of Protectionism: Environmental Concerns and Three Facets of Trade Policy Preferences." *Review of International Political Economy* 19(5): 837–66. https://doi.org/10.1080/09692290.2011.611054.
37. Davies, Rob. 2023. "Navigating New Turbulences at the Nexus of Trade and Climate Change: Implications and Options for Africa." Available at: https://owinfs.org/2023/ACF_Carbon.pdf accessed in December 2024.
38. Meyer, Timothy. 2024. "Copernican Revolution or Green Protectionism?" In Kathleen Claussen and Geraldo Vidigal (Eds), *The Sustainability Revolution*

in International Trade Agreements. Oxford: Oxford University Press (2024), Duke Law School Public Law & Legal Theory Series 23 (2023).
39. European Commission. 2023, supra note 5.
40. Maimele. 2023, supra note 6.
41. Davies. 2023, supra note 37.
42. Clausing and Wolfram. 2023, supra note 28.
43. Meyer. 2024, supra note 38.
44. Davies. 2023, supra note 37.
45. Bechtel, et al. 2012, supra note 36.
46. Davies. 2023, supra note 37.
47. Persaud. 2003, supra note 34.
48. Davies. 2023, supra note 37.
49. Lamy, Pascal, Genevieve Pons, Colette van der Ven, and Claudia Azevedo. 2024. "Turning the EU's Carbon Border Adjustment Mechanism into a Green Development Tool." Europe Jacques Delors. Available at: https://www.europejacquesdelors.eu/publications/eu-cbam-a-green-development-tool, accessed in November 2023.
50. African Climate Foundation and The London School of Economics and Political Science. 2023. "Implications for African Countries of a Carbon Adjustment Mechanism in the EU." Available at: https://www.lse.ac.uk/africa/assets/Documents/AFC-and-LSE-Report-Implications-for-Africa-of-a-CBAM-in-the-EU.pdf, accessed in December 2024.
51. Rasool, et al. 2024, supra note 13.
52. European Commission. 2023. "A Green Deal Industrial Plan for the Net-Zero Age." Available at: https://eur-lex.europa.eu/legal-content/EN/TXT/PDF/?uri=CELEX:52023DC0062, accessed in December 2024.
53. Bechtel, et al. 2012, supra note 36.
54. Ibid.
55. Davies. 2023, supra note 37.
56. Persaud. 2003, supra note 34.
57. Tamiotti, Ludivine. 2011. "The Legal Interface between Carbon Border Measures and Trade Rules." *Climate Policy* 11(5): 1202–11. Available at: https://doi.org/10.1080/14693062.2011.592672 accessed in October 2024.
58. Bounds, Andy. 2024. "Global Carbon Pricing Needed to Avert Trade Friction, Says WTO Chief." September 16, 2024. Available at: https://www.ft.com/content/b2de8c00-a46b-41e3-ba8b-a1e9e0c8b975, accessed in November 2024.
59. World Trade Organization. 2024. "DDG Paugam: WTO System Prerequisite to Achieving Steel Decarbonisation, Climate Goals." June 2024. Available at: https://www.wto.org/english/news_e/news24_e/ddgjp_11jun24_e.htm, accessed in November 2024.
60. World Bank. 2024. "State and Trends of Carbon Pricing Dashboard." Excel Spreadsheet. Available at: https://carbonpricingdashboard.worldbank.org/about#download-data, accessed in October 2024.
61. Maimele. 2023, supra note 29.

62. Clausing and Wolfram. 2023, supra note 28.
63. Rasool, et al. 2024, supra note 13.
64. CSIR Centre for Robotics and Future Production. 2024. "Greenhouse Gas Observatory Proof of Concept."
65. Ramos. 2023, supra note 3.
66. Ibid.
67. Ibid.
68. van der Ven, Colette and David Luke. 2023. "Africa in the World Trade Organisation." In David Luke (Ed.), *How Africa Trades*, 117–40. London: LSE Press. https://doi.org/10.31389/lsepress.hat.e.
69. The Bridgetown Initiative. 2023. "The Bridgetown Initiative and the Transformation of the Global Financial Architecture." The Parliamentary Network on the World Bank and the International Monetary Fund.
70. Clausing and Wolfram. 2023, supra note 28.
71. Maimele. 2023, supra note 6.
72. Ismail, Faizel. 2022. "Trade and Climate-Resilient Development in Africa: Towards a Global Green New Deal." Forum on Trade, Environment & the SDGs (TESS). Available at: https://tessforum.org/latest/trade-and-climate-resilient-development-in-africa-towards-a-global-green-new-deal, accessed in October 2024.
73. Ibid.
74. European Commission. 2023. "Questions and Answers – An Adjusted Package for the Next Generation of Own Resources." Text. European Commission – European Commission. June 2023. Available at: https://ec.europa.eu/commission/presscorner/detail/en/qanda_23_3329, accessed in October 2024.
75. Rasool, et al. 2024, supra note 13.
76. Parry, Ian, Simon Black, and James Roaf. 2021. "Proposal for an International Carbon Price Floor Among Large Emitters." IMF, 2021. Available at: https://www.imf.org/en/Publications/staff-climate-notes/Issues/2021/06/15/Proposal-for-an-International-Carbon-Price-Floor-Among-Large-Emitters-460468, accessed in October 2024.
77. Ibid.
78. Ibid.

7. EU CBAM implementation challenges

Stefan E. Weishaar

1. INTRODUCTION

The EU's Carbon Border Adjustment Mechanism (CBAM) came into effect on 1 October 2023 and is an integral part of the EU's so-called 'Fit for 55' package, which delivers on the 2019 European Green Deal. The CBAM is an environmental measure putting a price on embedded emissions of certain goods imported into the EU.

The object and purpose of the CBAM regulation[1] is to address carbon leakage at the same time as the free allocation of emission allowances under the EU Emissions Trading Scheme (EU ETS) is phased out for production within the EU. Both measures are essential to incentivise EU industry to transition towards the EU's ambitious climate change goals of reducing emissions by 55% by 2030 and reaching net zero by 2050.

The CBAM is implemented in two stages. The first stage (October 2023–December 2025) is a transitory phase where only a reporting requirement exists. Importers of goods will only have to report greenhouse gas (GHG) emissions embedded in their imports (direct and indirect emissions), without making any financial payments or adjustments. During this transitional period, the CBAM will apply to imports of certain goods and selected precursors whose production is carbon-intensive and at most significant risk of carbon leakage: cement, iron and steel, aluminium, fertilisers, electricity, and hydrogen. The transition period serves as a pilot and learning period for all stakeholders (importers, producers, and authorities) and also as a time to collect useful information on embedded emissions to refine the methodology for the definitive period.

As of the second phase, direct emissions of CBAM goods will be covered. Indirect emissions will be covered only for some sectors (cement and fertilisers). The Commission will lay down implementing rules on calculation

---

[1] Regulation 2023/956 of the European Parliament and of the Council establishing a carbon border adjustment mechanism, 10 May 2023, L130/52, 16.5.2023.

methods for embedded emissions in a separate implementing regulation before 2026.

A review of the CBAM's functioning during its transitional phase will be concluded before the entry into force of the definitive system. At the same time, the product scope will be reviewed to assess the feasibility of including other goods covered by the EU ETS into the scope of the CBAM mechanism, such as certain downstream products and those identified as suitable candidates during negotiations. The report should include a timetable setting out their inclusion by 2030. The CBAM will eventually – when fully phased in – capture more than 50% of the emissions in ETS-covered sectors.[2]

The second phase involves a fiscal obligation and enters into force in 2026, when embedded emissions in imports of CBAM goods should be covered by acquired CBAM certificates to be surrendered annually. The price of CBAM certificates will be equivalent to the ETS allowance price that domestic production in the EU faces. While the detailed legislative framework is still unfolding by way of secondary legislation, it is already becoming clear that the emerging legal package will be complex.

This chapter examines several implementation challenges relating to small consignments (section 2) and necessary data collection (section 3), verification of the embedded emissions (section 4), and the way the CBAM price will be set (section 5). Our aim is to identify practical shortcomings and offer policy suggestions for each implementation challenge. Concluding remarks will highlight relevant findings (section 6).

2. SMALL CONSIGNMENTS

During the transition period, importers under the CBAM are defined as either a person lodging a customs declaration for release for free circulation of goods in their own name and on their own behalf or, where the customs declaration is lodged by an indirect customs representative, the person on whose behalf such a declaration is lodged.[3] The definition, therefore, covers both importers (companies and natural persons) and indirect customs representatives (i.e., logistics companies such as DHL and Schenker). During the transitional period, indirect customs representatives are not obliged to file a CBAM report if the importer is established in an EU Member State. If not, they are obliged to file a report.[4]

---

[2] See https://taxation-customs.ec.europa.eu/carbon-border-adjustment-mechanism_en.

[3] See Regulation 2023/956, Article 3(15).

[4] See Regulation 2023/956, Article 32.

During the definitive periods, in principle goods can only be imported to the EU by an 'authorised CBAM declarant', entailing that the importer is duly established in an EU Member State and has received authorisation by the CBAM Authority in the Member State of establishment, demonstrating financial and operational capacity (applications are possible from 31 December 2024 onwards).[5] Also, indirect customs representatives can be authorised during the definitive period.

When a product is bought in a non-EU country and imported into the EU, VAT is payable on the purchase, irrespective of the value of the goods.[6] Pursuant to the 2019 amendment to the Union Customs Code, all imported goods up to 150 euros will have to be declared at the border using an electronic customs declaration that requires three times less data than a standard declaration.[7] In addition to VAT, the importer may also have to pay customs duties for goods above 150 euros and excise duty for specific goods.[8]

During the definitive period, any importer, including both companies and individuals, is obligated to pay for the embedded emissions of imported goods under the CBAM. Following the customary customs declaration processes, goods in excess of a value of 150 euros must be declared. The same threshold is thus applied for the purpose of CBAM imports. Consequently, a home owner that imports, for example an aluminium window frame in excess of 150 euros into the European Union, must file a report under the CBAM rules and declare the embedded carbon emissions. The administrative burden on imports of such small consignments is expected to be substantial. Evidently, the burden will substantially exceed the ordinary customs declaration for the purpose of paying VAT, for example where the tax due is based on the value of the product.

During the definitive period, small importers will have to purchase CBAM allowances at the common EU auction platform, provide a relevant verification report from an accredited CBAM verifier specifying embedded emissions according to the laid down methodology by the 31 May each year, and surrender CBAM certificates covering declared GHG emissions by the 31 May each year. Like any other importer, including small importers, they are allowed

[5] See Regulation 2023/956, Articles 4 and 5.

[6] See: https://taxation-customs.ec.europa.eu/buying-goods-online-coming-non-european-union-country_en#the-customs-declaration-in-detail.

[7] Commission Delegated Regulation (EU) 2019/1143 of 14 March 2019 amending Delegated Regulation (EU) 2015/2446 as regards the declaration of certain low-value consignments, C/2019/1979, OJ L 181, 5.7.2019, p. 2–12.

[8] See: https://taxation-customs.ec.europa.eu/buying-goods-online-coming-non-european-union-country_en#the-customs-declaration-in-detail.

to reduce an explicit carbon price that has already been paid in a third country.[9] Non-compliance with this statutory obligation is punishable by an 'effective, proportionate and dissuasive' penalty by the national CBAM Authority. Clearly, the administrative burden created by the CBAM will be felt more severely by smaller importers.

Individuals or companies importing products from third countries will also face additional administrative burdens. This must be monitored, especially since it cannot be expected that average citizens know about complex customs procedures and will require additional explanations and support from customs officials. Moreover, it is also not always clear where products bought, for example via the internet, are actually coming from. Sometimes products are ordered that are supposed to come from a seller in the EU, but they are actually shipped from a country outside the EU customs territory. Monitoring and ensuring compliance will thus constitute a weak point of the CBAM application.

Such challenges could be addressed by making it easier for importers to comply with CBAM rules by alleviating the administrative burden. Perhaps increasing the threshold of import values could also be considered. The Dutch Emissions Authority has recently proposed increasing the 150 euro threshold and to base the duty to declare CBAM imports on the weight of CBAM goods.[10] Another possible solution is to establish proxy values for CBAM values and free individual importers from obligations to submit verification reports or to link customs declaration procedures directly to payments of CBAM certificates. Such measures may not only alleviate the administrative costs falling most heavily upon small importers, small companies, and individuals but also thereby have a positive effect upon the distributional justice of the net-zero transition of the EU economy. Importantly, it may also have a positive effect on trade between EU actors (small EU importers, companies, and individuals) and small producers in third countries that otherwise might find it too burdensome to meet the information requirements under EU CBAM and find it difficult to export to the EU.[11]

---

9 See Article 3(23) of CBAM Regulation.

10 See Dutch Emissions Authority (2024), 'Nederlandse Emissieautoriteit pleit voor hogere deelnamedrempel voor CBAM,' Nieuwsbericht of 5th December 2024. Available at: https://www.emissieautoriteit.nl/actueel/nieuws/2024/11/28/nederlandse-emissieautoriteit-pleit-voor-hogere-deelnamedrempel-voor-cbam

11 Effects of the EU CBAM on developing countries are subject to an increasing number of studies. See, for example, the WB exposure index which allows the impact of the CBAM for particular sectors to be traced, available at: https://www.worldbank.org/en/data/interactive/2023/06/15/relative-cbam-exposure-index). See also Boqiang Lin and Hengsong Zhao (2024) Threatening the Poor? The Economic Impacts of Carbon Border Adjustment Mechanism on *Developing*

3. DATA COLLECTION

Reliable data is essential for the effective working of the CBAM mechanism. The data collection differs between the transition period and the definitive period.

For the transition period, the Implementing Regulation of the CBAM Regulation affords some flexibility in calculating embedded emissions.[12] Until the end of 2024, companies will have the choice of reporting based on using (a) full reporting according to the EU methodology; (b) reporting based on an equivalent method; and (c) reporting based on default reference values[13] (until 31 July 2024). As of 1 January 2025, only the EU methodology will be permissible in principle. Estimations of complex goods will be made available by the operators of the installations and can still be used if they account for less than 20% of the total embedded emissions.[14]

During the definitive period importers are obliged to surrender CBAM allowances in accordance with the embedded emissions of the imports. The legal burden of having and acting upon the data thus rests with importers. Since producers in third countries are the source of these data and subject to reporting and verification processes, it is clear that importers will depend on the cooperation within their supply chain.

Obtaining data from third-country producers is, however, not trivial. Producers may have some type of information, often at an aggregate level, but it will generally not be based on the fairly complicated EU methodology; instead, it will be calculated in a different way. While there is some flexibility in accepting data during the transitional period by employing default values, as of January 2026, the EU methodology must be followed. The Commission will lay down implementing rules on calculation methods for embedded emissions in a separate implementing regulation before 2026. The implementing act for Annex IV of the CBAM regulation will build inter alia upon existing legislation for the monitoring and verification of emissions and activity data for installations covered by Directive 2003/87/EC.[15] At the time of writing, the

---

Countries. Structural Change and Economic Dynamics, Volume 71, December 2024, pp. 582–593.

[12] See Article 4 Commission Implementing Regulation (EU) 2023/1773.

[13] See Default values for the transitional period of the CBAM between 1 October 2023 and 31 December 2025, Brussels, 22 December 2023. Available at: https://taxation-customs.ec.europa.eu/system/files/2023-12/Default%20values%20transitional%20period.pdf.

[14] See Article 5 Commission Implementing Regulation (EU) 2023/1773.

[15] See Article 7(7) CBAM regulation, in particular Commission Implementing Regulation (EU) 2018/2066 of 19 December 2018 on the monitoring and reporting

2026 rules are still unknown. The default values during the definitive period are thus expected to be different from those default values employed during the transition period, especially since they will include a mark-up and will be determined by an as yet unknown implementing regulation.

So the data that importers are currently compiling for the purpose of the 'learning by doing' exercise for calculating embedded emissions for the registration of CBAM allowances in the transition phase will need to be revisited and corrected for the definitive period.

Costs associated with following EU data collection standards may be prohibitively high and administratively burdensome for producers in third countries that only sell a few products to the EU. The costs may thus lead to an increase in the prices of goods imported to the EU.

A particular complexity in data availability is related to the data validation processes (also further discussed in section 4 below) and the requirement to obtain product-level data. The CBAM obligation relates to products that are imported into the EU while the EU ETS operates on the basis of installations rather than individual products. While it is necessary from a methodological perspective for the difference to be similar to the EU ETS, this also complicates the data-gathering process. EU measuring and monitoring standards, even if correctly applied in third countries, still need to be broken down to individual products. This can be especially challenging when different types of products (e.g., nuts as well as bolts) are produced at one installation. Decision-makers may enjoy some leeway and flexibility in attributing embedded emissions to specific final products, much in the same way that activity-based costing approaches in financial accounting can offer some discretion to managers in attributing costs to some processes and less to others.

In its legislation, the European Commission presupposes that third-country producers are willingly cooperating in the data-gathering and validation processes and happily reveal their data to importers. Cooperating in both elements, sharing production process information and detailed product data, may be considered sensitive from a business perspective. Some producers may not want to give the information because they are concerned about competition and may even claim business secrets. Compliance of declarants with the reporting obligation during the transition phase shall be ensured via the imposition of a penalty by the Member States ranging from 10 to 50 euros per tonne of unreported emissions during the transition period. This penalty applies if the reporting declarant has not taken the necessary steps to comply

---

of greenhouse gas emissions pursuant to Directive 2003/87/EC of the European Parliament and of the Council and amending Commission Regulation (EU) No 601/2012 (OJ L 334, 31.12.2018, p. 1).

with the obligation to submit a CBAM report or where the report is incorrect.[16] Default values are available under specific circumstances during the transitional period and thereby facilitate the reporting process.[17]

Nevertheless, reporting data is a challenge. There is a substantial degree of underreporting that seems to persist in early 2024.[18] even though the initial software issues have been resolved. This may also be exacerbated by the fact that many importers are responsible for few products with limited emissions and may not even be acutely aware of their obligation to follow CBAM rules.

Addressing this issue is non-trivial. Clearly, verifiers and businesses need to sit together so that importers can get the data, but perhaps the system for the definitive period could be simplified so that data is more readily available. That may, however, undermine environmental integrity by inadequately preventing carbon leakage, which the CBAM seeks to address.

4. VERIFICATION OF EMBEDDED EMISSIONS

Any ETS requires a robust, transparent, and credible system of monitoring, reporting and verification. The CBAM, which seeks to put a price on emissions and prevent carbon leakage, also requires adequate data and robust verification. This section will, therefore, first consider the data gathering and, subsequently, the verification process and verifiers themselves.

Verification requires the adequate collection of data. Under the CBAM regulation, there are several available ways to collect the data: (a) relying on embedded emissions data registered by operators in third countries in the CBAM registry; (b) actual values; and (c) default values.

(a) For data on embedded emissions in goods produced in third countries, authorised CBAM declarants may also choose to rely upon verified data of these producers that has been registered in the CBAM registry in accordance with Article 10 of the CBAM regulation.[19] The data registered by operators in third countries shall be sufficiently detailed to enable the verification of the embedded emissions and enable the review of the CBAM declarations.[20] The registration in the registry is valid for five years,[21] and operators are obliged to retain the verification report and

16 Article 16 CBAM Implementing Regulation (EU) 2023/1773.

17 See Articles 4(2), 4(3) and 5 of CBAM Implementing Regulation (EU) 2023/1773.

18 See https://practicalesg.com/2024/03/low-early-reporting-rate-for-cbam/.

19 See 2023/956, Article 8(1) and 8(2).

20 See 2023/956, Article 10(6).

21 See 2023/956, Article 10(3).

required information for the calculation of embedded emissions for four years.[22] Interestingly, there is no obligation for the operator to keep the information on embedded emissions in the CBAM registry up to date and accurate – that obligation seems to primarily refer to the general registration data of the operator.[23] So once data is in the system, it is not subject to continuous scrutiny but can nevertheless be relied upon by importers.

(b) Alternatively, instead of relying on embedded emissions data contained in the registry, importers can also rely upon actual embedded emission values. Calculation methodologies differ between simple goods and complex goods.[24] Under both calculation methodologies, direct and (where applicable) indirect emissions of the attributed emissions per unit of product are estimated. For complex goods, the emissions of input materials (the precursors) are also estimated.

(c) In the event that actual emissions cannot be determined adequately, Annex IV Article 4 allows for the use of default values for calculating embedded emissions. These default values are based on the average emissions intensity of each exporting country for each good (other than electricity) listed in Annex I and subject to a proportionately designed mark-up based on a share of the worst-performing EU ETS installations for that type of good.[25] The markup will be determined in future implementing acts.[26]

There are default values on imported electricity for specific default values for third countries, a group of third countries, or a region within a third country. There are also alternative default values for electricity based on EU emission factors in case adequate information cannot be obtained otherwise.[27] Default values for indirect emissions[28] are calculated on average emission factors of the electricity grid in the Union, the country of origin, the emission factor of price-setting sources in the country of origin, or based on the electricity used for the production of that good.[29] If reliable data demonstrates that the average values are more favourable, other default values can be used.[30] No later than 30 June 2025, the Commission will adopt an implementing act to specify the

---

22 See 2023/956, Article 10(5)(c).
23 See 2023/956, Article 10(4).
24 See 2023/956, Annex IV (4)(2) and (4)(3).
25 See 2023/956, Annex IV (4)(1).
26 See 2023/956, Article 7(7) and Annex IV (4)(1).
27 See 2023/956, Annex IV (4)(2).
28 Indirect emissions are the emissions arising from the generation of electricity used to produce the goods to which the CBAM Regulation applies.
29 See 2023/956, Annex IV (4)(3).
30 See 2023/956, Annex IV (4)(3).

calculation methods and build upon existing legislation for the monitoring, reporting, and verification of emissions and activity data for installations covered under the EU ETS.[31]

The CBAM verification system takes due note of the EU ETS methodology and is, in certain aspects, similar, but there are also differences. The EU ETS employs a monitoring, reporting, and verification process based on installations, while the CBAM operates on the basis of the product level. Both seek to take account of direct and indirect emissions. Importantly, the EU ETS takes into account process emissions, which the CBAM does not consider at all. Moreover, while the EU ETS adequately covers indirect emissions in terms of electricity prices, the CBAM relies on direct technical links or power purchase agreements.[32] The latter, in particular, may say little about the actual nature of the power generation of the electricity consumed by an installation. In the presence of a political will to cross-subsidise indirect emissions in exported goods to the EU, it would be easy to reduce the indirect emissions costs to those exporting producers by having them consume renewable energy on paper. In practice, this may add little to preventing carbon leakage or ensuring a level playing field between EU and third-country producers.

After examining the data gathering, we also need to examine the verification process and the verifiers themselves. This latter issue in particular has scarcely attracted attention in the CBAM debate and relates to the availability of verifiers and their accreditation. This undoubtedly constitutes an important lynchpin of the CBAM.

The CBAM requires qualified and certified verifiers to testify to the embedded carbon emissions and the measuring methodology that is employed in the various jurisdictions from where importers obtain goods and materials covered by the CBAM. According to the verification principles listed in Annex V of the CBAM regulation, verifiers shall visit the respective installation unless criteria for waiving the visit are met.[33] It remains, however, unclear what precisely these criteria are.

Besides some general verification principles and information on what is to be contained in a verification report, the CBAM rules offer little guidance as to how the verification process is supposed to be undertaken to ensure a consistent application across the various third-country jurisdictions and to prevent carbon leakage.

The EU ETS, which offered inspiration to the legislator for the development of the CBAM, may offer some insights into how the CBAM verification process

31 See 2023/956, Annex IV (4)(3) and Article 7(b).
32 See 2023/956, Annex IV (6).
33 See 2023/956, Annex V(1)c.

might be organised. Authorised CBAM declarants are obliged to ensure that the total embedded emissions declared in their submitted CBAM declarations are verified by a verifier accredited pursuant to Article 18 and based on the verification principles set out in Annex VI.[34] It should first be observed that pursuant to Article 18(1) of the CBAM regulation, persons accredited to verify under the EU ETS system are also accredited verifiers under the CBAM rules.[35] Moreover, national accreditation bodies may accredit verifiers that have the capacity to apply relevant provisions (Articles 8 and 10) and Annex VI of the CBAM regulation. The Commission may adopt delegated acts specifying the conditions for the granting of accreditation, the control and oversight of verifiers, the withdrawal of accreditations, and the mutual recognition and peer evaluation of accreditation bodies.[36]

Taking the current rules for the verification of data and for the accreditation of verifiers under the EU ETS as a yardstick for the CBAM,[37] it is clear that, under both rules, verifiers are obliged to provide a verification report that offers reasonable assurance that the operator's report is free from material misstatements.[38] In the EU ETS context, verifiers must assess the likely nature, scale, and complexity of the verification tasks within the framework of a strategic analysis and conduct a risk analysis on the design, planning, and implementation of an effective verification.[39] Such formulation is, however, absent in the context of the CBAM.

Moreover, in the context of the EU ETS, verifiers draft a verification plan, undertake verification activities, and verify data through analytical procedures but also through sampling and site visits. The reliability and accuracy of data are as critical as the adherence of the operators to the monitoring plans and monitoring methodology. Under the EU ETS, verifiers have to check the correct application and implementation of the monitoring methodologies, which

---

34 Reg 2023/956, Article 8(1).

35 Specifically, verifiers need to be accredited in accordance with the Commission Implementing Regulation (EU) 2018/2067 of 19 December 2018 on the verification of data and on the accreditation of verifiers pursuant to Directive 2003/87/EC of the European Parliament and of the Council, C/2018/8589, OJ L 334, 31.12.2018, pp. 94–134.

36 See 2023/956, Article 18(3).

37 See Commission Implementing Regulation (EU) 2018/2067 of 19 December 2018 on the verification of data and on the accreditation of verifiers pursuant to Directive 2003/87/EC of the European Parliament and the Council, L334/94 of 31.12.2018.

38 Article 7(1) Commission Implementing Regulation (EU) 2018/2067 and 2023/956, Annex VI (1)(b).

39 Articles 11 and 12 Commission Implementing Regulation (EU) 2018/2067.

have been approved by the competent authority in the monitoring plan.[40] Also, implementing acts adopted by the Commission concerning the calculation of embedded emissions have to build upon existing legislation for the monitoring and verification of emissions and activity data for installations covered by Directive 2003/87/EC, in particular Commission Implementing Regulation (EU) 2018/2066 and Implementing Regulation (EU) 2018/2067.[41]

The legislator thus seems to expect that similar methodologies can be easily applied in third countries by already accredited EU ETS verifiers and that the data is as robust as those gathered within the EU ETS context. It is, however, unclear if EU accreditors are equally competent to verify emission processes in all parts of the world, if they have the headcount to rise to this challenge, and who is competent to accredit the monitoring plans in third countries.

Bottlenecks in the data gathering and verification process are critical for the operation of the CBAM and the envisaged phase-out of the free allocation of emission allowances under the EU ETS. An assessment of the availability of verifiers and their potential to actually apply EU methodology at the product level in third countries needs to be evaluated. The current system seems to be motivated by the goal of ensuring the environmental integrity of the CBAM system, but it may not be cost-effective and practical enough in real-life applications. Perhaps a simplification guided by practical considerations would be necessary. In any event, speeding up the accreditation processes of verifiers is suggested to avoid a shortage of verifiers. Similarly, the rapid adoption of the delegating act with the necessary details for accreditation and verification methodology is suggested.

5. PRICE SETTING

Once the permanent CBAM system enters into force on 1 January 2026, importers will need to declare each year the quantity of goods imported into the EU in the preceding year and their embedded emissions. They are then obliged to surrender the corresponding number of CBAM certificates. The price of the certificates will be calculated depending on the weekly average auction price of EU ETS allowances expressed in euros per tonne of CO2 emitted. The phasing-out of free allocation under the EU ETS will take place in parallel with the phasing-in of CBAM in the period 2026–2034.

---

[40] See Commission Implementing Regulation (EU) 2018/2066 of 19 December 2018 on the monitoring and reporting of greenhouse gas emissions pursuant to Directive 2003/87/EC of the European Parliament and of the Council and amending Commission Regulation (EU) No 601/2012 (OJ L 334, 31.12.2018, p. 1).

[41] See Article 7(7b) Regulation (EU) 2023/956, also based on Commission Delegated Regulation (EU) 2019/331.

The price of CBAM allowances will thus directly reflect the price of EU emission allowances (EUAs). Since the CBAM regulation is part of the EU's decarbonisation efforts, the question arises what would happen if there was no EUA price as all emissions of covered entities have been phased out?

To address this question, it needs to be pointed out that the EU ETS directive, Directive 2003/87/EC, does not have an expiry date and that the United Nations Secretary-General António Guterres described the state of climate change in no uncertain terms as: '[...] a highway to climate hell with our foot on the accelerator'.[42] It is, therefore, conceivable that the current EU targets of attaining net-zero emissions by 2050 might be further strengthened in the future. This might indeed require further decarbonisation efforts, which potentially undermines the price-setting function of the EU ETS.

At the moment, however, EU greenhouse gas emissions are projected to decline over time and reach net-zero by 2050, with emissions stemming from agriculture, waste, and to a lesser degree, energy and industry (see Figure 7.1). To the extent that those emissions are related to covered entities, there would still be EUAs and a market price that could be used to determine the market price of CBAM certificates.

The price-setting function of the market, however, can however, be manipulated more easily if the size of the market becomes smaller as the number of allowances that are brought into circulation is reduced and market liquidity declines.

Market manipulation can take various forms: action-based, information-based, or transaction-based.

5.1 Action-based Manipulation

Large traders who enjoy a good or relatively better understanding of the EU ETS spot market can take advantage of a high degree of uncertainty in the market and buy allowances. They can thereby influence market expectations and, once prices are high, sell off their EUA holdings. Alternatively, they can sell allowances at high prices and buy them back after a price decline. This kind of action-based market manipulation can be described as 'pump and dump'.

42 António Guterres, Secretary-General's Remarks to High-Level Opening of COP27, Speech delivered on 7 November 2022. Available at: https://www.un.org/sg/en/content/sg/speeches/2022-11-07/secretary-generals-remarks-high-level-opening-of-cop27.

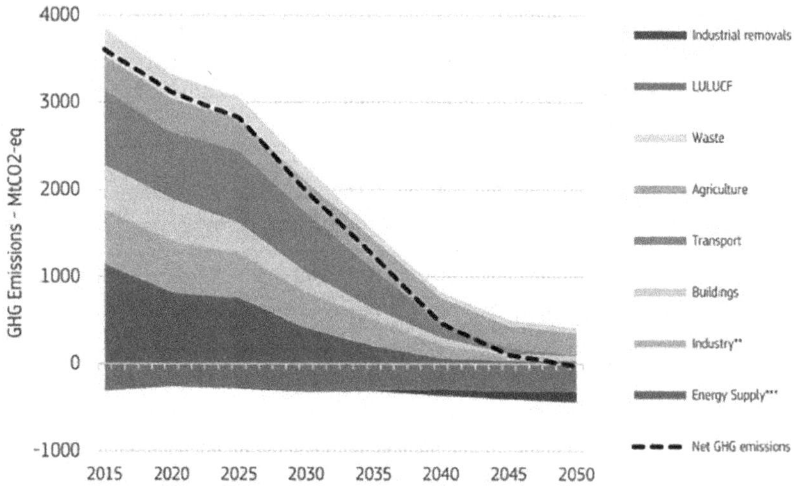

** Excluding non-BECCS industrial removals. *** Including Bioenergy with carbon capture and storage (BECCS).
Source: PRIMES, GAINS, GLOBIOM https://climate.ec.europa.eu/eu-action/climate-strategies-targets/2040-climate-target_en.

Figure 7.1 Greenhouse gas emissions by sector 2015–2050

5.2 Information-based Manipulation

Manipulation can also be based on information. Undertakings that enjoy better market insights or insider information can spread rumours that lead other market actors to expect a change in the EUA market price or in market demand or supply conditions. Besides information-based abuses, companies can use signalling strategies to manipulate the market. Signalling strategies often occur in an opaque form that does not disclose the identity of the signalling party or the true source of information. One can, however, safely conjecture that, in order to impact the market, signals need to be received by many or – if the market is small – by relevant actors. Signals disseminated by prominent news sources could lead the market in a certain direction.

5.3 Trade-based Manipulation

Manipulations can also be trade-based. Market manipulation can, for example, be organised with the help of other parties that lead to a manipulation of the demand, supply, or the price of an asset. Companies may try to squeeze the market by taking a particular position on the derivative market, requiring sellers to deliver EUAs in the future while bidding up the EUA price on the spot market before the delivery date. In this way, manipulators are able to earn a profit by selling off their EUA holdings at a higher price.

Market manipulation will thus be a more prominent problem when the market for EUAs is getting less liquid, and manipulation strategies and market cornering may become easier. One important aspect that should not be underestimated from a security perspective is, of course, that imports of CBAM goods to the EU are closely linked with the EUA price. Unforeseen price spikes in the EUA price will thus expose importers to significant contractual risks similar to exchange rate risks. Depending on the magnitude of the price fluctuations, such fluctuations could affect the real economy strongly and quickly.

In light of the above, it is suggested that the EU critically examines its oversight mechanisms that in their approach currently differentiate between auction markets and financial markets. It is suggested that a holistic monitoring approach jointly covering auction markets, secondary markets, and financial markets as well as import streams will be important for identifying market manipulations.

6. CONCLUDING REMARKS

The EU has set itself the goal of becoming the first carbon-neutral 'continent' by 2050. From a climate change perspective, it is clear that global carbon emissions must be reduced substantially. European industry and energy generation must, therefore, reduce their GHG emissions, and it is not helpful if European consumers simply import carbon-intensive products from abroad – carbon leakage must, therefore, be addressed as well. The CBAM regulation is, therefore, an attractive approach to achieve emission reductions in the EU and to incentivise the carbon transition of the economy.

The challenges highlighted above, however, clearly show that substantial problems remain in the implementation and operation of the CBAM. The issues raised point to more than just teething problems, indicating that a lot of communication must take place and that the system may need to be simplified. Without adequate data, effective and robust verification processes, and timely publication of detailed rules, the system will not be operational. Similarly, verifiers themselves must be available to do the job. Also, the sheer number of small importers and the associated administrative costs of importing small consignments may render the importation of CBAM goods very expensive.

A revisiting of the CBAM rules with a clear focus on practicality and ease of implementation may be merited. Importantly, it is recommended that the current patchwork of market oversight should be changed towards a holistic approach that combines oversight over all relevant market aspects, including auctioning, secondary markets, financial markets, and trade flows.

PART III

Environmental taxes and the pursuit of climate justice

8. Brazil's 2023 tax reform and its environmental paradigm shift: a step towards the world's most environmentally progressive constitution

Arthur Maria Ferreira Neto

1. INTRODUCTION

In recent decades, tax systems around the world have been undergoing a profound paradigm shift,[1] gradually moving away from the traditional notion that taxation serves merely as a revenue-generating mechanism to fund the state apparatus and finance public services. Similarly, the relationships between tax authorities and taxpayers are evolving; they are no longer perceived as purely antagonistic and adversarial interactions, in which the tax authorities do everything to appropriate a portion of individuals' wealth and benefit from the productivity of companies, leaving taxpayers with no choice but to passively submit to state forces or seek sophisticated means to avoid tax liabilities at all costs. Today, taxation is increasingly viewed as a tool for shaping economic and social behaviours, aligning with broader goals such as environmental sustainability, social inclusion, and economic equity.

In reality, the value agenda that today animates the majority of foreign tax systems, especially in Europe, revolves around the ideas of neutrality, transparency, simplification (*i.e.*, rationalisation), and environmental sustainability (Freitas, 2011). In these more advanced legal contexts, the imposition of taxes

1 Here, we understand it to be possible to use the concept of a scientific paradigm shift in the detailed sense outlined by Thomas Kuhn (1970). For a more comprehensive view of the various paradigm shifts experienced within Brazilian tax law, see our work *Por uma ciência prática do direito tributário* (Ferreira Neto, 2016).

presupposes a new market development model, in which an interconnection between economic progress, social inclusion, and environmental preservation is necessary through the adoption of ecologically orientated extra-fiscal policies.[2] Therefore, there is also talk of an ecological transition in the field of taxation and economic development, projecting the construction of a solidarity or civil economy.[3] This economic development model does not advocate for a complete abandonment of the traditional/capitalist system but seeks an improved way of organising economic activity, no longer centred on self-interest and maximising profits at any cost, but rather aiming to achieve objectives that are simultaneously beneficial for the entrepreneur and social utility.[4]

Thus, the new tax paradigm is rooted in an ecological transition, where the interconnection between economic growth and environmental preservation is pivotal. Taxation is emerging as a key instrument for promoting a "green economy", one that balances profitability with social and environmental responsibilities.[5]

---

[2] For an encompassing understanding of this new international context involving environmental and sustainable taxation, see Comelli et al. (2023).

[3] Probably the best contemporary work to revive the medieval concept of "Civil Economy"—which today can be understood as an economic model based on reciprocity, fraternity, humanism, and community-building relationships, serving as an alternative to the modern idea of a market economy founded on individualism, self-interest, profit maximization, and efficiency at any cost—is by Bruni and Zamagni (2010).

[4] The social economy has been active for years in environmental protection and promoting circular economy models, well exemplified by the international network RREUSE, comprising organisations involved in the reuse, repair, and recycling of objects and materials. These social enterprises not only aim to contribute to legislative bodies and public institutions in the development of policies that foster the circular economy and product reuse but also facilitate the reintegration into the labour market of individuals affected by substance abuse, homelessness, disabilities, low qualifications, and long-term unemployment (https://rreuse.org [accessed 23/12/2023]). For this new vision of economy with social responsibility, see Ricardo Crespo: "La Responsabilidad social empresaria (SER) es una cuestión que, afortunadamente, já adquirido gran relevancia hoy en día. [...] El marco de este tema es la vocación hacia el bien común que há de abrazar toda persona e institución que forman parte de la sociedad. En este contexto, el fin de la empresa [...] va más allá de la empresa misma" (Crespo, 2012: 142–3).

[5] On this topic, see the Report of the European Commission, *The future of European competitiveness: a competitiveness strategy for Europe*, September 2024, at https://commission.europa.eu/document/download/97e481fd-2dc3-412d-be4c-f152a8232961_en.

Inspired by these global trends, Brazil has embarked on a transformative constitutional reform. Last year, after decades of academic and legislative discussions, it finally found sufficient political momentum to approve the long-awaited tax reform, which profoundly and comprehensively altered (and will continue to alter) the rationale underlying our tax system, culminating in the enactment of Constitutional Amendment No. 132/2023 (CA132/23).[6]

The tax reform promises to be a measure of great relevance to the country's economic development, as it aims to promote the "simplification" (*i.e.*, rationalisation), efficiency, and equity of the existing tax system, as already announced in the new set of principles contained in Article 145, § 3, of the Constitution, which states that the "National Tax System must observe the principles of simplicity,[7] transparency, tax justice, cooperation, and environmental protection". This landmark reform introduces profound changes to the Brazilian National Tax System, with a special emphasis on environmental taxation. By establishing a new framework for environmental taxes, incentivised regimes, and the distribution of tax revenues based on sustainability criteria, Brazil is aligning its tax system with the pressing contemporary demands for sustainability and socio-environmental responsibility.

In this context, this chapter examines the constitutional changes introduced by CA132/23, with a particular focus on the new framework for environmental taxation, which emerges as a key element in the reconfiguration of the traditional tax law paradigm in the country. The reform goes beyond the mere simplification efforts and efficiency of the tax system. It represents a commitment to a greener and more responsible economy, where tax instruments are strategic tools for encouraging sustainable practices and discouraging environmentally harmful activities.

---

6 Available at: https://planalto.gov.br/ccivil_03/constituicao/emendas/emc/emc132.htm (accessed 24/10/2024).

7 It must be noted that the intended simplification efforts of Brazilian tax law will likely remain a mere promise, as a close reading of the over 30 pages (74 pages in the official format) of constitutional text comprising EC 132/2023 reveals that legal practitioners, accountants, and business professionals will face even greater technical and operational challenges, with a risk of maintaining (or even increasing) the high volume of tax litigation and intensifying the difficulties for companies to ensure tax compliance. This is evident from the analysis of the new normative content introduced by the Amendment, which implements a highly complex legal regime for creating, managing, and collecting the Goods and Services Tax (IBS) (Article 156-A) and the Goods and Services Contribution (CBS) (Article 195, V), combined with the allowance for creating Selective Taxes (IS) (Article 153, VIII), as well as provisions for numerous differentiated and exceptional rate regimes, along with a prolonged transition period during which the old and new systems will coexist.

This research adopts an analytical-descriptive methodology, reviewing the newly established environmental taxation framework, analysing the impact of CA132/23 on the Brazilian National Tax System, exploring not all the aspects created by the approved tax reform, which would require a more extensive study, but specifically analysing the significant innovations that this constitutional change brings to the context of environmental taxation. Within the scope of Brazil's tax reform, this article intends to identify at least three different key areas of innovation:

I. The creation of new environmentally orientated taxes, which aim to directly encourage sustainable practices and discourage activities harmful to the environment;
II. The implementation of favoured tax regimes and incentives for green investments to stimulate both the tax legislator and companies/entities that adopt sustainable practices and invest in clean technologies; and
III. The innovation of mechanisms for the financial distribution of public resources based on environmental criteria.

2. THE NEW FRAMEWORK FOR ENVIRONMENTAL TAXATION INTRODUCED BY BRAZIL'S 2023 TAX REFORM

Before CA132/23, Brazil's National Tax System was marked by significant complexities and inefficiencies, particularly concerning environmental taxation. Understanding the pre-existing challenges is essential to grasping the full magnitude of the changes introduced by the new tax reform, which has set the stage for a profound transformation of the country's tax system. Beyond responding to economic demands—such as enhancing entrepreneurial activity, productivity, and efficiency—the reform also addresses broader societal principles, including social inclusion, fiscal justice, and environmental sustainability.

The previous tax system, now set to be gradually replaced, was characterised by a strong focus on normative formalism, prioritising the taxpayer's perspective, protecting individual freedoms, and safeguarding property. This focus on limiting the state's power to tax and clearly defining taxable economic bases provided a stable and predictable legal environment for managing tax relations (Greco, 2011). However, it often failed to engage with broader issues such as fiscal justice, the need to address social inequalities, and the promotion of sustainable policies.

In contrast, Constitutional Amendment 132, enacted in December 2023, brought significant changes to the National Tax System, especially by explicitly introducing a clear environmental orientation for taxation. More than a mere reorganisation, the reform creates a new set of guiding principles for tax law in Article 145, § 3, of the Constitution, which mandates that the National Tax System must observe the principles of simplicity, transparency, tax justice, cooperation, and environmental protection.

The new constitutional framework foresees several specific tax instruments and financial mechanisms that: (a) establish distinct environmental taxes, (b) create regimes and incentives to encourage environmental protection, and (c) outline rules for distributing public revenues based on sustainability actions and ecologically-driven policies.

This section delves into these new environmental taxation mechanisms introduced by CA132/23, assessing their merits and potential areas for improvement. Our analysis will follow the three thematic categories outlined earlier.

2.1 New Taxes with Environmental Characteristics

The tax reform introduced by CA132/23, which some viewed primarily as a reform of consumption taxation, extends beyond this scope by granting new tax competencies that enable the creation of environmentally orientated extra-fiscal taxes. This can be seen in the new constitutional provisions outlined in Articles 153, VIII, 155, § 6, 149-A, and 126 of the ADCT,[8] which empower various federative entities to institute taxes explicitly focused on environmental protection. Let us examine them.

2.1.1 The "Selective Tax": a new excise tax on activities harmful to health and the environment

Among these provisions, Article 153, VIII, stands out as it grants the Federal Union the power to impose a tax on the "production, extraction, commercialisation, or importation of goods and services harmful to health or the environment". Commonly referred to as the "Selective Tax" ("IS" in Portuguese),[9] this new excise tax is not primarily designed as a revenue-generating mechanism

---

8 ADCT is the Transitional Constitutional Provisions Act with normative constitutional status.

9 The reason for the popularity of this term is that, in earlier drafts of the Proposal for Constitutional Amendment n° 45, this tax was intended to fully replace the Federal Tax on Industrialised Products (IPI), which follows selectivity, and to help maintain the financial viability of the Manaus Free Trade Zone (ZFM), objectives that were later altered during the Tax Reform process, as will be discussed further with the retention of the Industrialised Products Tax charged with guaranteeing "IPI-ZFM".

but rather as a tool to promote extra-fiscal purposes by discouraging environmentally harmful activities (Ferreira Neto and Kronbauer, 2020).

The legislator adopted a preventive approach here, intending to use taxa tion as a means to deter unsustainable practices (Ricci, 2015). Article 153, VIII, provides the Federal Union with a mechanism to influence market behaviours and reduce negative environmental externalities. It is noteworthy that the legislator opted for a preventive approach, aiming to curb harmful practices through taxation. However, the implementation of this tax will require a complementary law (LC), signalling the need for careful legislative deliberation to define the scope and specifics of the tax base.

Additionally, the rates for the Selective Tax will be established by ordinary law (LO), allowing flexibility in adjusting the tax burden based on the environmental impact of specific goods and services. This flexibility could prove essential in achieving the extra-fiscal goals of the tax. Yet, the exemption of exports and certain sectors (such as electricity and telecommunications) from the "IS" raises questions about the potential inconsistency in applying environmental protections globally. The current immunity for exports[10] of environmentally harmful products may warrant further debate, as it limits the tax's global environmental impact.

Finally, the inclusion of the Selective Tax (IS) in the calculation base of other taxes such as the "ICMS",[11] "ISSQN",[12] and "CBS"[13] introduces concerns about the cumulative burden of consumption taxes, potentially exacerbating the regressive nature of these levies. It is evident that IS will face the widely discussed tax issue of the illegitimate inclusion of a consumption tax in the base of another tax of the same nature, which ends up increasing the perverse regressivity of this type of tax, imposing disproportionate burdens on the consumer.

---

[10] § 1 of the same article establishes an immunity rule for the Selective Tax by stating that it "will not apply to exports or transactions involving electricity and telecommunications", which clearly indicates that the Constituent intended to exempt certain strategic economic operations from this extra-fiscal tax, either to preserve our trade balance or to avoid impacting the consumption value of certain priority goods and services, thereby aiming not to harm international competitiveness and the preservation of strategic economic sectors.

[11] ICMS (in Portuguese) is the current State Tax on Commerce.

[12] ISSQN (in Portuguese) is the current Municipal Tax on Services.

[13] CBS (in Portuguese) will be the new Federal Social Contribution on Goods and Services.

2.1.2 Environmental tax on ownership of vehicles

Article 155, § 6, II, introduces significant innovations regarding the state tax on motor vehicle ownership ("IPVA" in Portuguese). CA132/23 empowers states to set differentiated "IPVA" rates "based on the environmental impact of vehicles", offering a clear path for states to incentivise the use of more sustainable vehicles. This extra-fiscal function of the new "IPVA" is expected to promote greener transportation choices, making it a key instrument in reducing pollution and fostering sustainability. It can also function as an incentive for the acquisition of more ecologically orientated vehicles.

In a certain sense, this inclusion is not entirely innovative, as the Constitution, since 2003, had already provided for the possibility of setting selective rates for "IPVA" based on the type and use of the vehicle (Paulsen, 2023, p. 428).

This innovation, therefore, represents a deeper and more sophisticated approach to vehicle ownership taxation (Mamede, 2002, p. 94), being a measure that not only encourages the acquisition of more sustainable vehicles but also recognises the different negative environmental externalities associated with various types of automobiles, encouraging the choice of less polluting vehicles and promoting sustainability in the transportation sector. As such, the "IPVA" becomes not only a revenue tool but also an important mechanism for environmental protection.

2.1.3 Municipal contribution for public space preservation

Thirdly, CA132/2023 expanded the tax competence rule established in Article 149-A, which, originally through EC 39/2002, granted municipalities and the Federal District the power to impose contributions for the funding of public lighting services (Paulsen, 2023, p. 151). This rule also directs taxes towards financing, expanding, and improving the "monitoring systems for the security and preservation of public spaces". This measure grants greater autonomy to municipal federative entities to address local environmental challenges, aligning taxation with the promotion of services that contribute to quality of life and urban sustainability.

In fact, this decentralisation in environmental contributions—taxes with a specific revenue destination (Ferreira Neto, 2006)—at the municipal federative level also reflects a constitutional view that understands the importance of local authorities in efficiently and effectively managing resources aimed at sustainability and urban environmental preservation.

2.1.4 Maintenance of the Federal Tax on Industrialised Products to economically preserve the Manaus Free Trade Zone

One of the more surprising elements of CA132/2023 is the partial retention of the Federal Tax on Industrialised Products ("IPI" in Portuguese), which was expected to be abolished by this recent tax reform. The constitutional purpose of preserving the collection of this federal tax was to create an indirect mechanism for environmental preservation, specifically in the economic region of the Manaus Free Trade Zone ("ZFM" in Portuguese). This measure ensures that the ZFM continues to comparatively benefit from tax incentives designed to support sustainable development in the Amazon region, but it does this by continuing to charge IPI from other companies located in all other Brazilian states.[14]

This provision caused some astonishment among tax law professionals who were awaiting the approval of the tax reform, as the IPI was expected to be one of the taxes abolished with the implementation of the new tax system, on the basis that this old tax would be replaced by the previously analysed Selective Tax.

Nonetheless, a charitable reading of the mechanism introduced by Article 126 of the ADCT clearly shows that its intention was to preserve the competitive advantage of economic sectors operating in the Manaus Free Trade Zone. This zone is known to be a free-trade area established to create an industrial, commercial, and agricultural centre within the Amazon with incentivised economic conditions that allow for sustainable and harmonious development with the biodiversity of the Amazon rainforest, encouraging environmental conservation and reducing the appeal of pursuing other economic activities that could potentially be harmful to this ecologically significant region.

Despite all its environmental relevance, one cannot help but question whether there are potential risks in using such an extravagant taxation technique, through which, on one hand, a supposed general rule of "IPI" exemption is announced via a zero rate, but on the other hand, an exception rule is established that is not only very broad in scope (*i.e.*, all "products with incentivised industrialisation in the Manaus Free Trade Zone") but also quite indeterminate in defining which products might suddenly become taxable. Furthermore, it should be noted that this constitutional rule, which will extend the life of the "IPI" after 2027, creates a curious situation where the emergence of new IPI incidences will depend on the potential productive choices of economic agents located in the Manaus Free Trade Zone, as well as potential local and regional political decisions in Manaus and the State of Amazonas.

Such factors could trigger the resurgence of new IPI taxation scenarios across the national territory. If this scenario materialises, it could undoubtedly generate problems of insecurity and unpredictability for the industrial sector

---

14 This is due to the introduction of Article 126 in the ADCT, which establishes that: "From 2027 [...] the tax provided for in Article 153, IV, of the Federal Constitution (IPI) [...] will have its rates reduced to zero, except with respect to products that have incentivised industrialisation in the Manaus Free Trade Zone, according to criteria established by complementary law."

in other parts of Brazil. Clear and precise regulation will be essential to ensure that the IPI continues to align with environmental goals while avoiding unnecessary complexity in the tax system.

2.2 Favourable Tax Regimes and Environmentally-motivated Tax Benefits

As explored earlier, the evolution of global awareness of environmental challenges has catalysed the adoption of tax instruments geared towards achieving sustainable fiscal practices. The recent tax reform in Brazil sought to align with this paradigm not only by creating new environmental taxes, as covered previously, but also by establishing guidelines focused on sustainability and environmental protection in the allocation of tax benefits and favoured tax regimes.

This environmental commitment has been embodied in several constitutional provisions, including Articles 43, § 4, 155, § 1, VII, 225, § 1, VIII, of Brazil's Federal Constitution, and Articles 8 and 9 of CA132/2023. Each provision reflects a conscious effort to integrate fiscal incentives with environmental objectives.

2.2.1 Regional incentives and environmental sustainability

First, Article 43, § 4, emphasises the role of regional incentives in promoting sustainable practices by mandating, whenever feasible, that tax incentives consider environmental criteria and carbon emission reductions. This directive reflects a deliberate strategy to align regional economic development with environmental sustainability, encouraging industries to adopt cleaner technologies and implement low-emission practices.

However, the qualification "whenever possible", though arguably necessary from a legislative perspective, might reduce the practical impact of this provision if exploited as a loophole. Legislators could potentially bypass environmental conditions in cases where they might prove inconvenient.

Therefore, it will be essential for the judiciary to play an active role in ensuring that future regional incentives adhere to these environmental guidelines, preventing misuse and safeguarding against incentives that could lead to environmental harm (Guimarães, 2022).

2.2.2 State tax on donations: immunity for donations to environmental non-profit organisations

The reform introduced a new immunity under Article 155, § 1, VII, targeting the state inheritance and donation tax ("ITCMD" in Portuguese) to exempt donations made to non-profit entities that advance public and social goals, including environmental objectives. By exempting donations to non-profits engaged in environmental, scientific, and social causes, this measure could significantly boost philanthropic support for NGOs and organisations devoted to ecological protection and sustainability.

This initiative builds on the immunity introduced by CA126/2022, which already exempted donations from ITCMD if they were earmarked for socio-environmental projects within the Federal Executive or gifted to federal educational institutions aimed at climate change mitigation.

Consequently, a foundational environmental framework has emerged within the ITCMD context, recognising the essential contribution of non-profit entities in fostering social and ecological health. However, this immunity is not self-executing and will necessitate complementary legislation to establish specific conditions and implementation guidelines.

2.2.3 A favourable tax regime for biofuels and low-emission hydrogen

Article 225, § 1, VIII, introduces a preferential tax regime for biofuels and low-carbon hydrogen, designed to establish a comparative advantage over fossil fuels. This initiative not only aims to foster a transition to cleaner energy alternatives but also enhances the competitiveness of sectors committed to reducing greenhouse gas emissions.

By prioritising these renewable energy sources, the Brazilian tax reform endorses a shift towards a sustainable energy matrix that can contribute substantially to the nation's climate goals.

2.3.4 National Basic Grocery Basket and zero taxation

To uphold the constitutional social right to food established in Article 6, Article 8, and its sole paragraph in CA132/2023, the creation of a "National Basic Grocery Basket" (*Cesta Básica Nacional* in Portuguese) may be necessary. This basket will encompass food items deemed essential for human consumption based on factors such as regional and cultural significance, nutritional value, and health benefits.

By granting zero-rate taxation on "IBS" and "CBS" (the two new main taxes on consumption created by CA132/23) for products in this basket, the provision seeks to make nutritious, culturally relevant food more accessible. Additionally, this measure underscores the goal of fostering sustainable agriculture and promoting regional diversity in agricultural practices, further aligning with the broader environmental ethos of the reform.

2.3.5 Differentiated tax regimes and urban rehabilitation incentives

Lastly, Article 9 of EC 132/2023 enables the establishment of differentiated tax regimes, specifically allowing for exemptions or reductions of up to 100% to support urban rehabilitation efforts in historic zones and regions marked by environmental degradation.

By fostering urban renewal, these incentives aim to harmonise development with the preservation of cultural heritage and ecological restoration, contributing to more resilient and environmentally responsible urban landscapes.

2.3 Mechanisms for the Financial Distribution of Public Resources Based on Environmental Criteria

The inclusion of environmental considerations in the distribution of public revenue under Brazil's 2023 tax reform, specifically through Constitutional Amendment 132/2023, marks a significant step towards aligning fiscal policy with sustainability goals. Though primarily rooted in financial rather than strictly tax law, these mechanisms incentivise sustainable practices at local and regional levels.

By bridging economic development with environmental preservation, these measures underscore Brazil's commitment to a more balanced, sustainable future. This shift is operationalised through provisions in Article 158, § 2, III, and Article 159-A of the Constitution, as well as Article 92-B of the Transitional Constitutional Provisions Act (TCPA), which prioritise sustainable development and environmental protection in public resource distribution.

2.3.1 Revenue shares for municipalities and environmental preservation indicators

Article 158, § 2, III, introduces an innovative approach to revenue distribution for municipalities, mandating that 5% of distributed resources be allocated based on environmental preservation indicators established by state law. This provision aims to encourage municipalities to adopt sustainable practices, acknowledging the critical role of local governance in environmental stewardship.

However, implementing this framework poses challenges, particularly in standardising the criteria and metrics used to assess each municipality's success in sustainability policies. The effectiveness of this initiative depends on transparent, consistent indicators that reflect local efforts in conservation and sustainable development.

Additionally, delegating the determination of "environmental preservation indicators" to state law allows for regional adaptation but requires careful oversight to ensure consistency and fairness in how municipalities are evaluated.

2.3.2 National Fund for Regional Development and environmental sustainability

Article 159-A establishes the National Fund for Regional Development with a notable emphasis on environmental sustainability. Designed to address social and regional disparities, the fund prioritises projects in the states and federal districts that incorporate sustainability and carbon reduction measures.

By aligning regional funding with environmental goals, this approach fosters a model of development that respects local ecological dynamics while addressing socio-economic challenges, incentivising the creation of projects with measurable, positive impacts on both the environment and regional prosperity.

2.3.3 Fund for the sustainability and economic diversification of the State of Amazonas

Article 92-B, §§ 2 and 3, of the ADCT establishes a fund for the State of Amazonas, financed by federal resources to support economic diversification and sustainable development. This fund, created to assist Amazonas in offsetting tax revenue losses, represents a strategic initiative to support both local economies and the conservation of the Amazon.

It allows for a coordinated effort between federal and state authorities, with the state's direct involvement in policy-setting, ensuring that the fund's use aligns with regional conservation priorities. The fund thus provides a flexible financial instrument to mitigate the economic impact of systemic tax changes while preserving one of the world's most critical ecological areas.

2.3.4 Sustainable Development Fund for the Western Amazon and Amapá

Similarly, § 6 of Article 92-B of the ADCT introduces a Sustainable Development Fund for the Western Amazon and Amapá, with similar goals of economic diversification and sustainable growth. By empowering these states to manage the fund and define their own policies, this provision reinforces the importance of regional autonomy in developing tailored, sustainable solutions that address local environmental and economic needs. This decentralised approach acknowledges the ecological and socio-economic uniqueness of each state, allowing for solutions that are both adaptable and regionally responsive.

In essence, these fiscal mechanisms integrate sustainability as a key criterion in public resource allocation, creating a robust framework for incentivising environmentally conscious governance across all levels of administration. The measures enacted under Constitutional Amendment 132/2023 not only enhance Brazil's fiscal architecture but also reflect a progressive model that other nations might look to as a benchmark for aligning fiscal policy with environmental sustainability.

3. CONCLUSION

This chapter aimed to explore the paradigm shift introduced by Brazil's tax reform through Constitutional Amendment 132/2023, particularly in terms of integrating tax instruments that explicitly support the constitutional principles of environmental protection and sustainable economic development.

By analysing the transformation within the National Tax System, this research has outlined various tax and financial mechanisms designed to foster policies that align with modern imperatives of sustainability and quality of life. The introduction of these new taxes and fiscal provisions transcends the traditional goal of revenue generation, adopting a proactive role in shaping sustainable practices and behaviours. By positioning taxation as a lever for influencing economic and political choices, Constitutional Amendment 132/2023 underscores the extra-fiscal potential of tax law as a tool to nurture a more environmentally responsible society, dedicated to safeguarding natural resources.

In essence, Constitutional Amendment 132/2023 signifies more than a formal restructuring of Brazil's tax system. It extends beyond a mere shift in the consumption tax model—through the establishment of the IBS and CBS—and embodies a genuine commitment to sustainability. This amendment marks a proactive stance by the state in fostering an eco-conscious economy, where taxation becomes a strategic instrument to guide both corporate and individual decisions towards a greener future. As a result, this reform positions Brazil at the forefront of environmental fiscal policy, setting a potential model for other nations seeking to integrate sustainability at the core of their economic frameworks.

BIBLIOGRAPHY

Bruni, Luigino and Zamagni, Stefano. *Economia civil: Eficiência, equidade, felicidade pública*. São Paulo: Cidade Nova, 2010.

Comelli, Alberto, Milne, Janet, Andersen, Mikael, and Ashiabor, Hope. *Taxation and the green growth challenge*. Cheltenham: Edward Elgar, 2023.

Crespo, Ricardo. *Filosofía de la economía*. Navarra: EUNSA, 2012.

European Commission Report. *The future of European competitiveness: a competitiveness strategy for Europe*, September 2024. Available at https://commission.europa.eu/document/download/97e481fd-2dc3-412d-be4c-f152a8232961_en.

Ferreira Neto, Arthur Maria. *Natureza jurídica das contribuições na Constituição de 1988*. São Paulo: MP, 2006.

Ferreira Neto, Arthur Maria. *Por uma ciência prática do direito tributário*. São Paulo: Quartier Latin, 2016.

Ferreira Neto, Arthur Maria and Kronbauer, Eduardo Luís. Princípio da seletividade: duas concepções rivais de essencialidade. *Economic Analysis of Law Review*, Brasília, 2020, v. 11, p. 30, 2020.

Freitas, Juarez. *Sustentabilidade: direito ao futuro*. Belo Horizonte: Fórum, 2011.

Greco, Marco Aurélio. Crise do formalismo no direito tributário brasileiro. *Revista da PGFN*, Brasília, ano 1, n. 1, 2011.

Greco, Marco Aurélio. Solidariedade social e tributação. In Greco, Marco Aurélio and Godoi, Marciano Seabra de (Colab.). *Solidariedade social e tributação*. São Paulo: Dialética, 2005.

Guimarães, Bruno A. François. *Limites à concessão de benefícios fiscais:* dos controles formais aos controles materiais. Rio de Janeiro: Lumen Juris, 2022.

Kuhn, Thomas. *The structure of scientific revolutions*, 2nd ed. Chicago, IL: University of Chicago Press, 1970.

Mamede, Gladston. *IPVA: Imposto sobre Propriedade de Veículos Automotores*. São Paulo: Ed. RT, 2002.

Paulsen, Leandro. *Constituição e Código Tributário comentados à luz da doutrina e da jurisprudência*. 19th ed. São Paulo: Saraiva, 2023.

Ricci, Henrique Cavalheiro. *Direito tributário ambiental e isonomia tributária: Extrafiscalidade, limitações, capacidade contributiva, proporcionalidade e seletividade*. Curitiba: Juruá, 2015.

9. How excise taxes can contribute to a fair transition: a discussion on the progressive or regressive character of excise duties on energy products

Sébastien Wolff

1. INTRODUCTION

Until recently, the primary purpose of excise taxes on energy products has been to raise revenue for state expenditures without investigating the impact on citizens' available income and consumption decisions. Additionally, excise duties were often collected without regard for the personal situation of the taxpayer. With the adoption of regional and national transition plans, excise duties on energy products have taken on a new role: that of discouraging the use of energy sources that are harmful to the environment and accelerating the adoption of more planet-friendly technologies. However, low-income households may not have enough available revenue to invest in transitioning and may be caught out by excise duties on fossil fuels.

Excise duties are usually categorised as a production tax and, consequently, fairness among taxpayers was only a remote preoccupation at the time of their design and adoption by governments. In this research, the question of whether excise duties on energy products are currently increasing the social equality of a determined tax system or, on the contrary, are a more significant part of the tax burden on low-income households is investigated. Section 2 is dedicated to the gathering of worldwide academic research on the progressive or regressive character of excise duties in the real economy. The third section presents examples of measures taken by governments to limit the effects of increased energy prices, whether due to tax reform or increased prices in raw materials markets. It examines the contribution excise duties can make to a just transition, highlighting the necessary design features. Finally, the fourth section brings together the key points for designing excise duties on energy products that contribute to maintaining a fair energy transition and to limiting energy poverty.

2. THE USE OF EXCISE DUTIES FOR POLICY REASONS

2.1 The Impact of Excise Taxation on Available Income

Consumption taxes and excise duties are usually associated with a heavier burden for low-income individuals because, despite being lower in absolute terms, they represent a higher share of their expenses. Additionally, due to their limited access to energy-saving technologies, low-income households must consume a higher quantity of energy products and pay more taxes to cover their basic energy needs.[1] Their carbon footprint for having their basic energy needs covered is higher than that of richer households for instance. In the next paragraphs, different national experiences are analysed to identify the effects of excise duties on welfare and how governments can mitigate the budget effect on vulnerable populations.

In *Tax by Design*,[2] Mirrlees *et al.* discuss two different channels through which taxes can influence behaviour and welfare. The first is the *income effect*, where taxation changes cause a reduction or an increase in the available income. The implications are numerous, ranging from consumption patterns to work demand. If the tax reduces the income that people receive for a given number of hours of work, it will encourage them to work more to limit any decline in living standards. This is also true when an increase in indirect taxation on all or a limited number of products is planned. Second, the *substitution effect* will lead to increasing taxation on goods or incomes to make an hour of work or a unit of a certain good less attractive relative to an hour of leisure or another good than had previously been the case, encouraging people to work less or to purchase goods not subject to the same tax increase. Mirrlees noted that

> [T]the two effects work in opposite directions. For any individual tax change, it is impossible to say *a priori* which will dominate. But for revenue-neutral changes to taxes, income effects will tend to roughly balance out on average: money given

---

[1] S. Okushima, "Energy poor need more energy, but do they need more carbon? Evaluation of people's basic carbon needs" [2021], *Ecological Economics*, 187, pp. 1–14.

[2] J. Mirrlees, S. Adam, T. Besley, R. Blundell, S. Bond, R. Chote, M. Gammie, P. Johnson, G. Myles and JM Poterba, *Tax by Design* (Oxford: Oxford University Press, 2011) pp. 21–46.

> away to some people must be matched by money taken from others, so a positive income effect for one group will be offset by a negative income effect for another (though it is possible that one group might be more responsive than the other). Substitution effects will not necessarily balance out in this way.[3]

From a tax design perspective, a fixed tax rate on consumption could be assimilated to an income tax for households dedicating a major share of their income to consumption.[4] Since general consumption expenditures increase in volume but decrease in percentage of income with revenue, excise duties can be seen, based on tax design and the nature of the product, as regressive or progressive.

2.2 The Progressive, Regressive and Redistributive Effects of Excise Taxation

In 2018, Adachi measured the burden of indirect taxation, including consumption and excise taxes, in Japan by income group.[5] This study identifies that indirect taxes are regressive,[6] more particularly consumption tax, and that it is causing a serious problem for the poorest households. In 2018, Japanese excise taxes on liquor, tobacco, oil, and other products accounted for around 3.5% of national income, which is lower than the average European country. The results are that low-income earners are exposed to a relatively high burden of indirect taxation compared to others. For instance, the first decile will support an overall indirect tax burden that is three times greater than the economic impact on the tenth decile. The simulations conducted by Adachi show that, even when accompanied by policies aiming at mitigating this regressivity, such as setting lower rates on consumption and excise products, consumption taxes remain regressive.[7]

---

[3] Ibid., p. 29.

[4] Ibid., p. 149: "A tax on consumption levied at a uniform rate on goods and services is economically equivalent to a flat-rate expenditure tax."

[5] Y. Adachi, *The Economics of Tax and Social Security in Japan* (Singapore: Springer, 2018), p. 65. See also on the same theme: Y. Adachi, T. Uemura and Y. Saitoh, "Measuring the burden of indirect taxation including consumption tax in Japan by income group" [2017] *Public Finance and Management,* 17(3).

[6] The author proposes the following definition of a regressive tax: "A regressive tax is a tax that takes a larger burdens percentage of income from low-income earners than from high-income earners. It is in opposition with a progressive tax, which takes a larger percentage from high-income earners" (Y. Adachi, *The Economics of Tax and Social Security in Japan* (Singapore: Springer, 2018) p. 66).

[7] Y. Adachi, *The Economics of Tax and Social Security in Japan* (Singapore: Springer, 2018) 66.

In general, authors recommend counterbalancing the regressivity of excise taxes on energy products by the adoption of policy measures limiting income effects.[8] In a paper on tax shift presented in 2006, the European Commission noted the following:

> The policy simulations of these studies show that increasing the EU energy taxes, while reducing the employers' social security contributions by the corresponding amount (revenue neutrality), leads to higher employment (compared with the reference scenario) and better environment at the same time. The latter effect is shown by the reduction of CO_2 and other energy-related emissions (NOx, SO2, VOC, PM). The size of both effects depends on the size of the tax increase. Higher energy taxes

---

[8] See for instance: A. Brunetti and M.G. Calza, "Redistributive effects of changes in indirect taxation" [2015] *Rivista di statistica ufficiale*, 2015(2). The authors state as follows: "changes in indirect taxes do not directly affect household incomes but they affect the amount of consumption and consequently they can affect the general level of economic welfare of the household. However, a better assessment of the distributional impacts of tax reforms requires the measurement of the impacts both on household expenditure and income. To this effect it would be important to integrate in a comprehensive database detailed survey information on household expenditure and on household disposable income" (p. 9); E Biorn, "The distributive effects of indirect taxation: an econometric model and empirical results based on Norwegian data" [1975] *Swedish Journal of Economics*, 7(1), pp. 1–11. The author nuanced the need for income compensation measures for alcohol and tobacco: "Empirical results based on Norwegian data indicate that, from a distributive point of view, there are certain differences between excises on tobacco and alcohol and subsidies on food. Tentative results with regard to the degree of overestimating the 'true' income compensation when using the Laspeyres price index formula are also reported." See as well: Y. Adachi, *The Economics of Tax and Social Security in Japan* (Singapore: Springer, 2018) 88; A. Decoster and G. Van Camp, "Redistributive effects of the shift from personal income taxes to indirect taxes: Belgium 1988–93" [2001] *Fiscal Studies*, 22, pp. 457–487; M. Palme, 'Income distribution effects of the Swedish 1991 tax revision: an analysis of a microsimulation using generalised Kakwani decomposition' [1996] *Journal of Policy Modelling*, 18(4), pp. 47–69. The European Commission declared also: "A reduction in income taxes coupled with an increase in VAT tends to reduce the tax burden on higher incomes while increasing it on poor or middle-income households. The redistributive properties of direct income taxes have indeed been, historically, an important reason for their introduction and considerable expansion during the XX century" (European Commission (2006) "Macroeconomic effects of a shift from direct to indirect taxation: a simulation for 15 EU Member States", Note presented by the European Commission services (DG TAXUD) at the 72nd meeting of the OECD Working Party No. 2 on Tax Policy Analysis and Tax Statistics, Paris, 14–16 November 2006, available at: https://www.oecd.org/tax/tax-policy/39494151.pdf, accessed 22 October 2024, p. 12).

> would, however, also affect the competitiveness of energy-intensive industrial sectors negatively, (also shown in the studies), which so far has been an obstacle to a wider use of environmental tax reforms in the Member States.[9]

On the last consequence of increased excise duties on energy, the statement of the Commission could be nuanced to accommodate the beneficial effect of reduced activity in energy-intensive industrial sectors.

Flues and van Dender note in this respect that: "while richer households are affected more by an increase in taxes on domestic energy in absolute terms, such taxes are still likely to be regressive if no additional policy measures are implemented. Lump-sum transfers can mitigate regressive impacts, while income-tested transfers can result in a progressive impact of the tax reform".[10] Furthermore, in developed economies, due to limited access to technological innovation reducing the carbon footprint, low-income households will require more carbon to meet their basic energy needs.[11]

The regressive effect was also observed by Cnossen: "A problem with excisable products, especially if they are addictive, is that the demand is generally inelastic. As a result, people on lower incomes with the same quantitative level of consumption as people on higher incomes will pay more tax as a percentage of income than those on higher incomes." The author noted also a progressive effect under certain circumstances: "people on lower incomes will benefit relatively more from an internal-cost internalising excise duty [...] if they consume

---

9 European Commission (2006), "Macroeconomic effects of a shift from direct to indirect taxation: a simulation for 15 EU Member States", Note presented by the European Commission services (DG TAXUD) at the 72nd meeting of the OECD Working Party No. 2 on Tax Policy Analysis and Tax Statistics, Paris, 14–16 November 2006, available at: https://www.oecd.org/tax/tax-policy/39494151.pdf, accessed on: 22 October 2024.

10 F. Flues and K. van Dender, "The impact of energy taxes on the affordability of domestic energy" [2016] *OECD Taxation Working Papers*, 30, p. 34.

11 S. Okushima, "Energy poor need more energy, but do they need more carbon? Evaluation of people's basic carbon needs" [2021] *Ecological Economics*, 187(1–14). The study carried out in Japan concludes on the higher carbon intensity required for the poorest households to meet their basic energy needs: "The results show the greater carbon needs of the energy poor due to the higher carbon intensity of their domestic energy services use than the more affluent population. This means that the energy poor need to generate more carbon emissions to attain their basic energy needs (BEN) than the wealthy population in Japan. It also implies that decarbonization policy such as higher carbon pricing, which may be introduced in the near future, will place a severe burden on people in EP [energy poverty]. Carbon pricing would exacerbate EP" (p. 12).

relatively more than higher-income groups and the price elasticity is higher for them".[12]

The results can be slightly different for economies in development. Indeed, not all citizens have access to the same technologies, due to revenue but also geographical constraints. In India, gas or electricity is not available everywhere, and only a small portion of the population has access to motorised transportation. The poorest households are then *per se* untouched by a rise in taxes on fossil fuels. In 2020, Ohja, Pohit, and Ghosh concluded their research with five lessons on the reform of excise duties on energy products in this country:

(1) A carbon tax, no matter how it is recycled, cannot be a promoter for inclusive green growth and development without further measures.
(2) When carbon tax revenues are recycled specifically towards the development of the clean energy sectors, there are no perceptible gains in economic growth.
(3) Fears of major GDP losses from carbon taxes are exaggerated since the increase remains neutral in most of the scenarios.
(4) Whenever GDP gains are garnered by recycling carbon tax revenues into additional investment in all sectors, it is not carbon emission abatement that suffers, but inclusiveness.
(5) Finally, it is the policymakers' priorities about growth and inclusiveness which will decide whether the carbon tax revenues are to be recycled exclusively towards additional investment in all sectors or whether these revenues are to be shared between additional overall investment and extra cash transfers to households.[13]

For emerging economies, due to the limited access to fossil fuels for low-income households, mitigating measures can be less relevant than the proper use of additional revenues. However, the main observation remains that an increase in indirect taxation will have a negative impact on inclusiveness and could lead to adverse effects on the country's development under the GDP growth approach. Under the prism of sustainability, however, increasing the price of fossil fuels could lead to an accelerated transition to renewable energy and ensure a safer future.

---

[12] S. Cnossen, "Excise taxation for domestic resource mobilisation" [2022] *CESifo Working Papers*, 8842, p. 11.

[13] V.P. Ohja, S. Pohit and J. Ghosh, "Recycling carbon tax for inclusive green growth: a CGE analysis of India" [2020] *Energy Policy*, 144, pp. 11–12.

3. MITIGATING THE SOCIAL CONSEQUENCES OF EXCISE TAXATION WHEN CONTRIBUTING TO ENVIRONMENTAL PROTECTION

3.1 Tax Shift and Potential Consequences on (Energy) Poverty

Shifting from income taxes to excise taxes is a common method to enhance environmental protection. However, to avoid increasing poverty among low-revenue households, a tax shift from income to excise taxes requires compensating for the loss in purchasing power caused to low-income households.[14] A possibility would be to lower the impact of higher energy taxation by granting relief of income tax. However, it will also affect savings. The European Commission summarises this paradox as follows:

> In principle, revenue taxation affects both the consumption and the savings component of revenue (even though in practice the taxation of the savings component is much less heavy). Reducing direct taxation and increasing consumption taxation should normally stimulate savings, which would become comparatively less taxed. In the short run, this could, in theory, have a contractionary effect on GDP given that consumption demand, unlike savings, translates one-to-one in aggregate demand.[15]

Including savings taxation in the analysis deserves interest since private investment in transitional activities can lead to a spillover effect for environmentally friendly economic activities. Conversely, savings are susceptible to hampering environmental and social protection policies if invested in non-sustainable activities. In this respect, the recent framework developed at the European level for redirecting investments to sustainable economic activities can help greatly.[16] The additional reporting requirements for investment in sustain-

---

[14] The European Commission indeed notes as well that: "[C]oncentrating taxation on consumption would spare from taxes the highest income taxpayers who are likely to have a very low propensity to consume. Their accumulated wealth is likely never to be consumed but rather bequeathed to future generations" (European Commission (2006), "Macroeconomic effects of a shift from direct to indirect taxation: a simulation for 15 EU Member States", Note presented by the European Commission services (DG TAXUD) at the 72nd meeting of the OECD Working Party No. 2 on Tax Policy Analysis and Tax Statistics, Paris, 14–16 November 2006, https://www.oecd.org/tax/tax-policy/39494151.pdf, accessed 22 October 2024).

[15] Ibid., p. 13.

[16] European Commission (2018), Communication of 8 March 2018 from the Commission: "Action Plan: Financing Sustainable Growth", COM/2018/097 final;

ability set the investor in a position to evaluate for himself the sustainable objectives—including the activities responding to environmental, climate, and social concerns—to which he wants to contribute.[17] This potential building block for excise policies will not be further elaborated but could be a cornerstone for convergence and a powerful tool to mobilise private investment for environmental protection.

3.2 Step 1: Determining the Optimal Level of Taxation from an Environmental and Social Perspective

The first key point for policy intervention is to identify the optimal level of taxation for society and to ensure an adequate level of protection for the environment. For energy products, this optimum may be difficult to calculate and, if determinable, seems complicated to reach in real life.[18] Indeed, despite precise climate and environmental impact, levels of taxation and subsequent emissions limits cannot easily be set in a predictable way. One reason is that the prices for energy products on global markets are not as stable as other commodities and that, sometimes, excise taxes are used to moderate shocks

---

Regulation (EU) 2019/2089 of the European Parliament and of the Council of 27 November 2019 amending Regulation (EU) 2016/1011 as regards EU Climate Transition Benchmarks, EU Paris-aligned Benchmarks and sustainability-related disclosures for benchmarks. *OJ* L 317 of 9 December 2019, p. 17; Regulation (EU) 2019/2088 of the European Parliament and of the Council of 27 November 2019 on sustainability-related disclosures in the financial services sector. *OJ* L 317 of 9 December 2019, 1; Regulation (EU) 2020/852 of the European Parliament and of the Council of 18 June 2020 on the establishment of a framework to facilitate sustainable investment and amending Regulation (EU) 2019/2088. *OJ* L 198 of 22 June 2020, p. 13.

[17] Regulation (EU) 2019/2089 of the European Parliament and of the Council of 27 November 2019 amending Regulation (EU) 2016/1011 as regards EU Climate Transition Benchmarks, EU Paris-aligned Benchmarks and sustainability-related disclosures for benchmarks. *OJ* L 317 of 9 December 2019, p. 17; Regulation (EU) 2019/2088 of the European Parliament and of the Council of 27 November 2019 on sustainability-related disclosures in the financial services sector. *OJ* L 317 of 9 December 2019, 1; Regulation (EU) 2020/852 of the European Parliament andof the Council of 18 June 2020 on the establishment of a framework to facilitate sustainable investment and amending Regulation (EU) 2019/2088. *OJ* L 198 of 22 June 2020, p. 13.

[18] For a discussion on the optimal taxation, see: J.A. Mirrlees, "Optimal commodity taxation in a two-class economy" [1975] *Journal of Public Economics* 4, 27–33; J.A. Mirrlees, "Optimal tax theory: a synthesis" [1976] *Journal of Public Economics*, 6, pp. 327–358.

on energy markets and to fill revenue gaps in national budgets.[19] The OECD discouraged this practice during the 2022 European energy crisis:

> The key message emerging from this policy brief is that governments will need to shift from policies that directly seek to limit price increases to those that cushion their impact through targeted income support. This approach will ensure that the support provided is fair and effective, while limiting its effects on government budgets and maintaining price signals to encourage the transition to carbon neutrality.[20]

Additionally, since excise duties are usually considered a production tax, limiting companies' profit from fossil fuel energy can be seen as a way to avoid overinvestment or reinvestment in such activities. Limiting available profit coming from fossil-fuel-linked activities can be justified by climate objectives but also by adequate security of supply, a concern brought to light in the recent aggression of Ukraine by Russia.[21] Furthermore, fossil fuel rents tend to concentrate wealth within a very limited number of hands, leading to a counter-productive outcome from a social perspective.[22]

---

19 It was particularly the case as a first response to the energy crisis experienced in 2022. See: Belgium Federal Government (2022), "A federal crisis plan to combat soaring energy prices", available at: https://www.belgium.be/en/news/2022/federal_crisis_plan_combat_soaring_energy_prices, accessed 22 October 2024. The answer from the Belgian government states as the first reaction: "Excise duties on petrol and diesel are lowered"; G. Garavatti, S. Tagliapietra and G. Zachmann (2021), "National policies to shield consumers from rising energy prices", Bruegel Datasets, first published 4 November 2021, https://www.bruegel.org/dataset/national-policies-shield-consumers-rising-energy-prices accessed 22 October 2024; OECD (2022), "Why governments should target support amidst high energy prices", 30 June 2022, available at: https://www.oecd-ilibrary.org/docserver/40f44f78-en.pdf?expires=1669129619&id=id&accname=guest&checksum=3E437909B97A2CDDA8E6C3DE64BF89AC, accessed 22 October 2024.

20 OECD (2022), "Why governments should target support amidst high energy prices", 30 June 2022, available at: https://www.oecd-ilibrary.org/docserver/40f44f78-en.pdf?expires=1669129619&id=id&accname=guest&checksum=3E437909B97A2CDDA8E6C3DE64BF89AC, accessed 22 October 2024.

21 L. Wenar, *Blood Oil: Tyrants, Violence and the Rules that Run the World* (Oxford: Oxford University Press, 2017).

22 T. Bergstrom, "On capturing oil rents with a national excise tax" [1972] *American Economic Review*, 72, no. 1, p. 201. The author enumerates several worrying risks: "It has been argued by some that most of the 'rents' received by major oil producing nations accrue to a small and extremely wealthy ruling class. Such concentrated wealth may be used in capricious and dangerous ways, such as in financing terrorism. Furthermore, the concentration of enormous mineral wealth

3.3 Step 2: Determining Accompanying Measures and Collecting Previous Experiences

Another feature of tax policy from a social perspective is whether it includes measures to encourage progressivity—or, at least, limit regressivity—and how past experiences have been analysed to assess the real impact of a policy change. Different elements could be considered when reforming excise duties on energy products to avoid a regressive effect, achieve the sought environmental impact, and maintain equality and fairness among taxpayers.

When designing an increase in excises on energy products, the subsequent losses in sales for energy suppliers should also be considered: due to the decrease in quantities sold, the losses in profit would be passed on to consumers by increasing their prices beyond the increase in taxation. This is advantageous from an environmental perspective and enhances the appeal of sustainable energy sources. However, it may restrict overall access to energy if certain groups of citizens lack the financial means to invest in more sustainable technologies.

In developed economies, high-income earners redirect more of their revenue to investment and less to consumption. It is then necessary to maintain a progressive design for lawmakers to envisage counterbalancing tax measures when elaborating policies. In Japan's Comprehensive Revision, the purpose of increasing consumption tax and excise duties was to fund social security expenses due to the ageing population. Behind social objectives can be hidden difficult economic realities for certain categories of the population. Adachi concludes with the following alarming statement:

> In order to lower the tax regressivity accompanying any increase in the consumption tax, instead of measures such as lowering tax rates, setting zero tax rates, or providing tax refunds to all income earners, social security policies closely targeting low-income earners are required.[23]

---

in a militarily and politically unstable portion of the world is extremely tempting to potential invaders and increases the likelihood of war."

[23] Y. Adachi, *The Economics of Tax and Social Security in Japan* (Singapore: Springer, 2018), p. 88. This statement was also supported in the Mirrlees review (see *supra*) when stating one of the main principles for effective taxation: the need to think of the tax system as just that – a system. "The way that different taxes fit together matters, as does being clear about the role of each tax within the system." J. Mirrlees, S. Adam, T. Besley, R. Blundell, S. Bond, R. Chote, M. Gammie, P. Johnson, G. Myles and J.M. Poterba, *Tax by Design* (Oxford: Oxford University Press, 2011), p. 45.

The study corroborates previous studies on Japan, mainly those conducted by Poterba in 1991 on gasoline. These showed that the burden caused by a gasoline tax—a tax on quantity of a certain energy product—as a share of total expenditure was less regressive than a tax on a share of household income. In his paper, Poterba proposed different policy techniques to avoid regressivity on carbon taxes:

> Several policies would reduce the burdens on low-income and low-expenditure households. First, many transfer programs are already indexed for price changes. Since the carbon tax will be paid by consumers in the form of higher retail prices, indexed components of income will partly adjust to offset the tax burdens. [...] A second approach to ameliorating the distributional burdens of the carbon tax is increased use of redistributive income taxes. [...] [A] third approach to reducing regressivity would be an explicit policy of tax credits for energy expenditures. Allowing each household a tax credit equal to the first one or two percent of income devoted to purchasing energy would enable the tax authorities to alter the average price of energy, hence blunting the carbon tax's redistributive effects, while preserving the marginal price effects of the tax.[24]

On the design of compensation measures, Belgium decided in the 1990s to switch an important part of the income tax to indirect taxation. It included a substantial increase of excise duties on fuels and tobacco, compensating for a reduction in the top rates of personal income taxes. As expected, the economic evaluation concluded that:

> The positive redistributive impact of the personal income tax system has been eroded by the tax revision. The negative redistributive impact of the indirect tax system increased. Evidently, for the joint tax system, this implies that the redistributive impact has also decreased.[25]

The increase in indirect taxation was used to increase pensions and work incentives for unemployed workers, ultimately resulting in a positive impact for the lower deciles.

> The fiscal consolidation in the nineties was more targeted to higher incomes and the poor were hit relatively less. In the 2001–2007 period, all income deciles gained

24 J.M. Poterba, "Tax policy to combat global warming: on designing a carbon tax" [1991] *NBER Working Papers Series*, 3649, p. 24.

25 A. Decoster and G. Van Camp, "Redistributive effects of the shift from personal income taxes to indirect taxes: Belgium 1988–1993" [2000] *KU Leuven Center for Economic Studies Discussion Paper Series*, No. 00.07, p. 47. See also the final version of the paper: A. Decoster and G. Van Camp "Redistributive effects of the shift from personal income taxes to indirect taxes: Belgium 1988–93" [2001] *Fiscal Studies*, 22, pp. 79–106.

from the large personal income tax revision. Increases in unemployment benefits and social assistance especially benefited the lower deciles. From 2007 to 2012 disposable incomes of lower deciles grew relatively stronger thanks to the welfare adaptations of public pensions.[26]

In the evaluation of the Czech revision of excise taxation, observers note that:

> One significant distortionary reaction of the market is the process of over-shifting the tax burden, when the price of taxed goods rises by more than the tax rate or its increase; this means that the end consumer not only bears the full cost of taxation but is also paying for the future loss of the supplier from decreased demand as a response to increased prices.[27]

Then they conclude that the Pigouvian principle underlying excise duties based on the environmental impact of the consumption of a certain good has been violated.

> This undesired market reaction does not correspond with the baseline policy that targets the pollution reduction. As shown by empirical analysis, the price of transport fuels tends to increase overall by more than the tax rate, affecting the welfare of final consumers. This practice of over-shifting represents a concealed form of overcharging the final consumers.[28]

The medium of redistribution in the case of a rise of excises seems not relevant, as long as it helps contribute to increasing the real revenue of households belonging to the bottom deciles. Therefore, compensation measures do not need to be inserted into the excise tax structure, but can come from other taxes.

---

26 A. Decoster, S. Perelman, D. Vandelannoote, T. Vanheukelom and G. Verbist, "A bird's eye view on 20 years of tax benefit reforms in Belgium" [2010] *Euromod Working Paper Series*, 15(10).

27 D. Nerudova and M. Dobranshi, "The impact of tax burden overshifting on the Pigovian taxation" [2016] *Procedia – Social and Behavioral Sciences*, 220, pp. 302–311.

28 Ibid., pp. 302–311. Nerudova and Dobranshi go further in their observations and conclusions by stating that the overshifting hampers not only Pigouvian taxation but also the Pareto optimality in resource distribution. As a consequence, "The violation of [the] Pigouvian Principle through overshifting increases the regressivity of environmental taxes, reduces the overall welfare and increases the distortionary costs of corrective taxation beyond the social benefits of pollution reduction" (p. 309).

3.4 Step 3: Find the Right Balance between Compensation Measures and the Polluter Pays Principle

By mitigating the revenue effect, the incentive character of environmental taxation is compromised. The public authorities would have to find the right balance between supporting low-income households and sending a consistent message in the direction of more environmental protection to every citizen. Simulations of policies can be informative on the economic impact of the reform borne by every citizen and on possible loopholes of a surge in energy taxation.

In Germany, simulations of three reforms were compared to a reference scenario: a revenue-neutral, carbon-harmonised fuel tax, a carbon tax, and, finally, a combination of the two. The results were as follows:

- The progressive tax on diesel has a lower tax level than the regressive tax on petrol and seems to hamper less low-income household revenue.[29]
- The authors find no evidence that a carbon price on transport fuels does, on average, disproportionately burden low-income households.

> If the goal is to avoid an increase in inequality, then our results for a carbon tax provide little argument against a further increase in the German carbon price on transport fuels. If one also wants to ensure social acceptance among the revision losers, then the additional tax revenues can be redistributed through targeted social benefits and subsidies that enable low-emission mobility.[30]

- Finally, the experience identifies that income is not necessarily the relevant criterion in case of a tax specifically targeting non-sustainable fuel.

> Although, from an environmental perspective, it appears reasonable that heavy users (which belong to the group of "revision losers" in our analyses) are penalised by these reforms, it might be worthwhile to address cases of hardship especially during a transition period. Specific groups of households might neither be able to adjust to a less carbon-intense mobility behaviour in the short run nor to bear the additional tax burden. This could apply to households with lower incomes, but also commuters, families, and households located in rural areas.[31]

These results are not easily transferable to a general rise of excises on all fossil energies, targeting fossil products purchased for heating purposes or by industries.

---

[29] L Jacobs, L. Quack and M. Metchel, "Distributional effects of carbon pricing by transport fuel taxation" [2022] *Energy Economics*, 114, pp. 1 and 14.

[30] Ibid., p. 14.

[31] Ibid., p. 15.

The design and application of compensative measures will be critical in asserting the right balance between the polluter pays principle and reducing budget inequalities among consumers of energy products. With regard to the polluter pays principle, it seems normal that the release of an additional unit of pollutant leads to the payment of a similar amount of tax since the restoration of the environmental damage will cost a similar amount. On the other hand, social justice calls for two different aspects: first, the implementation measures should make environmentally friendly technologies more accessible for households with limited or insufficient revenues; second, the amount paid by the polluter could be considered mandatorily progressive since it remains difficult to be entirely green or environmentally sustainable and every additional unit of pollutant spared should be correlated to an improvement of the tax situation. These two dimensions cannot easily be reconciled without the help of several measures: to avoid a regressive effect in case of a broad increase in excise taxes, the measure should be accompanied by tax credits or compensative measures on other direct and/or indirect taxes. Developing scenarios and performing simulations on a national budget can help to calibrate the envisaged changes.

4. CONCLUSION

Excise duties on energy products, like other excise taxes, are inherently regressive, as evidenced by multiple examples from both developed and developing economies. However, their regressive nature can be mitigated at the time of the adoption of the increase. Within the same policy, a portion of the revenue collected by the state can be allocated to alleviating the impact on low-income households, provided such redistribution is implemented alongside the increase in indirect taxation through complementary tax measures. The careful design of these accompanying measures is, therefore, critical to ensuring the success of environmental tax policies for both environmental protection and societal well-being.

From an environmental perspective, the evidence suggests that the quality of the environment improves when higher excise taxes are levied on goods with significant environmental implications. On the redistributive front, however, the results are mixed: the contribution to social equity depends heavily on how public authorities allocate the tax revenue. The so-called "double dividend"—where increased excise taxes on energy products both accelerate the environmental transition and enhance revenue distribution—can only be realised if revenues are strategically reinvested in environmentally friendly goods or activities.

In general, the authors recommend counterbalancing the regressive nature of energy excise taxes through policy measures that limit adverse income effects. Excise taxes on goods such as tobacco, alcohol, and fossil fuels can yield benefits by discouraging their consumption, particularly among low-income households that dedicate a significant share of their income to these items. While dedicating tax revenues to social policies can enhance equity and support vulnerable groups, this approach may inadvertently diminish environmental benefits by reducing incentives to lower energy consumption. Taxpayers receiving compensation may lack sufficient motivation to decrease their use of energy products significantly due to the transfer.

One potential solution is to direct the increased tax revenue towards closing the gap between low- and high-income households in access to sustainable technologies. On the positive side, this approach could simultaneously support social equity and environmental goals, creating a strong incentive for the adoption of cleaner technologies. On the negative side, focusing on specific technologies risks channelling household consumption strictly towards investments, without addressing the reduction in day-to-day disposable income.

10. Global minimum income taxation (OECD) and environmental taxation: implications for South American countries

Rodolfo Salassa Boix and Paloma García Córdoba

1. INTRODUCTION

The Global Anti-Base Erosion (GloBE) Rules[1] established in 2021 as a part of the Two-Pillar Solution led by the Organisation for Economic Co-operation and Development's (OECD) Inclusive Framework on Base Erosion and Profit Shifting (BEPS)[2] stands as an unprecedented international agreement supported by almost 150 countries and jurisdictions.[3] These rules aim to deal with the tax challenges arising from the digitalisation of the economy and profit shifting. By allowing jurisdictions to tax the profits of large multinational enterprises (MNEs), irrespective of physical presence, the GloBE Rules seek to establish a minimum tax rate of 15% on corporate profits.[4] As a result, this prevents the erosion of tax bases and artificial profit shifting, with potentially far-reaching consequences extending beyond corporate tax strategies.[5] This paradigm shift in corporate income taxation necessitates a thorough review of existing tax incentives,[6] particularly those related to environmental taxation.[7]

Through environmental taxes and tax incentives, respectively,[8] environmental taxation plays a critical role in promoting environmentally responsible practices and discouraging polluting activities.[9] Although the primary objective of environmental taxes is linked to environmental preservation, they remain fundamentally tax measures, encompassing both direct and indirect taxation. Notably, corporate income tax (CIT) is typically considered a direct tax. Nonetheless, the distinction between direct and indirect taxes has been widely debated.[10]

The complex relationship between the GloBE Rules and the use of environmental tax incentives underscores the significance of examining this topic, particularly within the context of developing countries.[11] Concerns about the possible weakening of environmental tax incentives have emerged following the implementation of the GloBE Rules, especially in developing countries where tax incentives are frequently used to attract investments and promote economic growth.[12] These investments include those that aim to promote sustainable development. The lack of coordination between tax policies and sustainable development goals could lead to an impractical implementation of global tax reform.[13] In light of this, understanding the implications for environmental tax policy in South American countries is significant.

Considering the impact of the OECD's GloBE Rules on corporate taxation and their potential effect on environmental taxation, especially in developing countries reliant on tax incentives, this chapter will present a preliminary approach concerning the impact of these new rules on environmental taxation. Special emphasis will be placed on understanding the implications for environmental tax policies in developing countries within the evolving landscape of international tax regulations. Although this chapter does not address the broader issue, we find it important to consider the fiscal policy implications of restricting states' ability to offer tax incentives.[14] In this context, we focus only on certain specific types of tax incentives. This chapter is framed within the research project *Environmental taxation and climate change: a new tax competence scheme for ecologically and financially more sustainable Autonomous Communities*, funded by the Institute d'Estudis d'Autogovern de Catalonia (PRE197/24/000023).

This chapter will be structured as follows: first, a brief overview of Pillar Two and the GloBE Rules will be provided. The complex relationship between tax incentives and environmental taxes will then be discussed. Subsequently, case studies of South American countries' corporate tax laws will be presented. Finally, closing remarks and recommendations will be presented.

2. GLoBE RULES AND TAX INCENTIVES

2.1 An Introduction to the GloBe Rules

Pillar Two is the cornerstone of the ongoing project led by the OECD. The OECD/G20 Inclusive Framework Agreement on the "Two-Pillar Solution to Address Tax Challenges from the Digital Economy", also known as BEPS 2.0, is the result of work which began in 2013.[15] The goal of the GloBE Rules is to reduce tax competition between jurisdictions in all situations. This stands in contrast to BEPS 1.0, which mainly focused on abusive tax structures that lead to tax evasion and avoidance.[16]

The GloBE Rules aim to establish a global minimum tax rate of 15% for MNEs. A detailed explanation of the operation of these rules would far exceed the purpose and scope of this chapter, but their operation will be briefly explained.

To begin with, these rules only apply to corporate tax and they ensure that MNE Groups with annual revenues at or above EUR 750 million (in at least two of the four fiscal years preceding the fiscal year being assessed) are subject to a minimum level of taxation in each of the jurisdictions in which they operate.[17] The GloBE Rules propose a "top-up tax" on foreign-sourced profits of MNEs that have an Effective Tax Rate (ETR) below the minimum of 15%.[18] To achieve this, the GloBE Rules are structured as an interconnected and coordinated system of rules designed for integration into the domestic laws of each jurisdiction.[19]

The calculation of the ETR involves a meticulous comparison of an MNE's income generated within a specific jurisdiction compared to the corresponding tax payments made therein. The Income Inclusion Rule (IIR) allows companies to specify the domiciled country of a parent or intermediate holding company to impose top-up taxes on MNEs where the ETR falls below the 15% threshold.[20] The Under Taxed Payments Rule (UTPR) works as a supplementary measure, limiting deductions to prevent MNEs from using low-tax jurisdictions if the IIR fails to capture specific income sources.[21] An additional provision, the Qualified Domestic Minimum Top-up Tax (QDMTT), has also been introduced by the GloBE Rules.[22] This provision grants the source jurisdiction (where the income arises) the primary right to levy taxes on profits taxed below the 15% minimum.

The 15% minimum rate may seem low compared to the current global average statutory corporate income tax rate of 23.45% among 181 jurisdictions.[23] This minimum rate is especially significant given the difficulties of reaching extensive multilateral agreements. The implementation of Pillar Two, however, still faces several kinds of obstacles despite the improvements made.[24]

2.2 Interaction between GloBE Rules and Tax Incentives

Tax incentives are targeted measures that lower the tax burden for certain activities or investments.[25] These incentives can take various forms, such as tax holidays, credits, or reduced rates, and are intended to boost economic activity, address market inefficiencies, encourage beneficial investments, and attract foreign direct investment. Different countries implement tax incentives in diverse ways, leading to significant variations in their application.

The interaction between these rules and tax incentives is significant, and the OECD has recognised this by releasing a special report on the subject.[26] The GloBE Rules do not explicitly prevent the offering of reduced tax rates or incentives.[27] However, they create significant restrictions since a jurisdiction's ETR must not fall below the GloBE Rules' minimum of 15%.

Since these rules apply exclusively to CIT, tax incentives related to other taxes, such as property or payroll taxes, remain unaffected.[28] An important feature of the GloBE Rules is that they apply uniformly to all tax incentives, regardless of their policy goals.[29] For instance, tax credits for renewable energy projects are treated no differently than those for fossil fuel initiatives.[30] Whether the incentive aims to promote sustainable development, green investments, or other goals, the GloBE Rules remain consistent.

As a result, jurisdictions may need to design their tax incentive programmes carefully to ensure compliance with the GloBE Rules. The impact of the GloBE Rules on tax incentives is expected to differ based on the specific type of incentive, the entity, and the jurisdiction involved.[31] This variability requires a case-by-case analysis to fully understand its implications. However, several general scenarios have been posited depending on the specific type of incentive.

For instance, tax incentives that involve low or zero corporate tax rates, or that partially or fully exempt income from taxation (like special regimes), are likely to be significantly impacted by the GloBE Rules.[32] In contrast, tax incentives related to the immediate or accelerated depreciation of assets are less likely to be affected by the GloBE Rules. This is because the rules allow for adjustments of the GloBE income to account for temporary differences, with a limit of five years, and jurisdictions may aim to maintain or even expand these types of incentives.

If these incentives cause an MNE's effective tax rate to fall below 15%, they could trigger top-up taxes under Pillar Two, diminishing their appeal. As a result, countries may need to reevaluate their tax incentive strategies, potentially shifting towards other investment promotion tools. However, certain incentives, like accelerated depreciation or VAT exemptions, can still be leveraged to attract investment.

The OECD additionally addresses the design and use of tax incentives in a post-Pillar Two world. Countries are encouraged to reassess their existing tax incentives to align with GloBE Rules and rethink their environmental strategies. This might involve shifting from tax-based incentives to alternative forms of support, such as cash grants or subsidies, to promote sustainability.

The implementation of GloBE Rules may drive a transition from traditional tax incentives towards more targeted and effective policy instruments. In this sense, the emerging GloBE Rules are reshaping the corporate tax landscape. According to the OECD, this is an opportunity to reassess tax incentive programmes, which involves identifying and eliminating inefficient tax incentives.

Another important aspect is the potential revenue generated, which the OECD highlights as a significant benefit of adopting the GloBE Rules. In this sense, the OECD suggests that jurisdictions could strategically allocate the revenues from Pillar Two to strengthen non-tax factors that attract investors, such as improving physical infrastructure and enhancing labour force skills.[33] Additionally, these funds present an opportunity to support environmental initiatives, aligning them with broader sustainable development goals.

3. ENVIRONMENTAL TAXATION: SPECIAL FOCUS ON ENVIRONMENTAL TAX INCENTIVES

For decades, tax law has been employed as a complementary mechanism to protect the environment by guiding the behaviours of taxpayers,[34] it has demonstrated its effectiveness in this regard.[35] This is accomplished through measures that, within the field of environmental taxation, combine elements of both environmental law and tax law, creating an interdisciplinary approach.

Environmental taxation consists of two major groups of measures aimed at protecting the environment through taxes. On the one hand, there are environmental taxes that do not primarily aim to generate revenue[36] but rather to incentivise polluting behaviours to internalise the cost of environmental damages.[37] For this to be effective, it would be advisable for taxpayers to have an alternative that provides them with a genuine opportunity to change their behaviour. However, this is not always the case. Thus, the key to these taxes lies in the configuration of the taxable event and the elements for calculating the tax liability,[38] rather than the ecological allocation of the collected funds.[39] While environmental taxes can serve specific purposes, their primary feature is their deterrent function.

On the other hand, there are environmental tax incentives which aim to encourage environmentally friendly behaviours by providing tax benefits to taxpayers that would otherwise be less likely to occur.[40] These benefits are quite varied.[41] The most common include eliminating (exemption), reducing (deductions or reduced rates), or deferring the tax burden (deferral).[42] Although environmental taxes have received more academic attention, tax incentives have been more commonly implemented in practice as tools for environmental protection.[43] This is likely due to the higher political costs (but lower fiscal costs) associated with environmental taxes compared to incentives.[44]

Tax incentives are always related to a specific tax that is generally either not paid or paid at a reduced quantity,[45] which is why they are considered tax measures. Subsidies, on the other hand, are usually not linked to any tax. As a result, tax incentives typically lead to a reduction in revenue since the administration stops receiving all or part of the income from the levy linked to the incentive.[46] Conversely, subsidies involve the administration directly giving money to individuals. In the first case, it is money that the administration stops receiving from individuals, while in the second case, it is public money that the administration gives to individuals. Each strategy has different implications for public finances.[47] To highlight this distinction, some authors refer to indirect financial aid (tax incentives) and direct financial aid (subsidies).[48]

Considering that environmental tax incentives generally eliminate or reduce the tax burden of existing taxes for environmental purposes and that many of these incentives impact the CIT burden, our work will focus on these incentives. The fact that subsidies are not part of our research does not mean we disregard their role in environmental protection, as they are also valuable tools for guiding taxpayer behaviour, whether in favour of or against the environment (if they aim to promote another general interest). This is important because the environmental message conveyed by some tax measures can be neutralised by the contradictory messages of anti-environmental subsidies, which may support polluting activities.

4. CORPORATE INCOME TAXES IN SOUTH AMERICAN COUNTRIES: RATES AND ENVIRONMENTAL TAX INCENTIVES

Before examining each corporate income tax (CIT) regime, it is important to highlight that South America has the highest regional average statutory CIT rate, standing at 28.38% in 2023.[49] This disparity suggests that the OECD's proposed 15% minimum tax rate could significantly impact CIT regimes within the region.

It is worth noting that environmental tax incentives often exist in various types of legislation, including CIT laws, environmental laws, and investment laws. In addition, another relevant piece of information is that Colombia[50] and Brazil[51] Colombia and Brazil were the only South American countries with regulations in place as of 2023 to comply with the GloBE Rules.[52]

In the following sections, we will present a preliminary analysis of CIT regimes in South American countries, with a specific emphasis on their CIT and the availability of environmental tax incentives that may reduce the overall tax burden and whether these incentives might impact the GloBE Rules. We conducted an examination of each country's CIT regime, as well as any applicable environmental or investment regulations, to identify potential environmental tax incentives.

4.1 Argentina

In Argentina, CIT is regulated by Law 20.628 of 1973, as amended by Decree 824/2019. This tax applies a mixed progressive scale (fixed amount and percentage) on the taxable net income of corporations.[53] This tax is applied using a mixed progressive scale, combining a fixed amount and a percentage on the taxable net income of corporations. However, the overall tax burden may be reduced through various tax incentives designed to encourage environmentally sustainable practices. Some examples of these incentives include:

- Total exemption of income derived from the disposal of waste and all types of activities related to environmental sanitation and preservation, including consultancy services, provided income is reinvested in these purposes.[54]
- Total exemption from the payment of tax on the distribution of dividends or profits distributed by companies holding investment projects that benefit from the National Promotion Regime for the use of Renewable Energy Sources for Electricity Production if these are reinvested in new infrastructure projects in the country.[55]
- Accelerated depreciation for investments included in the National Promotion Regime for the use of Renewable Energy Sources for Electricity Production, starting from the fiscal period in which the asset is commissioned, for investment projects that have effectively commenced between 1 January 2018 and 31 December 2025.[56]

4.2 Bolivia

In Bolivia, all companies are subject to a 25% CIT, which is calculated based on their profit after tax adjustments.[57] There is one CIT incentive aimed at environmental protection. It enables non-profit organisations, such as civil associations and foundations engaged in ecological activities, to apply for recognition as income-tax-exempt entities through the Tax Administration.[58]

4.3 Brazil

CIT in Brazil was established by Law 9430 of 1996[59] and is regulated by the Annex of Decree 9580/18 (Annex).[60] The tax rate is defined as 15% on the actual, presumed, or arbitrated income in general. Additionally, the portion of income that exceeds the result of multiplying 20,000 reais by the number of months in the period is subject to an additional 10% rate.[61] Therefore, this additional rate will always apply to MNEs under the GloBE Rules.

To promote investments in forestry projects, a 50% bonus on the value of this tax is established for amounts invested in afforestation or reforestation. These investments can be made in forest species, fruit trees, and large trees. Investments are related to the fiscal year in which the tax is collected.[62]

4.4 Chile

The CIT in Chile is levied on the annual business income of legal entities resident in the country.[63] Currently, the standard CIT rate is 25% for SMEs and 27% for larger entities under the Partially Integrated System (PIS).[64] Until 2014, Chilean tax legislation did not incorporate taxes with an extra-fiscal purpose aimed at environmental protection. Although there are no tax incentives specifically targeting environmental protection, certain generic incentives may be applicable.

Incentives provide certain benefits in geographically extreme zones.[65] For instance, in the Arica and Parinacota provinces, there is a 30–40% tax credit against the First Category Tax (FCT) for investments in fixed assets for businesses. A 10–40% tax credit is in place against CIT for investments in production or service provision in Region XI and Palena Province. In addition, there is a 50-year exemption from CIT for businesses in the Magallanes and Chilean Antarctica Region engaged in specific industries that ensure sustainable practices.

4.5 Colombia

The Tax Statute, which is regulated by Decree-Law 624 of 1989 (articles 158 to 676), regulates the CIT in Colombia. The general CIT rate (applicable to national corporations and their equivalents, permanent establishments of foreign entities, and foreign legal entities with or without residence in the country) is 35%.[66] The rate is above the 15% minimum set by the GloBE Rules, meaning that tax incentives should be carefully considered.

The tax burden of this levy can also be influenced by the application of various tax incentives related to the promotion of environmentally friendly behaviours. Some of them include a total exemption from income derived from the sale of electricity generated from wind energy, biomass or agricultural waste, or solar, geothermal, or marine energy, exclusively by generating companies, for a term of 15 years (starting from 2017), provided that certain requirements are met. Among these requirements are carbon dioxide emission certificates and the condition that at least 50% of the proceeds from the sale of these certificates are invested in social benefit projects in the region where the generator operates.[67]

In addition, there is a 50% tax credit on the total investment, made within a period not exceeding 15 years (starting from the taxable year following the year in which the investment became operational), for the development and utilisation of non-conventional energy sources, energy storage systems, and efficient energy use, primarily from renewable sources, within the national energy system. The deductible amount for this cannot exceed 50% of the taxpayer's net income, determined before deducting the value of the investment.[68]

4.6 Ecuador

The Internal Tax Regime Law (LRTI) of Ecuador establishes the rules and regulations governing taxes. It covers various taxes, including CIT.[69] Ecuador's CIT has a standard rate of 25%. However, this rate can fluctuate between 22% and 28% based on factors such as the company's ownership structure, shareholder location, and transparency in disclosing ownership details. Additionally, new investments may qualify for a reduced tax rate.

The rate is above the minimum set by the GloBE Rules, meaning that environmental tax incentives should be carefully evaluated. In Ecuador, tax incentives are not explicitly detailed within the tax legislation but are scattered across various other laws and norms.

New investments in sectors that contribute to changes in the energy matrix, strategic import substitution, export promotion, and rural and urban development can receive a total income tax exemption for five years.[70] These investments could be considered environmental tax incentives and could also benefit from the income tax exemptions and additional deductions on annual depreciation costs or expenses.

4.7 Paraguay

CIT in Paraguay is regulated by Law 6380/2019, which establishes a tax rate of 10% on net income.[71] Thus, the rate does not reach the minimum set by the GloBE Rules. Nevertheless, there are very few incentives related to the environment. For example, a tax exemption may apply to income earned by nonprofit entities engaged in social welfare or public interest activities, including environmental protection.[72] However, this measure does not impact the GloBE Rules due to the entity type.

4.8 Peru

In Peru, the CIT framework varies depending on the company's residency status. Resident companies face a 29.5% CIT on their worldwide net income, with deductions permitted for eligible expenses. Conversely, non-resident companies are subject to a 30% tax on their gross Peruvian-sourced income, without expense deductions.

The rate is above the 15% minimum set by the GloBE Rules, meaning that tax incentives should be carefully considered. Nevertheless, Peru does not offer any tax incentives for environmental protection under the CIT.

4.9 Uruguay

In Uruguay, Title 4 of Decree 101/2024 provides a 25% tax rate on corporate net income.[73] The tax burden of this levy can be influenced by several tax incentives related to the promotion of environmentally friendly behaviours, some of which are included in this regulation while others are not. Some examples include:

- Total exemption of income derived from the holding or transfer of assets paid or made available by investment fund management companies, provided these assets are from values designated by the Executive Power intended to finance activities in areas categorised as priorities. Among these areas is, for example, environmental management.[74]
- Total exemption of income derived from the treatment and final disposal of solid waste. This activity was declared promoted by Decree 411/2011, under the powers granted by the Investment Promotion Law.[75]
- Accelerated depreciation for movable assets intended for the elimination or mitigation of negative environmental impacts or for restoring affected environmental conditions, as well as for fixed improvements related to the treatment of environmental effects from industrial and agricultural activities.[76]
- Partial exemption (up to 90% depending on the fiscal period) of income derived from the generation of electricity through non-traditional renewable sources and the conversion of solar energy into thermal energy. This activity was declared promoted by Decree 354/2009, under the powers granted by the 1998 Investment Promotion Law.[77]
- Partial exemption (up to 90% depending on the fiscal period) of income derived from activities related to the generation of biotechnological products, services, and processes within the national territory, applicable to strategic production sectors, including the environmental sector. This activity was declared promoted by Decree 11/2013, under the powers granted by the Investment Promotion Law.[78]

4.10 Venezuela

Venezuela's CIT is a tax levied on the profits of corporations operating within the country. It applies to both resident and non-resident corporations, with the latter being taxed only on income sourced from Venezuela or attributable to a permanent establishment within the country. The general CIT rate ranges from 15% to 34%, but there are specific rates for certain industries, such as oil and mining, which can be significantly higher.

The tax rate exceeds the 15% minimum established by the GloBE Rules, highlighting the need for a cautious approach when considering tax incentives. However, Venezuela currently offers no tax incentives specifically aimed at environmental protection related to the CIT.

5. CONCLUDING REMARKS AND RECOMMENDATIONS

This chapter provided a preliminary approach to the impact of the GloBE Rules on environmental taxation, with a particular focus on their implications for environmental tax incentives in South American countries. The chapter was structured into three main sections to address the topic. The first examined the context of the GloBE Rules and their relationship with tax incentives; the second addressed environmental taxation measures, with particular emphasis on environmental tax incentives; and the last discussed current CIT regulations in South American countries, with special attention to tax rates and the environmental tax incentives that may influence the overall fiscal burden.

In the first section, we observe that the primary objective of the GloBE Rules is to reduce tax competition between jurisdictions by allowing countries to tax the profits of large MNEs, irrespective of physical presence, with a minimum corporate tax rate of 15%. Even though the GloBE Rules do not explicitly prohibit jurisdictions from implementing tax incentives, they establish parameters for their application by ensuring that the effective tax rate does not fall below the 15% threshold. These rules do not provide any exceptions for tax incentives aimed at specific policy goals, such as environmental protection. Consequently, countries must carefully reconsider the design of their tax incentive programs, even when intended to promote environmental sustainability. This may involve shifting from tax-based incentives to alternative forms of support, such as direct cash grants. Furthermore, the additional revenue generated by higher tax rates under the GloBE Rules could be directed towards environmental goals, potentially offsetting the limitations on tax incentives.

The second section of the chapter emphasised environmental taxation as an effective instrument for environmental protection. Environmental taxation influences taxpayer behaviour. Environmental taxes discourage polluting activities by increasing tax burdens, while environmental tax incentives (which work differently from subsidies) promote ecological activities by eliminating, reducing, or deferring tax payments. Developing countries have more frequently employed tax incentives, as environmental taxes tend to incur higher political costs. Tax incentives weaken fundamental fiscal principles such as generality, equality, and the ability to pay. Incentives should be applied in exceptional circumstances and supported by constitutional principles like environmental protection. Moreover, while tax incentives are linked to specific taxes, leading to reduced tax revenue, subsidies do not affect taxes directly as they involve direct financial transfers from the state. Consequently, environmental subsidies can be an alternative means of promoting environmental sustainability without violating the GloBE Rules. Tax incentives must be carefully evaluated on a case-by-case basis to determine their potential impact under the GloBE Rules.

The third section draws three main conclusions regarding the CIT regulations in South American countries. First, Colombia and Brazil are the only countries in the region that have explicitly incorporated the GloBE Rules. Second, except for Paraguay, which has a standard corporate tax rate of 10%, most South American countries have set their corporate tax rates above 15%, with 25% or higher being the prevailing standard. Third, several South American countries, particularly Argentina, Colombia, Bolivia, Ecuador, and Uruguay, have implemented various environmental tax incentives that could lower the effective corporate tax rate below the 15% threshold, potentially conflicting with the GloBE Rules.

In summary, the GloBE Rules will undoubtedly influence environmental taxation, particularly concerning tax incentives that reduce the effective CIT rate. As a result, South American countries will need to reassess their environmental tax incentive strategies, one of the main alternatives being the replacement of some tax incentives with environmental subsidies. Achieving the dual goals of preventing base erosion and profit shifting while ensuring environmental protection is a global challenge that remains unresolved and requires careful coordination.

NOTES

1. Organisation for Economic Co-operation and Development (OECD), 2021, *Tax Challenges Arising from the Digitalisation of the Economy – Global Anti-Base Erosion Model Rules (Pillar Two): Inclusive Framework on BEPS*, OECD Publishing, Paris. See https://doi.org/10.1787/782bac33-en (accessed 16 October 2024).
2. OECD, *BEPS Project Explanatory Statement: 2015 Final Reports*, 2016, *OECD/G20 Base Erosion and Profit Shifting Project*, OECD Publishing, Paris. See http://dx.doi.org/10.1787/9789264263437-en (accessed 16 October 2024).
3. OECD, *Members of the OECD/G20 Inclusive Framework on BEPS* (updated 28 May 2024). See https://www.oecd.org/content/dam/oecd/en/topics/policy-issues/beps/inclusive-framework-on-beps-composition.pdf (accessed 16 October 2024).
4. Article 10.1 of GloBE Rules.
5. International Monetary Fund (IMF), 6 February 2023, *International Corporate Tax Reform* (Fiscal Affairs Dept, Policy Papers, vol 2023, issue

001. See https://doi.org/10.5089/9798400232558.007 (accessed 16 October 2024).

6. OECD, *Tax Incentives and the Global Minimum Corporate Tax: Reconsidering Tax Incentives after the GloBE Rules*, OECD Publishing, Paris, 2022. See https://doi.org/10.1787/25d30b96-en (accessed 16 October 2024) and Belisa Ferreira Liotti et al. 2022, "The Treatment of Tax Incentives under Pillar Two", *Transnational Corporations Journal* 2(2).
7. Lyne Latulippe. 2023, "Globalisation, International Tax Policy and the OECD", in Christoph Scherrer, Ana Garcia, and Joscha Wullweber (eds), *Handbook on Critical Political Economy and Public Policy*, Edward Elgar Publishing, Cheltenham, 369 and Nupur Jalan. 2021, "BEPS 2.0: Pillar 2, Tax Incentives and Its Interplay – Can Subsidies Replace Tax Incentives?" *Journal of International Taxation* 32(10), 6.
8. Janet Milne. 2018, "A Bird's-eye View of Environmental Taxation", in Roberta Mann and Tracey Roberts (eds), *Tax Law and the Environment: A Multidisciplinary and Worldwide Perspective*, Lexington Books, New York, 1–16.
9. Melissa Castello. 2008. "Contribuido de Intervengo no Dominio Econômico sobre os Combustíveis: Um Superfund Brasileiro?" *Revista de Direito Ambiental* 44, 100.
10. Helmuth Cremer, Pierre Pestieau, & Jean-Charles Rochet. 2001, "Direct Versus Indirect Taxation: The Design of the Tax Structure Revisited" *International Economic Review* 42(3), 781–782.
11. Thomas Erhag, Katarina Nordblom, & Pernila Rendahl. 2023, "Attaining Decent Work and Economic Growth — What Role Does Taxation Play?" *Nordic Tax Journal* 1, 96–110.
12. Cathy Koch & Barbara Angus. 2023, "How a Global Minimum Tax Will Affect Sustainability Tax Incentives", Ernst & Young Global. See https://www.ey.com/en_gl/insights/tax/how-global-minimum-tax-affects-sustainability-tax-incentives (accessed 16 October 2024).
13. Tarcísio Diniz Magalhães & Ivan Ozai. 2021, "A Different Unified Approach to Global Tax Policy: Addressing the Challenges of Underdevelopment" *Nordic Journal on Law and Society* 4(1), 20.
14. Aitor Navarro Ibarrola. 2021, "Consideraciones de Política Fiscal sobre la Propuesta GloBE de Tributación Mínima (Pilar 2) y su Implementación" *Crónica Tributaria* 179, 63.
15. OECD, *Tax Challenges Arising from the Digitalisation of the Economy – Consolidated Commentary to the Global Anti-Base Erosion Model Rules (2023): Inclusive Framework on BEPS (OECD/G20 Base Erosion and Profit Shifting Project)*, OECD Publishing, Paris, 2024. See https://doi.org/10.1787/b849f926-en (accessed 16 October 2024).
16. Liotti *et al.* (note 6), 26.
17. Article 1.1 of GloBE Rules.

18. Joachim Englisch. 18 April 2021, *International Effective Minimum Taxation – Analysis of GloBE (Pillar Two)*. See http://dx.doi.org/10.2139/ssrn.3829104 (accessed 16 October 2024).
19. OECD. 2024, *Tax Challenges Arising from the Digitalisation of the Economy – Administrative Guidance on the Global Anti-Base Erosion Model Rules (Pillar Two)*, OECD Publishing, Paris. See http://www.oecd.org/tax/beps/administrative-guidance-global-anti-base-erosion-rules-pillar-two-june-2024.pdf (accessed 16 October 2024).
20. Article 2.1 of GloBE Rules.
21. Article 2.4 of GloBE Rules.
22. Article 10.1 Defined Terms of GloBE Rules.
23. Tax Foundation. 2023, "Corporate Tax Rates Around the World, 2023", Tax Foundation. See https://taxfoundation.org/data/all/global/corporate-tax-rates-by-country-2023/ (accessed 16 December 2024).
24. See Vikram Chand, V., Alessandro Turina, & Kinga Romanovska. 2022, "Tax Treaty Obstacles in Implementing the Pillar Two Global Minimum Tax Rules and a Possible Solution for Eliminating the Various Challenges" *World Tax Journal: WTJ* 14(1), 3–50.
25. Centro Interamericano de Administraciones Tributarias (CIAT), *Design and Assessment of Tax Incentives in Developing Countries, CIAT*, Panamá, 2018. See https://www.ciat.org/Biblioteca/Estudios/2018_design_assessment_tax_incentives_UN_CIAT.pdf (accessed 16 October 2024).
26. OECD, *Tax Incentives and the Global Minimum Corporate Tax* (note 6), 11.
27. Liotti et al. (note 6), 30.
28. European Parliament, *Tax Incentives after the Minimum Corporate Tax ("Pillar Two") – At a Glance*. See https://www.europarl.europa.eu/RegData/etudes/ATAG/2023/749793/EPRS_ATA(2023)749793_EN.pdf (accessed 16 October 2024).
29. OECD, *Tax Incentives and the Global Minimum Corporate Tax* (note 6), 36.
30. European Parliament (note 28).
31. OECD, *Tax Incentives and the Global Minimum Corporate Tax* (note 6), 29.
32. Ibid., 38.
33. Ibid., 6.
34. There is a consensus that Environmental Taxation originated in the 1990s with the environmental taxes implemented by Nordic countries, which primarily targeted air pollution (Jean-Phillippe Barde. 1994, *Economic Instruments in Environmental Policy: Lessons from the OECD Experience and their Relevance to Developing Economies*, OECD Publishing, Paris).
35. Castello (note 9), 79–101.
36. Charles Patterson. 2000, "Environmental Taxes and Subsidies: What is the Appropriate Fiscal Policy for Dealing with Modern Environmental Problems?" *William & Mary Environmental Law and Policy Review*, 24, 136. Although in practice they will always generate some revenue, which makes these measures economically less costly for states compared to fiscal incentives, where revenue is foregone (Christian Valenduc, "Carbon Pricing Versus

Environmental Tax Incentives: Is It 'Or' or 'And'?", *Reflets et perspectives de la vie économique* VIII, 43). See https://doi.org/10.3917/rpve.594.0039 (accessed 16 October 2024).

37. Ana Carrera Poncela & Alejandro Movellán Vázquez. 2000, "Aspectos económico-jurídicos y análisis descriptivo de la tributación ambiental en Latinoamérica" *Observatorio de la Economía Latinoamericana* 88, 7. See http://www.eumed.net/cursecon/ecolat/la/07/cpmv.htm (accessed 16 October 2024).
38. Carolina Rozo Gutiérrez. 2003, "Las funciones extrafiscales del tributo a propósito de la tributación medioambiental en el ordenamiento jurídico colombiano" *Revista de Derecho* 1, 170.
39. Janet Milne. 2011, "Environmental Taxation in the United States: The Long View" *Lewis & Clark Law Review* 15(2), 439.
40. Some authors distinguish between an environmental incentive and an environmental tax benefit (María Teresa Soler Roch, *Incentivos a la inversión y justicia tributaria*, Civitas, Madrid, 1983, 50–52).
41. Antonio Vaquera García. 1999, *Fiscalidad y medio ambiente*, Lex Nova, Valladolid, 57–58.
42. Rodolfo Salassa Boix. 2020, "De la sopa verde al mar de cristal: una propuesta tributaria para revertir la eutrofización del Mar Menor en tiempos de Covid-19" *Revista Catalana de Dret Ambiental* II (2), 11.
43. Violeta Ruiz Almendral. 2005, "La compleja compatibilización del establecimiento de beneficios fiscales por motivos medioambientales con el principio de igualdad tributaria: (a propósito de la Sentencia del Tribunal Constitucional alemán de 20 de abril de 2004, sobre los impuestos ecológicos 'Ökosteuer')" *Crónica* Tributaria, 114, 175–190 and Angela Köppl & Margit Schratzenstaller. 2021, *Aspects of Environmentally Beneficial Tax Incentives*, WIFO Working Papers 621/2021, Vienna, 2.
44. Comisión Económica para América Latina y el Caribe (CEPAL)/Oxfam Internacional, "Los incentivos fiscales a las empresas en América Latina y el Caribe" (2019), *Documentos de Proyectos LC/TS.2019/50*, Santiago, 10.
45. Tomás García Luis. 1990, *Impuesto sobre Sociedades: Desgravaciones por Inversión y Creación de Empleo*, Lex Nova, Valladolid, 35.
46. This will entail a financial adjustment in the state budget due to the revenue foregone, with various available alternatives (Yvette Lind. 2023, "The Fundamentals of Tax Incentives" *Skatterett* 42(1), 17).
47. Songa Li and Wen Yating. 2023, "Financial Subsidies, Tax Incentives and Technological Innovation in China" *Journal of Innovation & Knowledge* 8(3), 100406.
48. Lind (note 46) 17.
49. Tax Foundation. 2023, "Corporate Tax Rates Around the World, 2023", Tax Foundation. See https://taxfoundation.org/data/all/global/corporate-tax-rates-by-country-2023/ (accessed 16 December 2024).
50. Law 2277, enacted by the Colombian Executive Branch on 13 December 2022 and effective on 1 January 2023, introduced a tax reform that includes a 15%

Minimum Effective Tax Rate for Colombian-resident corporations, with certain industry-specific exceptions.

51. Provisional Measure No. 1.262/24 and Normative Instruction No. 2.228/24, published on 3 October 2024.
52. Article 10 of Law 2277 of 2022.
53. Article 73 of ITL (recently modified by Law 27630 of 2021).
54. Article 26, letter w), of LIG.
55. Article 9.5 of Law 26.190 of 2007.
56. Article 6 of Law 27.191 of 2015.
57. Law No. 843/1986, of 20 May 1986. Tax Reform Law. Title III Corporate Income Tax. Honorable National Congress (Bolivia).
58. Article 49 of Law No. 843.
59. We could also include the Social Contribution on Corporate Profits (SCCP), intended for the financing of social security (Art. 1), regulated by Law 7689 of 1988. Its calculation is based on the value of the result of the fiscal year before the provision for income tax (Art. 2), applying a rate of 9% (Art. 3).
60. Articles 158 to 676.
61. Article 225 of the Annex.
62. Article 1.3 of Law 5106/1966.
63. Article 1 of Law Decree Nº 824, referring to the First Category Tax (FCT).
64. See Circular SII N° 52 (10.10.2014): https://www.sii.cl/ayudas/aprenda_sobre/3072-1-3080.html (accessed 16 October 2024).
65. María Pilar Navarro Schiappacasse. 2020, "Protección del medio ambiente y Derecho tributario: una revisión de la Ley 21.210 en esta materia" *Revista de Derecho Ambiental* 14, 127–153.
66. Article 240 of Tax Statute (modified by Article 10 of Law 2277 of 2022).
67. Article 235-2, point 3, of the Tax Statute.
68. Article 11 of Law 1517 of 2014.
69. Article 2 of the Organic Law of the Internal Tax Regime is in accordance with Article 1 of the Regulations for the application of the Internal Tax Regime Law.
70. Paragraph 2.2 of the second reforming provision of the Organic Code of Production.
71. Article 21 of Law 6380 of 2019.
72. Article 25.2, letter c), of Law 6380 of 2019.
73. Article 23 of Title 4 of ordered text approved by Decree 101/024.
74. Article 66, letter X), of Title 4 of ordered text approved by Decree 101/024.
75. Article 6 of Decree 411/2011.
76. Article 86, letters A) and B), of Title 4 of ordered text approved by Decree 101/024 and article 9, letter B), of Law 16906/1998.
77. Article 3 of Decree 354/2009.
78. Article 4 of Decree 11/013.

11. Personal carbon allowances: an idea whose time has come?

Steve Dwyer

1. INTRODUCTION

In the 2015 Paris Agreement, almost all nations committed to "limiting global temperature increase to well below 2 degrees Celsius, while pursuing efforts to limit the increase to 1.5 degrees".[1] The world is failing to meet this commitment. "August 2024 ... was the 13th month since July 2023 in which the global-average surface air temperature exceeded 1.5°C above pre-industrial levels"[2] and "actions outlined in existing NDCs [Nationally Determined Contributions] are on track for a catastrophic 2.5–2.9 degrees C (4.5–5.2 degrees F) of warming by 2100",[3] even worse, "current policies would deliver up to 3.1°C of warming".[4]

There is abundant commentary on the failure of both governments and companies[5] to reduce greenhouse gas (GHG) emissions (Emissions) either sufficiently or at all. However, there has been less discussion about the role of individuals in reducing Emissions, or the policy instruments that could empower individuals to reduce their Emissions and advocate for societies to do the same. Governments, companies, and individuals need to work together to prevent a climate change "catastrophe":

> the Government, business and individuals cannot crack the problem acting on their own. The Government have to take a lead, not least by getting their own house in order. Business must make a contribution … [and] individuals can play an important part, too.[6]

This extract is from a 2006 speech by David Miliband, who was the United Kingdom (UK) Minister in charge of the Department for Energy, Food and Rural Affairs (Defra). He then went on to suggest a way to achieve this: "personal carbon allowances … could help individuals to see how they can make a contribution that will help the environment and themselves".[7]

Personal carbon allowances (PCAs) were first mooted in the 1990s as a system that could involve individuals in helping to reduce Emissions. Most early PCA models envisaged a trading element called personal carbon trading (PCT), enabling individuals to trade allowances amongst themselves. Then, between 2006 and 2008, Defra oversaw a consultation on the feasibility of introducing a PCT scheme for the UK, resulting in a final synthesis report.[8] While the report praised various aspects of PCT models, such as their progressive nature, the overall conclusion was that "the concept is … currently ahead of its time".[9]

Many organisations and academics disagreed with Defra's conclusion and emphasised the potential benefits of introducing PCAs, but over time the concept gradually disappeared from public discourse and policy consciousness. Academic interest in PCAs was galvanised by an influential article, 'Personal carbon allowances revisited',[10] published in 2021. Subsequently, scholarly literature has been advancing a range of PCA models and emphasising the benefits that might flow from such models.

This chapter summarises the history of PCA ideas over the last thirty years. It then goes on to consider a holistic but simplified approach that avoids the complexity of individuals trading Emission allowances by removing the requirement for a PCT system. The proposal involves combining Emissions taxes (carbon pricing) that are comprehensive and uniform (i.e., based on one rate multiplied by the estimated amount of carbon dioxide equivalent (CO_2e) Emissions) with monetary payments, recycling all or part of the additional carbon pricing receipts through the benefit or tax system. A potential example is a carbon universal basic income (CUBI).

No country has yet introduced such an overarching PCA system. However, "carbon fee and dividend" schemes have been implemented on a smaller scale.[11] The UK has been chosen as this chapter's theoretical guinea pig to explore how a more extensive scheme might fit into the country's existing environmental tax and Emissions landscape. Perhaps one day, the UK can become a real-life PCA policy experiment. Has PCAs' time finally arrived?

2. PCAs: WHAT THEY ARE, AND WHY INTRODUCE THEM

First, it is important to understand what PCAs are. PCAs were envisaged as the way to "link personal action with global carbon reduction goals"[12] and thus support the third leg of the government, business, and individual triage aiming to fix the climate crisis. In high-income countries, individuals' direct Emissions (e.g. heating, lighting, and travel) combined with the Emissions embedded in the goods and services (e.g., food and internet provision) supplied to individuals, can represent more than three-quarters of a country's total consumption Emissions (77% was one recent estimate for the UK).[13] PCA schemes aim to encourage individuals to reduce their Emissions, with most of them containing the common feature of allocating Emission allowances to individuals or family units, combined with economic incentives to minimise Emissions. Monetary incentives to encourage individuals to reduce Emission consumption can be delivered by carbon pricing or using a PCT system that facilitates Emissions allowance trading, where individuals whose Emission usage is lower than their allowance can sell their surplus allowances to those who want to exceed their allocated allowance, effectively an emission trading system (ETS) for individuals. At least one commentator[14] has proposed that the "individual ETS" should be linked to business ETSs.

Second, it is important to understand why PCAs are relevant. Carbon pricing, in its many forms, aims to provide economic incentives to change behaviour in order to reduce Emissions, but further reduction advantages are put forward for PCAs. These include:

> Raised visibility of personal carbon footprints. Raised awareness of personal carbon limits to sustain the transition to a net-zero-carbon society ... New definition of a fair share of personal emissions. Setting of acceptable levels of personal emissions.[15]

One further argument advanced for PCAs is related to equity. A broad application of carbon pricing may disadvantage lower-income individuals disproportionately, as they are the least able to pay the higher ensuing prices for such necessities as heat, light, travel, and even food (if embedded Emissions are taxed). PCAs could form part of a "just transition" as per-capita- or per-household-based PCAs would, in many cases, provide higher relative benefits to lower-income individuals, as they generally have a lower-than-average consumption of Emissions (this is not an invariable rule as each individual's consumption Emissions will vary depending on their particular consumption patterns).

3. PCAs: A BRIEF HISTORY OF THEIR DEVELOPMENT

The main development stages for PCAs and PCT (nomenclature that is sometimes confusingly used interchangeably) can be divided into four distinct phases. These phases pivot around PCAs' "highwater mark" of UK political attention (i.e., the 2006–8 Defra initiative) and then the resurgence of interest in PCAs from 2021. The four phases can be (reasonably) grouped as follows: pre-2006, 2006–8, 2009–20, and post-2020.

3.1 Developments in PCAs before 2006

PCAs were first proposed in the 1990s to persuade individuals to participate actively in reducing Emissions. Most early PCA models included a trading component, which allowed individuals to trade carbon allowances, thereby encouraging people to be interested in their individual Emissions consumption as an economic concern.

One early PCA concept was the "Tradeable Consumption Quotas",[16] which proposed the creation of a carbon market involving both manufacturers and individuals. Another version proposed a cap-and-trade model focusing on household energy use and travel consumption,[17] while "Tradeable Transport Carbon Permits"[18] was a French-originated idea that applied a cap-and-trade system specifically to private transportation.

3.2 Developments in PCAs 2006–8

During this period, discussion concerning PCAs entered the political arena as the UK Labour Government of that time considered the possibility and practicality of introducing a PCT system. David Miliband's 2006 speech was the starting point for that process.

3.2.1 The 'Great Stink' speech

In David Miliband's 2006 speech entitled "The Great Stink" (referencing the 1858 closure of Parliament due to the foul smell from the Thames and the emergency response that resulted in the construction of London's sewerage system), he proposed PCT as a bold, albeit untested, solution to the climate crisis; "we need to test our solutions against the scale of the problem, and specifically test them against the most radical options … such as tradeable personal carbon allowances".[19]

3.2.2 The Defra review period

During the Defra review period additional PCA models were proposed, including "Cap and Share",[20] "Tradeable Energy Quotas",[21] and "Household Carbon Trading".[22] Defra itself commissioned reports on different aspects of PCT, including "Social Acceptability",[23] "Economic and Technical Feasibility",[24] and "Equity and Distributional Impacts",[25] as well as producing its own report on "Effectiveness in the Policy Landscape".[26] Defra then produced a final report summarising the main findings from the consultation period.

3.2.3 Synthesis report on the findings from Defra's pre-feasibility study into PCT

This report[27] highlighted several important conclusions:

- Cost-Benefit Analysis: The results were negative, with upfront costs estimated between £700 million and £2 billion and annual costs from £1 to £2 billion.
- Equity and Distributional Impacts: While the policy was progressive from a tax perspective, some low-income individuals would still lose out. Urban areas were likely to benefit more than rural ones.
- Public Acceptability: Public support was minimal due to concerns about fairness, low government trust, and a lack of interest in trading. One respondent stated, "Have you really time to start bartering on the markets with credits, if you've got three children and a household to run and to work?"[28]
- Final Verdict: The high costs, combined with limited CO_2 reduction benefits, indicated that the policy costs outweighed the benefits by a factor of 15. Despite some positive comments, the report concluded that PCT "is an idea currently ahead of its time in terms of its public acceptability and the technology to bring down the costs".[29]

3.3 Developments in PCAs 2009–20

Many commentators and activists felt that Defra had written the idea off too easily; the UK's own Environmental Audit Committee (EAC) stated in 2008 that they thought it was a "missed opportunity",[30] the Sustainable Development Commission (SDC) in 2009 nominated it as the "breakthrough idea for the 21st century",[31] and the journal *Climate Policy* in 2010 devoted a whole issue to the idea, declaring that it "embodies specific and explicit ideas about equity … it is a policy idea which raises many of the right questions for climate change mitigation".[32] Meanwhile, at the grassroots level in the UK, the confluence of PCA ideas and the impact of the financial crisis helped spark the establishment of "Carbon Reduction Action Groups[33] and "Transition Towns",[34] with the former aimed at implementing community-level PCA systems on a voluntary basis and the latter focused on keeping consumption as local as possible by creating towns' own local currencies that citizens could spend only on local produce or in local shops.

Interest in PCAs in the UK declined after that, but there was still some residual academic interest in the UK regarding both the behavioural aspects[35] and distributional issues.[36] International interest expressed itself on the topics of labelling[37] and whether PCA schemes could be applied to low-income nations in specific markets.[38]

3.4 Developments in PCAs after 2020

In 2021, a significant paper by Nerini et al. reiterated the potential benefits of PCAs.[39] The paper highlighted how improvements in technology, particularly in Artificial Intelligence, along with the global drive for a low-carbon economic recovery following the COVID-19 crisis, presented a new opportunity for PCAs to re-enter policy discussions.

All that was needed was a "guinea pig"; "PCAs could be trialled in selected climate-conscious technologically advanced countries, mindful of potential issues around integration into the current policy mix ... and distributional impacts".[40] The remaining sections consider how introducing one specific type of PCA model (PCAM) for the UK might fit with the UK's current Emissions, environmental taxes, and income distributions.

4. PCAM: A PCA MODEL THAT COMBINES UNIFORM AND COMPREHENSIVE CARBON PRICING WITH A CUBI

Many countries, along with many multinational enterprises (MNEs), are required to voluntarily gather and disclose CO_2e Emission measurements related to their activities. Countries frequently use the categories of residency, territoriality, and consumption, while MNEs often provide CO_2e information that complies with the GHG Protocol[41] that categorises Emissions into Scope 1, 2, and 3. While direct Emissions (Scope 1) and Emissions like electricity (Scope 2) can be calculated based respectively on physical volumes of fossil fuels and kilowatt-hours,[42] indirect Emissions (Scope 3) are often estimated by reference to monetary amounts using transformational datasets (e.g., Classification of Individual Consumption According to Purpose (COICOP)[43]) to transform those amounts into CO_2e Emissions measurements.

4.1 Constituent Elements of the PCAM

Existing methodologies can estimate the CO_2e amounts for almost all Emissions consumed, and therefore, carbon pricing is theoretically applicable to almost all those Emissions. Although a few countries (such as South Africa and Republic of Korea) have carbon pricing that covers over 80% of their Emissions, the pricing is often modest;[44] most countries have much lower percentage coverage.

While some academics have argued for the introduction of innovative types of carbon pricing based on "E-Liabilities"[45] or a VAT-style Carbon Added Tax, the current carbon pricing instruments are mainly in the form of either carbon taxes or ETSs. For several countries (such as the UK and EU members), their ETSs will shortly be augmented by a Carbon Border Adjustment Mechanism (CBAM). As ETSs are extended to cover more entities, products, services, and embedded Emissions (such as those from transportation), the closer they come to establishing comprehensive carbon pricing systems.

An ETS model can target the level of Emissions (often referred to as "cap and trade") as it allows the country or region to set the total level of allowances available and thus "cap" permitted Emissions for a particular period. Those allowances can then be reduced over time. Auction prices for the allowances determine the level of government receipts while permitting businesses to "trade" those allowances, facilitating efficient Emission reduction solutions. A system that employs carbon taxes to reduce Emissions requires an estimation of the rate of carbon tax per t/CO_2e needed to generate the targeted Emissions reduction.

In the proposed PCAM, the PCA element is introduced by recycling the whole or part of the receipts from the expansion of carbon pricing to designated individuals (e.g., adults or adults and adults on behalf of their children) or clusters of individuals (e.g., families or households). For simplicity, the term "individual" will be used hereafter to encompass all such recipients. The equal allocation of the receipts compensates (albeit disproportionately in almost all cases) each recipient for the rise in prices due to carbon pricing. The government is then effectively acting as the price-setter for a carbon allowance "market" for each recipient, without them having to trade between themselves.

The intention of a PCA system is to encourage individuals to have a greater awareness of their carbon footprint and its relationship to the national (if not global) average. Receipt of an annual CUBI set by reference to the targeted CO_2e Emissions level (for each CUBI unit) would reinforce the idea of the "fair" consumption of Emissions. This can be augmented by additional measures to raise awareness of the impact on Emissions of consumption choices. These measures might include:

- Carbon content awareness at point-of-sale: While individuals can estimate their carbon footprints, awareness at the point of sale is also critical. Few retailers provide carbon content information, and simply displaying CO_2 or CO_2e Emission content may not be that powerful.
- A traffic-light system for Emissions: A more effective approach might combine Emissions data with a traffic-light system, flagging high-Emission products. A reported success is Norway's Oda[46] supermarkets, where a traffic light system (low, middle, high, and very high) has influenced shopping habits, reducing meat sales and increasing purchases of low-emission products like lentil soup.

- Automated carbon footprint calculators: While individuals or households have numerous carbon footprint counters to choose from, they often require manual inputs. Advances in gathering corporate Emission data are now "spilling over" into the personal sphere, with new techniques such as smartphone apps that can estimate the Emissions for individual travel and shop purchases, or – a very recent development in the UK – an automatic analysis of bank account expenditure transactions, which can then calculate the account holder's approximate carbon footprint.[47]

4.2 Is the PCAM Still a PCA System?

While the PCAM may initially appear to be radically different in concept from the early PCA and PCT models, especially as the individual is not required to actively participate in trading carbon allowances, the PCAM can be seen as a hybrid model that joins elements of PCAs with "carbon fee and dividend" type redistribution.

The interaction of the CUBI as a monetary payment to an individual based on a targeted Emissions allowance (multiplied by the government-set carbon price for each tonne of CO_2e Emissions) and the carbon pricing element of the price of goods and services paid by suppliers (as in an ETS) or end consumers (as in a CAT model) effectively replicates individual carbon trading. The government acts as the intermediary for each individual. It will pay for an individual's "unutilised" PCA when the CUBI received by an individual for a period exceeds that particular individual's carbon pricing payments for that same period (the carbon pricing is embedded in the payments for the goods and services that are subject to the carbon pricing charges). When the individual's carbon pricing payments exceed the CUBI for a period, the government is a net recipient.

So, the PCAM can be seen as both a PCA system setting an individual's target (and economically neutral) carbon consumption and a PCT "market" with "settlement" between the individual and the Government. There is, however, potentially a missing ingredient in relation to the informational element that allows the individual to be aware of their consumption Emissions. This "missing link" is where the CO_2e product labelling and carbon counting techniques are needed to fill this informational gap. If individuals are to be encouraged to make the behavioural choices to pick the lower-Emission alternatives at the point of sale or consider energy efficiency and lower-Emission lifestyle changes, then the CO_2e content or savings information needs to be easily accessible for each purchase, and reasonably accurate periodic carbon footprint estimates should be readily available for every adult with a minimum of cost and effort.

5. THE UK EMISSIONS AND ENVIRONMENTAL TAXATION LANDSCAPE

The UK contributes approximately 1% of global Emissions. Despite the UK's current low Emissions level, it carries a significant historical Emissions "debt" (in an ethical rather than legal sense). As the first industrial nation, the UK was the largest emitter during the 18th century and for much of the 19th century. Therefore, the UK's contribution to cumulative Emissions is significantly larger in percentage terms (i.e. around 4.4%)[48] than its current annual Emissions. So, while reducing UK Emissions won't significantly affect global levels, it could "pave the way" for other countries around the world to follow in its footsteps as part of repaying part of that moral "debt".

5.1 UK Emissions

UK Emission figures vary depending on the measurement techniques and definitions applied. Based on figures published by the Office for National Statistics (ONS) for 2021, territorial Emissions ("[E]missions that occur within the UK's borders")[49] were 421 MtCO_2e, just over half the 1990 level, and consumption Emissions (i.e., "consumption of all goods and services by the UK, sometimes referred to as *carbon footprint*")[50] had fallen much less, at 705 MtCO_2e ("a 36% reduction since 1990").[51] However, one consulting firm estimated that the consumption-based figure could be as high as 871 MtCO_2e for 2022.[52]

As of 2020, according to the UK 2021 Census,[53] the UK's population was 67.1 million (with around 52 million being over 18), clustered into 27.8 million households. So, per capita, the average UK carbon footprint is estimated to be between 10 and 13 tCO_2e, approximately twice the estimated global per capita amount of 6.8 tCO_2e.[54] Total consumption Emissions for all UK households are therefore estimated to be between 500 and 700 MtCO_2e. Carbon pricing for all UK consumption Emissions at £100 per t/CO_2e could thus result in receipts of up to £70–90 billion (the "non-household" element of around £20 billion would fall predominantly on national and local government).

5.2 UK Environmental Taxes

The UK's Emission figures set the background for an examination of the UK's current carbon pricing and "indirect" environmental taxes (i.e., taxes on goods and services that produce Emissions, but are not calculated by reference to the CO_2e Emissions that attach to them). The UK ETS and the Climate Change Levy (CCL) are categorised as carbon pricing because:

> the relationship between the tax base and emissions is reasonably direct: for example, the tax base for the UK ETS is auctioned allowances measured in tonnes of CO_2e, while the tax base for the CCL is the volume of gas, electricity and other fuels measured in kilowatt-hours.[55]

Indirect UK environmental taxes include Fuel Duties, Motor Vehicle Duties, Air Passenger Duties, and Renewable Energy Obligations. In 2023, the UK Government reported[56] UK ETS and CCL generated governmental receipts of £8.7bn, while for all "environmental taxes", the total receipts for that period were £52.5bn (of which nearly 50% arose from Fuel Duties (e.g., petrol and diesel)). The remaining receipts came from various other indirect environmental taxes beyond Fuel Duties.

For additional carbon pricing and CUBI payments to be both impactful and public exchequer "neutral", carbon pricing would need to rise significantly more than the existing £52.5bn. A £100 t/CO_2e additional carbon pricing on nearly all household consumption could generate revenues in the region of £50bn p.a. An alternative methodology would be to harmonise the existing direct and indirect environmental taxes based on their CO_2e Emissions at a uniform carbon price, but at such a level as to target the required additional receipts. An offsetting CUBI for each of the UK's approximate 50 million adults could, therefore, be initially set around the £1,000 p.a. mark (a four-digit sum may be sufficient to influence behaviour for lower-income, if not the higher-income groups). In this very convenient example, the break-even Emissions consumption level per adult would then be approximately 10 tCO_2e.

6. PCAs: GENERALLY PROGRESSIVE, WITH CAVEATS

A superficial analysis might consider environmental taxes (especially carbon pricing) to be "fair" since, generally, the consumption of goods and services increases with income such that those individuals or households with higher income levels consume more than those with lower incomes (and so would, on average, suffer higher environmental taxation). However, whether carbon pricing would be progressive (i.e., it "takes a larger percentage of income from high-income groups than low-income groups")[57] depends on the relationship between Emissions consumed and income levels. The Institute for Fiscal Studies (IFS) researched[58] this relationship for UK households grouped into "net equivalised[59] deciles. Selective findings from that research are shown in Figures 11.1 and 11.2.

Figure 11.1 shows that the estimated average UK household annual consumption-based Emissions (carbon footprint) in 2018 was nearly 20 t/CO_2e. The richest decile's carbon footprint was over 50% higher than the average,

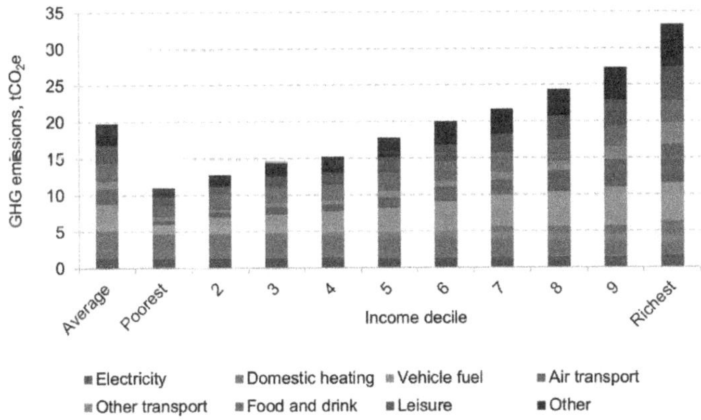

Note: Household incomes are equivalised using the modified OECD scale.
Source: IFS calculations using the Living Costs and Food Survey 2018 and Defra. IFS (2021), 'Tax Policies to Help Achieve Net-zero Carbon Emissions', *Institute for Fiscal Studies* at 357 (https://ifs.org.uk/sites/default/files/output_url_files/8-Tax-policies-to-help-achieve-net-zero-carbon-emissions-.pdf).

Figure 11.1 *Annual GHG consumption emissions by net household income group, 2018*

and the poorest decile's almost 50% lower (i.e., the carbon footprint of the former was approximately three times greater than the latter). However, since progressivity is related to income levels, then, based on the calculations contained in Figure 11.2, "lower-income households are associated with 22% more emissions per pound of spending, largely because a greater share of poorer households' spending goes on electricity, heating and food".[60]

Based on these findings (and assuming no change in consumption patterns), uniform and comprehensive carbon pricing would have a regressive impact on households. Recycling the additional carbon pricing receipts from households as equal monetary payments to each household, along with the carbon pricing, should produce a net progressive outcome. Ceteris paribus, the five lowest income deciles would receive a net benefit, and the four highest income deciles would be net losers, while the 6th decile is approximately break-even. Of course, these calculations are based on decile averages, so a proportion of low-income households in very specific circumstances will consume above-average Emissions (for instance, low-income households in rural locations that may have less energy-efficient homes or higher vehicle mileage). Mitigating this "unfairness" would require additional policy measures such as government

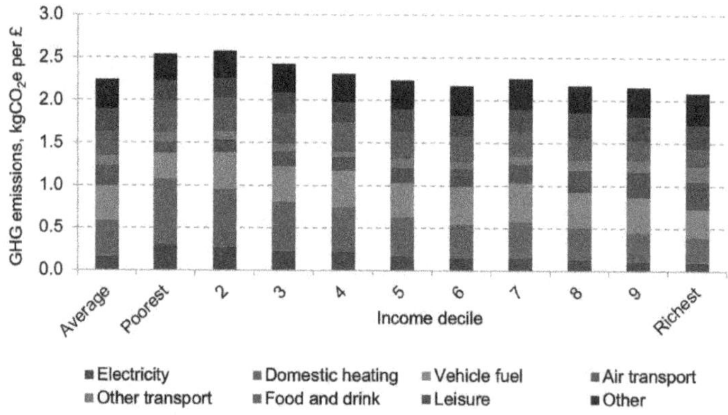

Source: IFS calculations. IFS (2021), 'Tax Policies to Help Achieve Net-zero Carbon Emissions', *Institute for Fiscal Studies* at 381 (https://ifs.org.uk/sites/default/files/output_url_files/8-Tax-policies-to-help-achieve-net-zero-carbon-emissions-.pdf).

Figure 11.2 Average GHG emissions per £ of spending by net equivalised income decile, 2018

subsidising the installation of insulation or heat pumps or providing discounts or interest-free loans to assist with the purchase of electric vehicles.

The degree of progressivity would depend on the exact nature of the CUBI system, whether given to each adult, taxpayer, household, or person (i.e., would children qualify for a full or partial CUBI payment or with a cap, at say two children maximum?). Further decisions would be required as to whether the CUBI should be made available to wealthier or higher-income groups (such as higher-rate income taxpayers). The importance of these different design choices would depend on the amount of additional carbon pricing and the size of the offsetting CUBI benefit (governments may not want to have full hypothecation, i.e., some of the extra tax receipts could be retained rather than recycled, either to meet the element of additional carbon pricing that would fall on national and local governments or to invest in 'green' initiatives).

Over time, the economic incentives and hoped-for behavioural changes are designed to assist in reducing Emissions to net zero (currently a 2050 target for territorial Emissions for the UK[61] but even if that is achieved, the UK's consumption Emissions are likely to stay above zero for many years after that). The receipts from carbon pricing would eventually be expected to diminish, even if there is an escalating carbon price. If 90% of Emissions are removed, then increasing the carbon price tenfold might be considered unachievable. Without sufficient carbon pricing receipts to recycle and assuming a government may not want to decrease the nominal CUBI payment (although its value in real terms would likely reduce due to inflation), then, eventually, the C for Carbon might become redundant, and so it might be converted into universal basic income. Another solution, or partial solution, to diminishing carbon pricing receipts would be to retain a percentage of the initial receipts (rather than fully recycle) to invest in a "sovereign wealth fund", the returns on which could help fund future CUBI payments. There is precedent for such a scheme in the Alaskan Permanent Fund Dividend (PFD)[62] where an element of that state's revenue from historic oil and gas exploration has been invested, with the returns used to provide annual dividends to its citizens.

7. CONCLUSION

Introducing a radical policy such as a PCA will require considerable political courage and deep commitment to addressing the climate change emergency. As with any taxation change, the "losers" are likely to be more vocal than the "winners". In the case of the UK, there is an element of synchronicity at play in that there has been a recent change of government, and, at the time of writing, the new Secretary of State for Energy Security and Net Zero is Ed Miliband, the younger brother of David. His opening address to his department provides some reasons to be optimistic regarding PCAs re-entering the policy arena:

> The reason I'm so excited to have been appointed to this role is because it speaks directly to the twin passions that continue to motivate me. First, resolving the economic inequality that scars the country, and second, tackling the climate crisis that imperils our world.[63]

PCAs have the potential to help deliver solutions to fulfil both passions. It would be a remarkable turn of events if the bold but rejected initiative of "Miliband the Elder" becomes UK policy under his sibling, "Miliband the Younger". An idea whose time is now!

NOTES

1. Paris Agreement to the United Nations Framework Convention on Climate Change (Dec. 12, 2015), T.I.A.S. No. 16-1104.
2. Copernicus Climate Change Service (2024), 'World's Warmest August Completes Hottest Boreal Summer on Record', available at: https://climate.copernicus.eu/worlds-warmest-august-completes-hottest-boreal-summer-record#:~:text=According%20to%20Samantha%20Burgess%2C%20Deputy,hottest%20boreal%20summer%20on%20record.

3. World Resources Institute (WRI) (2024), 'What Are Nationally Determined Contributions (NDCs) and Why Are They Important?', available at: https://www.wri.org/insights/nationally-determined-contributions-ndcs-explained.
4. United Nations Environment Programme (2024), 'Emissions Gap Report No More Hot Air ... Please!', available at: https://www.unep.org/resources/emissions-gap-report-2024#:~:text=The%20future%20of%20our%20planet,2.6%C2%B0C%20and%20beyond.
5. B. Kenza and A. Mooney (21 June 2024), 'How Companies Are Starting to Back Away from Green Targets', *Financial Times.*
6. D. Miliband (2006), 'House of Commons Debate 19 July 2006', vol 451, col 88. Hansard.
7. Ibid.
8. Defra (2008), 'Synthesis Report on the Findings from Defra's Pre-feasibility Study into Personal Carbon Trading', London.
9. Ibid, 21.
10. F. Nerini, T. Fawcett, Y. Parag et al. (2021), 'Personal Carbon Allowances Revisited', *Nat Sustain* 4, 1025–1031, https://doi.org/10.1038/s41893-021-00756-w.
11. See: Citizens' Climate Lobby, https://canada.citizensclimatelobby.org/carbon-fee-and-dividend/. "Climate Income (a.k.a. Carbon Fee and Dividend) is the policy proposal … to internalise the costs of burning carbon-based fuels …Canada's Greenhouse Pollution Pricing Act is a form of Climate Income." Austria has a Klimabonus and Switzerland has a similar scheme.
12. Nerini et al., note 10, p. 1025.
13. IFS (2021), 'Tax Policies to Help Achieve Net-zero Carbon Emissions', *Institute for Fiscal Studies*, p. 356, https://ifs.org.uk/sites/default/files/output_url_files/8-Tax-policies-to-help-achieve-net-zero-carbon-emissions-.pdf.
14. R. Ayres (1997), 'Environmental Market Failures: Are There Any Local Market-based Corrective Mechanisms for Global Problems?', *Mitigation and Adaptation Strategies for Global Change* 1, 289–309.
15. Nerini et al., note 10.
16. Ayres, note 14.
17. M. Hillman and T. Fawcett (2004), *How We Can Save the Planet*, Penguin, London.
18. C. Raux and G. Marlot (2005), 'A System of Tradable CO_2 Permits Applied to Fuel Consumption by Motorists', *Transport Policy* 12, 255–265.
19. D. Miliband (2006), 'The Great Stink: Towards an Environmental Contract' (Speech to the Audit Commission, 19 July 2006), p. 11. Available at: https://www.darkoptimism.org/DavidMiliband.pdf.
20. FEASTA (2008), 'Cap and Share: A Fair Way to Cut Greenhouse Gas Emissions', The Foundation for the Economics of Sustainability, www.feasta.org/documents/energy/Cap-and-Share-May08.pdf.
21. D. Fleming (2007), *Energy and the Common Purpose: Descending the Energy Staircase with Tradable Energy Quotas (TEQs)*, 3rd ed. The Lean Economy Connection, London, UK.

22. D. Niemeier et al. (2008), 'Rethinking Downstream Regulation: California's Opportunity to Engage Households in Reducing Greenhouse Gases', *Energy Policy* 36, 3436–3447.
23. L. Owen et al. (2008), 'Personal Carbon Trading: Public Acceptability', Report to Defra, London.
24. C. Lane et al. (2008), 'An Analysis of the Technical Feasibility and Potential Cost of a Personal Carbon Trading Scheme', Report to Defra, Accenture, with the Centre for Sustainable Energy (CSE), Defra, London.
25. J. Thumim and V. White (2008), 'Distributional Impacts of Personal Carbon Trading', Report to Defra, London.
26. Defra (2008), 'An Assessment of the Potential Effectiveness and Strategic Fit of Personal Carbon Trading', Defra London.
27. Defra, note 8.
28. Ibid, 15.
29. Ibid, 4.
30. EAC (2008), 'Personal Carbon Trading', The Stationery Office, London.
31. SDC (2009), 'Breakthroughs for the 21st Century', London.
32. Y. Parag and T. Fawcett (2010), 'An Introduction to Personal Carbon Trading' *Climate Policy* 10, p. 334.
33. R. Howell (2012), 'Living with a Carbon Allowance: The Experiences of Carbon Rationing Action Groups and Implications for Policy', *Energy Policy* 41, 250–258. These groups have now disappeared.
34. P. North (2010), *Local Money: How to make it Happen in Your Community*, Transition Books, Totnes. The 'Lewes Pound', established in 2008 in East Sussex, is currently the longest surviving UK local currency. Its motto is: "We have it in our power to build the world anew", Thomas Paine, Lewes resident 1768–1774.
35. Y. Parag et al. (2011), 'Policy Attribute Framing: A Comparison Between Three Policy Instruments for Personal Emissions Reduction', *Journal of Policy Analysis and Management* 30(4), 889–905.
36. M. Burgess (2016), 'Personal Carbon Allowances: A Revised Model to Alleviate Distributional Issues', *Ecological Economics* 130, 316–327, https://www.sciencedirect.com/science/article/abs/pii/S0921800916303354.
37. I. Satoh (2014), 'IT-enabled Personal-level Carbon Emission Allowance', *Procedia Computer Science* 32, 665–672.
38. F. Al-Guthmy and W. Yan (2020), 'Mind the Gap: Personal Carbon Trading for Road Transport in Kenya', *Climate Policy* 20, 1141–60.
39. Nerini et al., note 10.
40. Ibid, 1025.
41. GHG Protocol (2013), 'Corporate Value Chain (Scope 3) Accounting and Reporting Standard', https://ghgprotocol.org/sites/default/files/standards/Corporate-Value-Chain-Accounting-Reporing-Standard_041613_2.pdf.
42. Electrons are fungible; therefore, unless there is a dedicated power supply to a site, the Scope 2 electricity calculations apply grid averages.

43. United Nations Statistics Division (2018), 'COICOP 2018', available at: https://unstats.un.org/unsd/classifications/unsdclassifications/COICOP_2018_-_pre-edited_white_cover_version_-_2018-12-26.pdf.
44. According to the World Bank, the USD carbon prices for South Africa and Republic of Korea in 2023 were respectively $10.09 and $6.30. See: Carbon Pricing Dashboard, https://carbonpricingdashboard.worldbank.org/compliance/price.
45. R. Kaplan and K. Ramanna (2021), 'Accounting for Climate Change', *Harvard Business Review*, https://hbr.org/2021/11/accounting-for-climate-change.
46. S. Webb (18 January 2022), 'Customers Shun Red Meat after Carbon Footprint Added to Weekly Shop Receipts' *The Independent*.
47. NatWest Group (2021), 'NatWest to Launch Free Carbon Footprint Tracker to App Users', https://www.natwestgroup.com/news-and-insights/news-room/press-releases/climate/2021/jul/natwest-to-launch-free-carbon-footprint-tracker-to-app-users.html.
48. Our World in Data, 'Historical CO2 Emissions by Country', available at: https://ourworldindata.org/co2-emissions-metrics.
49. ONS (17 October 2024), 'Measuring UK Greenhouse Gas Emissions', available at: https://www.ons.gov.uk/economy/environmentalaccounts/methodologies/measuringukgreenhousegasemissions.
50. Ibid.
51. Ibid.
52. S.W. Consulting (2024), 'National Parks Net Zero Report', available at: https://www.sw-consulting.co.uk/national-parks-net-zero-report.
53. ONS (25 February 2022), 'Overview of the UK Population 2020', available at: https://www.ons.gov.uk/peoplepopulationandcommunity/populationandmigration/populationestimates/articles/overviewoftheukpopulation/2020#:~:text=1.,the%20first%20time%20since%201976.
54. Our World in Data, 'Per Capita GHG Emissions', available at: https://ourworldindata.org/grapher/per-capita-ghg-emissions?tab=table#sources-and-processing.
55. Office for Budget Responsibility (2023), 'Working Paper No.18 Emissions and our Tax Forecasts', available at: https://obr.uk/docs/dlm_uploads/Emissions-working-paper.pdf.
56. ONS (2 May 2024), 'UK Environmental Taxes: 2023', available at: https://www.ons.gov.uk/economy/environmentalaccounts/bulletins/ukenvironmentaltaxes/2023.
57. Internal Revenue Service, 'Glossary: Progressive Tax', available at: https://apps.irs.gov/app/understandingTaxes/student/glossary.jsp#progressivetax.
58. IFS, note 13.
59. HM Treasury (2024), 'Impact on Households: Distributional Analysis to Accompany Autumn Budget 2024 and Spending Review 2025', Phase 1, "'Equivalised': … take[s] into account the fact that larger households will require a higher net income to achieve the same standard of living as a

household with fewer members … 'Net': household incomes are ranked after deductions from direct taxes, and after additions from welfare benefits", p. 13.

60. IFS, note 13, 357–8.
61. UK Government (2019), 'UK Becomes First Major Economy to Pass Net Zero Emissions Law', available at: https://www.gov.uk/government/news/uk-becomes-first-major-economy-to-pass-net-zero-emissions-law.
62. M. Berman (2024), 'A Rising Tide that Lifts All Boats: Long-term Effects of the Alaska Permanent Fund Dividend on Poverty', *Poverty & Public Policy* 16(2), 126–145. "We estimate that the PFD reduced the number of Alaskans with incomes below the US poverty threshold by 20%–40% … reduced poverty rates of rural Indigenous Alaskans from 28% to less than 22%, and has played an important role in alleviating poverty among seniors and children", p. 126.
63. UK Government (2024), 'Energy Secretary Ed Miliband Sets Out His Priorities for the Department', available at: https://www.gov.uk/government/news/energy-secretary-ed-miliband-sets-out-his-priorities-for-the-department.

12. Understanding distributional impacts of carbon pricing – insights from comparative analysis

Jules Linden, Herwig Immervoll, Cathal O'Donoghue and Denisa M. Sologon[1]

1. INTRODUCTION

A widely adopted and growing form of environmental taxation relates to the pricing of CO_2 emissions. Currently, some 40 national and 25 sub-national jurisdictions explicitly price carbon to curb emissions, and around a quarter of global emissions are covered by a carbon price, up from just 5% in 2010.[2] Measures include carbon taxes, cap-and-trade systems, and phase-outs of fossil-fuel subsidies to incentivise a reduction in emissions and the move from dirtier to cleaner fuels and technologies. In addition, governments have long taxed fossil fuels through specific excise taxes, which are economically related to explicit carbon prices. For each fuel type, their base (fuel use) is proportional to associated CO_2 emissions, although the tax rates are not directly determined by the carbon content of the fuels.[3]

1 This research was supported by the Luxembourg Fonds National de la Recherche (AFR individual, project id: 14614512) and the Erasmus+ Programme of the European Union (ecoMOD Project, project number: 2023-1-LI01-KA220-HED-000157594). The opinions expressed and arguments employed herein are solely those of the authors. In particular, they do not necessarily reflect the official views of the OECD or its member countries.

2 UNFCCC. About Carbon Pricing. Accessed 10/30/2024. https://unfccc.int/about-us/regional-collaboration-centres/the-ciaca/about-carbon-pricing#What-is-the-current-status-of-carbon-pricing-in-th.

3 Effective Carbon Rates 2023. (2023), OECD Series on Carbon Pricing and Energy Taxation. https://doi.org/10.1787/b84d5b36-en.

Carbon pricing is regarded as environmentally effective, economically efficient, and simple to administer, without being technologically prescriptive.[4] Carbon pricing also raises significant government revenues that can be used to support a just energy transition or to pursue other government objectives. Nonetheless, current prices often fall short of the levels needed to meet national and international reduction targets, with the Intergovernmental Panel on Climate Change (IPCC) warning that "coverage and prices have been insufficient to achieve deep reductions".[5] Numerous governments are therefore considering reforms to increase effective carbon rates by increasing prices in existing measures, broadening the share of covered emissions, or introducing new carbon-pricing instruments.

A key challenge for carbon-pricing initiatives relates to their impact on the cost of living and its distribution across different population groups. By charging producers and consumers for emissions, carbon pricing results in potentially sizable burdens for households, and these vary significantly across and within countries.[6] There is a risk that burdens are regressive,[7] creating obstacles to a just energy transition. The distributional impacts also affect public support and public discourse, shaping the political economy of carbon pricing schemes.[8]

While the literature on the distributional impacts of carbon pricing is growing, there is a lack of in-depth comparative analysis that accounts for both direct impacts on household budgets (due to emissions associated with domestic heating and transport fuel) and indirect impacts (due to emissions associated with the production of non-fuel goods and services). Household burdens

---

[4] High-Level Commission on Carbon Prices. (2017), "Report of the High-Level Commission on Carbon Prices." Washington, DC: World Bank. 1–61, https://openknowledge.worldbank.org/server/api/core/bitstreams/e49473de-ad98-5d26-8add-102687c9dc80/content#:~:text=To%20achieve%20the%20Paris%20temperature,%24100%2FtCO2e%20range%20by%202030.

[5] Lee, Hoesung, et al. (2023), "Synthesis report of the IPCC Sixth Assessment Report (AR6), Longer report. IPCC."

[6] OECD. (2024), "Who pays for higher carbon prices? Mitigating climate change and adverse distributional effects." *OECD Employment Outlook 2024: The Net-Zero Transition and the Labour Market.* https://doi.org/10.1787/9138d7e3-en.

[7] Linden, Jules, Cathal O'Donoghue, and Denisa M. Sologon. (2023), "The many faces of carbon tax regressivity—Why carbon taxes are not always regressive for the same reason." *Energy Policy* 192: 114210.

[8] Dechezleprêtre, Antoine, Adrien Fabre, Tobias Kruse, Bluebery Planterose, Ana Sanchez Chico, and Stefanie Stantcheva. (2022), "Fighting climate change: International attitudes toward climate policies." NBER Working Paper No. w30265. National Bureau of Economic Research.

are the result of complex interactions of numerous factors,[9] leading to substantially different impacts across population groups and countries. It remains difficult to anticipate household burdens in countries that may have broadly similar abatement commitments and climates but differ in other respects, including stage of development and population characteristics.

This chapter quantifies and discusses household burdens arising from a hypothetical (additional) carbon tax of €30 per ton of CO_2 in Finland and Lithuania. The stylised tax is levied on CO_2 emissions resulting from the combustion of fossil fuels (coal, natural gas, heating oil, petrol, and diesel) and biomass (firewood) by households, as well as those purchased by firms in each country, including for district heating and electricity generation.[10] Lithuania and Finland have comparable climates, especially in the most populous regions, but average income levels differ, as do experiences with environmental taxation. A comparison between these two countries therefore provides an instructive case study to discuss key drivers of the distributional impact of carbon pricing. The simulations consider multiple revenue recycling options and account for direct burdens from households' energy consumption, as well as indirect burdens associated with the impact of carbon charges on the prices of non-energy goods.

Consumption patterns and distributional impacts differ markedly across the two countries. In Lithuania, energy budget shares follow an inverted U-shape across income groups, but poorer households consume more carbon-intensive energy than higher-income groups. In Finland, energy budget shares increase with income, and wealthier households consume more carbon-intensive energy. As a result, a uniform carbon price is more regressive in Lithuania than in Finland (but it remains slightly regressive in Finland because poorer households spend larger shares of their income). Average impacts are also larger in Lithuania. Using revenues to compensate households can lead to progressive impacts in both countries, but the distributional impact depends strongly on the type of revenue recycling (e.g., per capita transfers, indirect tax reductions, etc.), and even simple reforms lead to different outcomes across the two countries.

This chapter first highlights country-specific driving factors that shape household burdens from carbon pricing. It then discusses the role of carbon-price coverage and design. Next, it illustrates the distributional mechanics,

9 Linden et al., note 7.

10 In our modelling, a carbon tax is imposed on the energy industries in relation to the carbon content of their output. We assume that the tax is forward shifted by the energy industries to producers of goods and services, who in turn forward shift the tax to the final consumer (i.e., the household). This implies that, in our modelling, the entire carbon tax is forward shifted and borne by households.

using Lithuania and Finland as case studies and explores options for using carbon-pricing revenues to compensate households. A final section concludes with a short discussion and considerations for future work.

2. CARBON PRICING ACROSS COUNTRIES

Energy consumption and associated carbon footprints are unequal across countries. A key insight from the cross-country comparative literature is that they vary by average income and development level.[11] Carbon footprints are much higher in high-income countries, but in some middle-income countries, households spend a larger share of their income on energy. Within countries, the distribution of energy expenditures is also related to the stage of development. This relationship between environmental footprints (in this case due to energy consumption) and income is commonly referred to as Environmental Engel curves.[12]

A large 2019 study covering 87 low- and middle-income countries identified a threshold of $US 15,000 per year (PPP-adjusted) below which a carbon tax is likely to be progressive.[13] This is explained by an inverse U-shaped relationship between average energy expenditure shares and average income, where average energy expenditure first increases faster than expenditure on other goods as countries and households within countries become wealthier, and then shrinks beyond a certain income level, as households start to prioritise other consumption. Average energy budget shares are therefore low in poor countries, increase as households transition to middle-income levels, and fall again as countries' national income rises further.

A related pattern also finds support in studies across high-income European Union (EU) countries, with EU-wide carbon pricing found to be regressive across countries, putting a higher burden on comparatively poorer (and primarily Eastern) EU countries.[14] Key driving factors behind this pattern include higher energy budget shares in poorer countries, along with more carbon-intensive production and consumption.

---

[11] Dorband, Ira Irina, Michael Jakob, Matthias Kalkuhl, and Jan Christoph Steckel. (2019), "Poverty and distributional effects of carbon pricing in low-and middle-income countries – A global comparative analysis." *World Development* 115: 246–257.

[12] Sager, Lutz. (2019), "Income inequality and carbon consumption: Evidence from Environmental Engel curves." *Energy Economics* 84:104507.

[13] Dorband et al., note 11.

[14] Feindt, Simon, Ulrike Kornek, José M. Labeaga, Thomas Sterner, and Hauke Ward. (2021), "Understanding regressivity: Challenges and opportunities of European carbon pricing." *Energy Economics* 103: 105550.

Country and region-specific characteristics other than income also shape household carbon footprints and the resulting incidence of a carbon tax. Relevant factors include average household size, climate, the energy mix, population density and car ownership, resource availability and access to infrastructure, the carbon-intensity of value chains, income inequality, and the housing stock.[15] Carbon price burdens are therefore highly context-dependent, with income levels an important determinant of energy use.

3. CARBON PRICING FOR A JUST TRANSITION: DESIGN OPTIONS FOR POLICYMAKERS

Regressive carbon prices, with disproportionate burdens on the poor and other low-income groups, can be due to multiple factors. First, energy consumption as a share of total expenditure (energy budget shares) may be higher at lower income levels (making energy a "necessity" as defined by economists).[16] In addition, the coverage of a carbon price affects its distributional impact.[17] When tax-exempt commodities are heavily consumed by low-income households, a carbon tax will tend to be less regressive. In practice, some products or commodities are exempt under carbon pricing schemes,[18] sometimes to protect households' living standards and sometimes to protect industries from foreign competition. Here, we focus on the impacts on households' living standards.

Carbon prices on domestic fuel and electricity are generally more regressive than for motor fuel,[19] as low-income households spend larger parts of their resources on heating and electricity. Levying carbon prices on motor fuels can,

[15] Ivanova, Diana, Gibran Vita, Kjartan Steen-Olsen, Konstantin Stadler, Patricia C. Melo, Richard Wood, and Edgar G. Hertwich. (2017), "Mapping the carbon footprint of EU regions." *Environmental Research Letters* 12, no. 5: 054013.

[16] In economics, "necessities" are defined as goods and services that have an income elasticity of less than one, i.e., the income share spent on the good or service declines with income. Conversely, goods and services are defined as "luxuries" if they have an income elasticity greater than one.

[17] See OECD, note 6. The empirical analysis in the present paper does not study how the specific scope and design of carbon-pricing measures shapes its distributional impacts.

[18] Sumner, Jenny, Lori Bird, and Hillary Dobos. (2011), "Carbon taxes: A review of experience and policy design considerations." *Climate Policy* 11, no. 2: 922–943.

[19] Flues, F., and Thomas, A. (2015). "The distributional effects of energy taxes." OECD Taxation Working Paper No. 23, OECD Publishing: Paris.

in fact, be progressive.[20] Taxing electricity and domestic fuels at different rates can have various distributional impacts depending on the energy mix and technology used to produce electricity. For instance, in China, the poorest spend a larger share of income on coal-based electricity while the wealthy spend more on heating fuel,[21] making taxation of electricity more regressive than taxation of heating fuels.

More granular differentiation of carbon prices by fuel type, across different types of heating or transport fuels, also affects distributional outcomes. For instance, in Ghana, the poorest predominantly use kerosene for transportation, and firewood and charcoal for heating.[22] In Germany, charges on diesel were found to be more progressive than on petrol as wealthier households consume diesel more heavily.[23]

In practice, carbon pricing schemes are indeed frequently designed to mitigate regressive impacts. For example, Mexico exempts natural gas from its (currently small) carbon tax to reduce its regressivity.[24] In the EU, a separate emission trading scheme was established covering the residential and transportation sectors, as higher carbon prices in these sectors have an immediate effect on households. Exempting "dirtier" fuels used by the poor, however, compromises abatement objectives, as it weakens incentives to switch to less carbon-intensive alternatives.

The majority of household spending is on non-fuel items. Embedded (indirect or upstream) emissions associated with the production of goods and services can therefore make up large shares of households' total emissions.[25] Because non-fuel spending also tends to be "flatter" across income groups than fuel spending, accounting for the indirect burdens can render carbon pricing significantly less regressive.[26] Pricing emissions associated with the

---

20 Vandyck, Toon, and Denise Van Regemorter. (2014), "Distributional and regional economic impact of energy taxes in Belgium." *Energy Policy* 72: 190–203.

21 Jiang, Zhujun, Xiaoling Ouyang, and Guangxiao Huang. (2015), "The distributional impacts of removing energy subsidies in China." *China Economic Review* 33: 111–122.

22 Cooke, Edgar F.A., Sarah Hague, Luca Tiberti, John Cockburn, and Abdel-Rahmen El Lahga. (2016), "Estimating the impact on poverty of Ghana's fuel subsidy reform and a mitigating response." *Journal of Development Effectiveness* 8, no. 1: 105–128.

23 Jacobs, Leif, Lara Quack, and Mario Mechtel. (2022), "Distributional effects of carbon pricing by transport fuel taxation." *Energy Economics* 114: 106290.

24 Renner, Sebastian. (2018), "Poverty and distributional effects of a carbon tax in Mexico." *Energy Policy* 112: 98–110.

25 OECD, note 6.

26 Ohlendorf, Nils, Michael Jakob, Jan Christoph Minx, Carsten Schröder, and Jan Christoph Steckel. (2021), "Distributional impacts of carbon pricing: A

production of imported goods (through a Carbon Border Adjustment mechanism, CBAM) can also make carbon pricing less regressive.[27] Carbon pricing schemes sometimes feature different rates for household-level or industrial emissions (e.g., in Denmark). In Europe, the EU Emission Trading Scheme (EU-ETS) first covered carbon-intensive sectors, exempting the transportation and residential sectors. At the same time, however, substantial free allocations enable industries to gradually transition to low-carbon energy sources and can make the EU-ETS effectively more regressive.[28]

While the discussion above focused on CO_2 emissions, the coverage of emissions of other greenhouse gases (GHGs), notably methane (CH_4) and nitrogen dioxide (N_2O), also shapes the distributional impacts of pricing measures. At the household level, CO_2 emissions result primarily from energy use, while a large part of CH_4 and N_2O emissions result from agricultural production. A study of the Netherlands found that a broader coverage of emissions beyond CO_2 reduced the regressivity of a carbon tax[29] (due to more equal food spending shares than energy spending shares across income groups), while studies in Mexico[30] and 16 Latin American and Caribbean countries[31] found that including CH_4 and N_2O emissions makes carbon pricing more regressive (due to particularly high food spending shares among the poor).

The existing literature therefore highlights the likely impacts of specific design choices. However, as incomes, energy consumption, and other expenditure patterns differ substantially across countries, it is difficult to use research results to make generalisations or to extrapolate from one country context to another.[32]

---

meta-analysis." *Environmental and Resource Economics* 78: 1–42.

27 Feindt et al., note 14.

28 Vandyck, Toon, Matthias Weitzel, Krzysztof Wojtowicz, Luis Rey Los Santos, Anamaria Maftei, and Sara Riscado. (2021), "Climate policy design, competitiveness and income distribution: A macro-micro assessment for 11 EU countries." *Energy Economics* 103: 105538.

29 Kerkhof, Annemarie C., Henri C. Moll, Eric Drissen, and Harry C. Wilting. (2008), Taxation of multiple greenhouse gases and the effects on income distribution: A case study of the Netherlands. *Ecological Economics*, 67, no. 2: 318–326.

30 Renner, note 24.

31 Vogt-Schilb, Adrien, Brian Walsh, Kuishuang Feng, Laura Di Capua, Yu Liu, Daniela Zuluaga, Marcos Robles, and Klaus Hubacek. (2019), Cash transfers for pro-poor carbon taxes in Latin America and the Caribbean. *Nature Sustainability* 2, no. 10: 941–948.

32 Steckel, Jan C., Ira I. Dorband, Lorenzo Montrone, Hauke Ward, Leonard Missbach, Fabian Hafner, Michael Jakob, and Sebastian Renner. (2021), "Distributional impacts of carbon pricing in developing Asia." *Nature Sustainability*, 4, no. 11: 1005–1014.

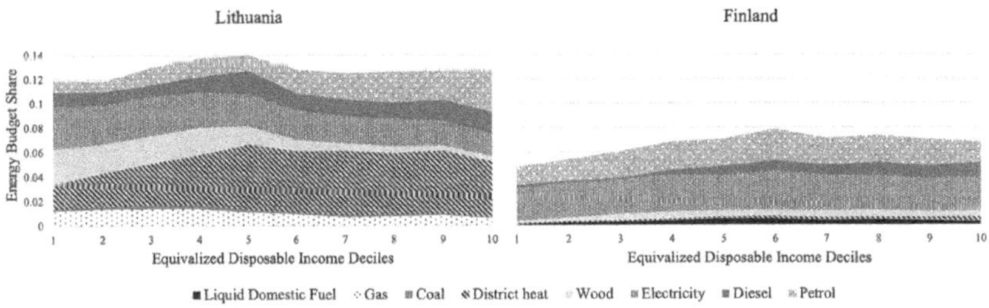

Source: Authors' own calculations. Based on 2015 EU-Household Budget survey data.

Figure 12.1 *The average energy expenditure as a share of the household budget by income group*

4. RESULTS

4.1 Results I: When Are Carbon Prices Regressive?

Comparisons between Finland and Lithuania illustrate that, even across countries in close proximity, energy budget shares can vary substantially, increasing with income for some types of energy while declining with income for others. Overall, Figure 12.1 shows that, in Lithuania, the share of household income devoted to energy consumption is almost twice as high as in Finland. Average energy consumption increases with income in Finland, while it follows an inverted U-shape in Lithuania. Motor fuel budget shares (diesel plus petrol) increase with income in both countries, but diesel expenditure is concentrated among wealthier households in Finland, whereas wealthier households in Lithuania spend significantly more on petrol.

The carbon content of energy varies markedly across fuel types and, for electricity, it also varies across countries. The energy mix therefore has a significant impact on carbon-price burdens. As shown in Figure 12.1, the mix varies markedly by income. In addition, other characteristics, such as location, also play an important role and tend to be correlated with income.[33] Households in urban areas are, for instance, more likely to have access to district heating networks, while poor and rural households may rely more heavily on traditional biomass or liquid fuels. Some households rely heavily on electric heating. Figure 12.1 shows that carbon-intensive wood and coal consumption is concentrated among low-income households in Lithuania, while wealthier households rely more heavily on comparatively low-carbon district heating. In

[33] OECD, note 6.

Finland, households appear to rely on electric heating to a significant extent. Higher energy budget shares for low-income groups and a carbon-intensive energy mix both suggest that carbon-price burdens will be larger, and likely more regressive, in Lithuania than in Finland.

Households also differ also in their capacity to absorb the costs of carbon pricing. Carbon charges are levied in relation to consumption (of carbon-intensive goods), while analysts and policymakers are often interested in carbon-price burdens relative to income. The difference between expenditure and income is given by savings. Households with higher savings rates will thus see smaller burdens relative to their income, and they will have a greater capacity to absorb higher energy prices and living costs. By contrast, for households that barely manage to save at all, or that dis-save, higher carbon prices are more likely to create binding constraints on their ability to purchase essential goods and services. The role of savings rates in the distributional impacts of carbon pricing is commonly recognised,[34] though often only implicitly so. Where savings rates vary strongly with income, carbon pricing tends to be more regressive.[35] Relatedly, savings also play an important role in investments in low-carbon heating systems and vehicles, as they are a prerequisite to investing for most households.

Accounting for differences in both consumption patterns and savings rates, Figure 12.2 shows a much more regressive distribution of carbon tax burdens in Lithuania than in Finland. Comparing with Figure 12.1 demonstrates that energy expenditures are not the only determinant; for instance, carbon tax burdens do not follow the same inverted U-shape as energy expenditure.[36] A higher-carbon energy mix in Lithuania, and negative savings rates among

---

[34] Poterba, J.M. (1991). "Tax policy to combat global warming: on designing a carbon tax." National Bureau of Economic Research, Working Paper No. 3649.

[35] Linden et al., note 7.

[36] A previous analysis of a carbon tax in Lithuania was published as a working paper (Immervoll, Herwig, Cathal O'Donoghue, Jules Linden, and Denisa Sologon. (2023), "Who pays for higher carbon prices? Illustration for Lithuania and a research agenda." *OECD Social, Employment, and Migration Working Papers* 283: 0_1-53). The distributional impact estimates presented in this chapter differ from those in the earlier working paper for several reasons. First, this chapter analyses a €30 per ton of carbon tax (€60 per ton in the working paper). Second, the base year is 2015 (2022 in the working paper). Third, the primary dataset is the Lithuania Household Budget Survey (Survey on Income and Living Conditions in the working paper, with expenditure patterns imputed rather than observed). Fourth, the working paper accounts for household behavioural responses, which are not included in this chapter.

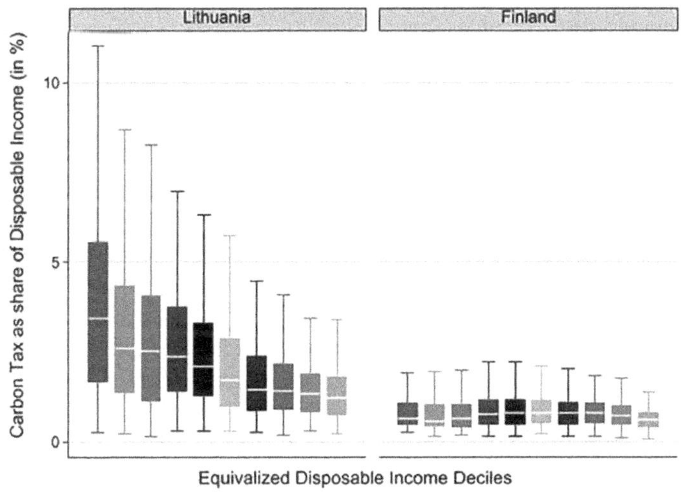

Notes: Simulation of a uniform €30 per ton CO_2 tax. The box represents the middle 50% (25th to 75th centile), light horizontal lines represent the median, and whiskers show the overall spread (2.5th to 97.5th centile). Household emissions, and thus carbon tax payments, include direct emissions (from household fuel consumption) and indirect emissions (from the production of non-fuel goods and services, including electricity.
Source: Authors' calculations. Based on 2015 EU-Household Budget survey data and World Input Output Data. For methodological details see Cathal O'Donoghue, Beenish Amjad, Jules Linden, Nora Lustig, Denisa Sologon, and Yang Wang (2025 forthcoming), "The Distributional Impact of Inflation in Pakistan: A Case Study of a New Price Focused Microsimulation Framework, PRICES." *International Journal of Microsimulation.*

Figure 12.2 Carbon tax burden as a share of household disposable income (direct and indirect emissions)

Lithuanian low-income households, explain the bigger impact on low-income groups, and the regressive overall impact.

Figure 12.2 shows a significant spread of burdens within income groups, indicating that they can differ as much, or more, within income groups as between them, and confirming findings from some earlier studies.[37] While the main attention here is on income groups, differences between demographic groups or regions can help to illuminate patterns of public support for, or

---

[37] Cronin, Julie Anne, Don Fullerton, and Steven Sexton. (2019). "Vertical and horizontal redistributions from a carbon tax and rebate." *Journal of the Association of Environmental and Resource Economists*, 6, no. S1: S169-S208.

resistance to, carbon pricing policies. They are also needed for targeting support to the most impacted groups, and for anticipating future emission trends and associated policy priorities, for example in the context of population ageing.

4.2 Results II: Using Carbon-pricing Revenues to Compensate Households

A key advantage of carbon pricing over other climate-change mitigation measures is that it raises revenues.[38] The use of these revenues, in turn, determines the net distributional impact of carbon price reforms and is likely to shape public support for it.[39] Revenues can be used for redistributive, environmental, or unrelated purposes.[40] Here, we focus on the impacts of revenue recycling on distributional outcomes.

A central insight from existing research on the distributional impact of carbon pricing is that, with full revenue recycling, the distributional impact of revenue use can outweigh that of carbon pricing itself.[41] Even a fraction of carbon-price revenues may be sufficient to make the overall impact of a carbon price progressive.[42] Whether net impacts are in fact progressive or regressive depends, however, on the specific design and targeting of household compensation. In designing compensation mechanisms, a fundamental challenge is that full compensation for everyone is not possible.[43] Consumption patterns and the resulting carbon price payments are diverse and correlate imperfectly with observable household characteristics that can be used to target payments. Reforms will necessarily create winners and losers, and the incidence of gains and losses is important for social equity and for political-economy reasons.

---

38 Revenues differ across carbon pricing schemes depending on their scope and design. Emission trading schemes in particular often include free allocations to specific industries, for instance, emission-intensive trade-exposed industries. Free allocations reduce the revenue collected.

39 Klenert, David, Gregor Schwerhoff, Ottmar Edenhofer, and Linus Mattauch. (2018), "Environmental taxation, inequality and Engel's law: The double dividend of redistribution." *Environmental and Resource Economics*, 71, no. 3: 605–624.

40 Steenkamp, Lee-Ann. (2021), "A classification framework for carbon tax revenue use." *Climate Policy* 21, no. 7: 897–911.

41 Cronin et al., note 37.

42 Vogt-Schilb et al., note 31.

43 Sallee, James M. (2019), *Pigou Creates Losers: On the Implausibility of Achieving Pareto Improvements from Efficiency-enhancing Policies*. No. w25831. National Bureau of Economic Research.

Environmental tax reform may involve shifting the tax burden from existing distortionary taxes, such as taxes on labour, to resources or pollution and may possibly achieve a "double dividend". Under the double dividend hypothesis, environmental taxation combined with reductions in existing taxes (income, corporate, consumption, or capital tax) could simultaneously improve economic and environmental conditions. The initial impact of reductions in income, consumption, and corporate taxes, however, may be regressive.[44] Analysis incorporating adjustments in employment, wages, and capital incomes find that income tax cuts may benefit low-income households sufficiently to turn regressive impacts into net progressive impacts.[45]

If the aim is to compensate households and avoid increases in inequality in the short-term, other revenue recycling options may be preferable. Per capita lump-sum transfers tend to turn net impacts progressive,[46] overcompensating most low-income households. Benefits targeted at the poor, the energy poor, or disproportionately affected regions also turn net impacts progressive and can do so at significantly lower fiscal cost than untargeted lump-sum transfers.[47] Similarly, proportional increases in existing social benefits will be progressive[48] if the underlying benefit system is.

Various countries have implemented some form of revenue recycling. South Africa uses carbon-tax revenues to finance a reduction of existing electricity generation levies. British Columbia uses revenues to cut other taxes and to provide for direct transfers to households. Switzerland uses one-third of revenues to support a green transition and reduce energy consumption, and the rest to lower health insurance premiums. Austria introduced a "climate bonus" paid to residents, a lump-sum payment whose level varies by region. At the EU level, countries are currently designing Social Climate Plans, detailing their plans to use EU-ETS revenues to compensate vulnerable households.

The impact of these different revenue recycling options differs across countries, however. Households with characteristics used to target payments may

---

44 Goulder, Lawrence H., Marc A.C. Hafstead, GyuRim Kim, and Xianling Long. (2019), "Impacts of a carbon tax across US household income groups: What are the equity-efficiency trade-offs?" *Journal of Public Economics* 175: 44–64.

45 Vogt-Schilb et al., note 31.

46 Berry, Audrey. (2019). "The distributional effects of a carbon tax and its impact on fuel poverty: A microsimulation study in the French context." *Energy Policy* 124: 81–94.

47 Ibid.

48 Immervoll, Herwig, Cathal O'Donoghue, Jules Linden, and Denisa Sologon. (2023), "Who pays for higher carbon prices? Illustration for Lithuania and a research agenda." *OECD Social, Employment, and Migration Working Papers* 283: 0_1-53.

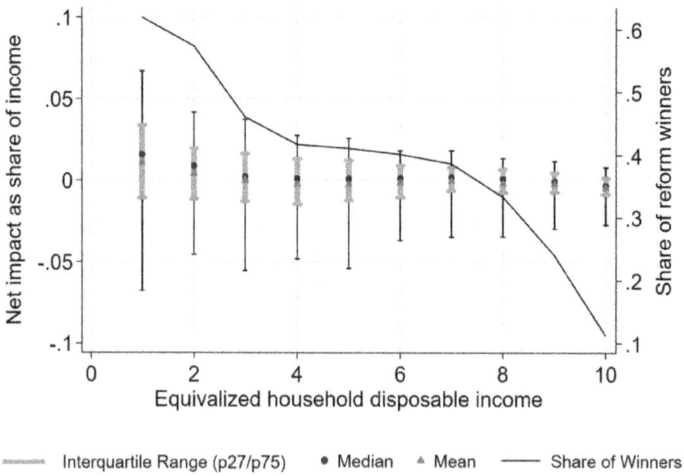

Figure 12.3a Lithuania: per capita transfers

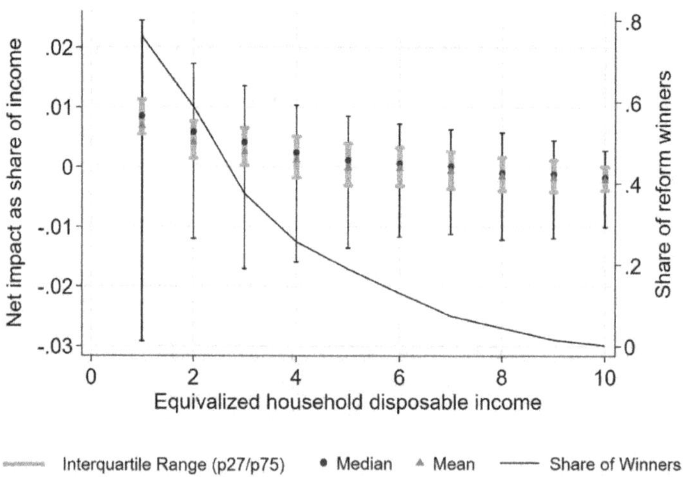

Figure 12.3b Finland: per capita transfers

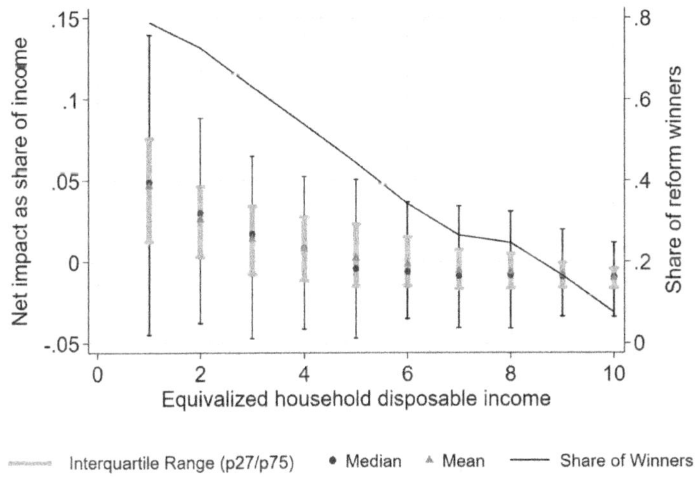

Figure 12.3c *Lithuania: 'Rural' per capita transfers*

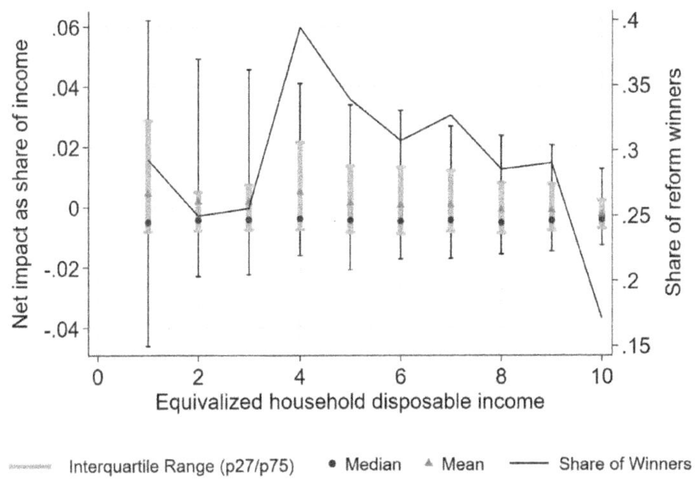

Figure 12.3d *Finland: 'Rural' per capita transfers*

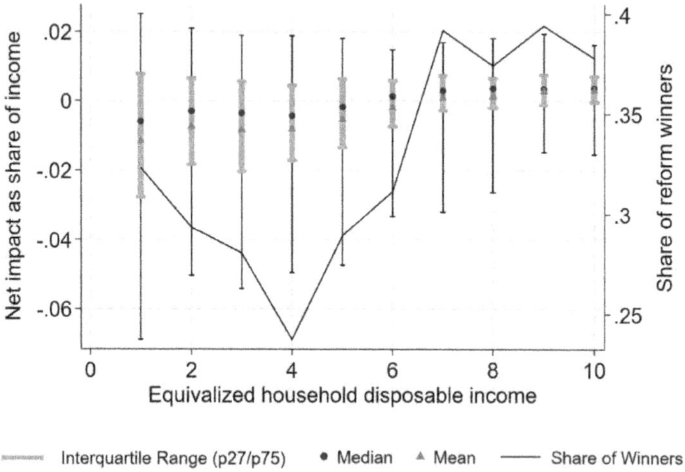

Figure 12.3e *Lithuania: Proportional reduction of indirect taxes*

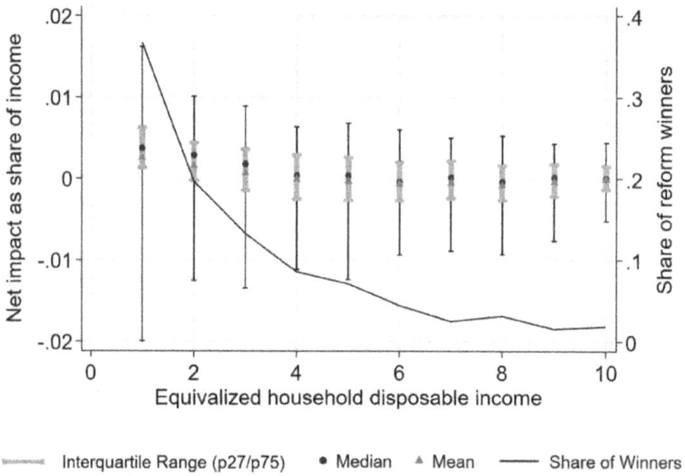

Note: Positive values represent net gains for the household (the household's revenue recycling payment exceeds its carbon tax payment) and negative values represent net losses (the household's carbon tax payment exceeds its revenue recycling payment).

Figure 12.3f *Finland: Proportional reduction of indirect taxes*

be wealthier or poorer in some countries than others. Figures 12.3a–f show the distributional impact of three reforms where all revenues are returned to households through transfers or lower indirect taxes. Unconditional per capita lump-sum transfers lead to progressive impacts in Lithuania and Finland, but the share of low-income households gaining from the reform is higher in Finland. Compared to Finland, a greater share of middle-income households in Lithuania gain from such a reform. In Lithuania, close to 15% (34%) of revenues would be sufficient to fully compensate the bottom two (four) deciles, while 8% (23%) would be sufficient in Finland. A version of the lump-sum, per capita transfers, where (all) revenues are returned to rural households only, is more progressive in Lithuania, as the correlation between location and carbon tax burdens is stronger in Lithuania than in Finland. Some countries, like France or Germany, and recently also Finland,[49] have lowered indirect taxes on energy commodities to limit the increase in energy prices due to carbon pricing.[50]

In our simulations, a simple proportional reduction in indirect taxes is overall progressive in Finland but regressive in Lithuania. These examples highlight that the distributional impact of revenue recycling programmes can dominate that of the carbon tax, and that even simple revenue recycling schemes can have very different distributional impacts across countries. Some other countries, like Portugal and Sweden, used revenues to reduce income taxes. This type of revenue recycling is not modelled here. As noted above, it likely results in more regressive initial impacts, though the medium-term impacts are unclear.[51]

5. CONCLUSION

This chapter reviewed the evidence on the distributional impact of carbon pricing and provided a comparison of its impact across two countries with comparable climates but different development levels, Lithuania and Finland. The distributional effects of carbon pricing result from complex interactions of numerous factors, leading to substantially different impacts across countries.

49 OECD. Effective Carbon Rates 2023, (2023), *Effective Carbon Rates 2023: Pricing Greenhouse Gas Emissions through Taxes and Emissions Trading*. OECD Series on Carbon Pricing and Energy Taxation. Paris: OECD Publishing, https://doi.org/10.1787/b84d5b36-en.

50 OECD, note 6.

51 For a simulation of this scenario, see also Immervoll, H., O'Donoghue, C., Linden, J. and Sologon, D.M. (2023). "Who pays for higher carbon prices? Illustration for Lithuania and a research agenda." OECD Social, Employment and Migration Working Papers, No. 283, OECD Publishing: Paris.

Relevant driving factors include the proportion of energy consumption relative to income across different groups, the types of energy consumed by these groups, the pricing of various energy sources, and how carbon-pricing revenues are allocated or utilised.

The results illustrate how expenditure patterns, notably on energy, and income levels in the two countries lead to markedly different burdens for households. Further, they show how differences in population characteristics and existing tax-benefit systems cause a divergence in the impact of even simple revenue recycling schemes. The findings highlight the complexity that drives short-term distributional outcomes of carbon pricing, and the need for timely country- and region-specific analysis.

The primary aim of a carbon price is to change the behaviour of individuals and firms so as to reduce emissions. In the medium and long run, these changes in behaviour have effects on production, investments, and jobs, and affect environmental quality, and thus people's health and exposure to climate damages. Short-term impacts on households are, however, an important consideration for social equity reasons, and they can be a decisive factor for the political feasibility of necessary climate mitigation efforts.

PART IV

Environmental tax reform case studies

13. Progress in environmental tax reform in Brazil

Roney Sandro Freire Corrêa and Denise Lucena Cavalcante

1. INTRODUCTION

This chapter addresses the relevant regulatory transition that Brazil is going through in 2024. The new legal guidelines arising from Constitutional Amendment No. 132 of 12/20/2023 (CA No. 132/2023), brought numerous changes to the Brazilian Tax System, mainly regarding taxation on consumption and innovation in relation to sustainability criteria and the recognition of environmental protection as a guiding principle of the tax system, as provided for in Art. 145, §3, of the Federal Constitution/88, in the following terms: "The National Tax System must observe the principles of simplicity, transparency, tax justice, cooperation and environmental protection."

In addition to the new principles, the Brazilian tax reform also stands out for the institution of the selective tax, a new tax under the jurisdiction of the Union, which will be levied on the production, extraction, commercialisation, or import of goods and services that are harmful to health or the environment (Art. 153, VIII, Federal Constitution). The selective tax will come into effect in 2027 and will be regulated by law (the bill is currently being processed in the National Congress[1] – PLP No. 68/2024).

The selective tax is equivalent to excise taxes, sin taxes, Pigouvian taxes, sugar taxes, among others. It was initially designed in Brazil solely to discourage the consumption of goods and services that generate negative externalities, such as cigarettes and alcoholic beverages.

[1] Available at: https://www25.senado.leg.br/web/atividade/materias/-/materia/164914. Accessed on August 25, 2024.

The issue of environmental protection was not contemplated in the initial text of the selective tax in Brazil. It was included later, after debates within the legislative power.[2]

Initially, the selective tax focused exclusively on health issues and generated regulatory challenges. Legislators had not considered the intersection of health and environmental protection and the need for different guidelines.

Despite the occasional criticism of this new taxation in the country, there is no doubt that the selective tax linked to environmental protection aligns with international guidelines. Further, it demonstrates that Brazil is one of the pioneering countries in Latin America by incorporating environmental criteria into its constitutional text and the National Tax System.

The recent constitutional changes in the Brazilian context, therefore, represent important advances for environmental tax reform, reinforcing the use of taxes as a fiscal instrument promoting environmental protection in the national debate, thus paving the way for a low-carbon economic transition.

2. THE EXTRA-FISCAL NATURE OF THE SELECTIVE TAX

Brazil is currently experiencing intense debates about the selective tax, reviving an old controversy in the tax sphere about the role of taxes in shaping the behaviour of taxpayers.

A variety of theories and empirical analyses have permeated the discussion in recent decades, especially in the dialectic between the paths that the State should adopt when it comes to taxes with predominantly regulatory or behaviour-inducing purposes. As Janet Milne rightly points out, this intervention differs from traditional command-and-control regulation, since environmental taxation, as an instrument of environmental policy, uses economic theory to achieve an environmental goal, without restricting freedom of decision, as in the case of regulation.[3]

---

2 Regarding the inclusion of environmental criteria in the Brazilian tax system, see: Cavalcante (2024).

3 "As an environmental policy instrument, environmental taxation differs radically from traditional command-and-control regulation. Acting through the government's fiscal apparatus, not its police power, environmental taxation harnesses economic theory, not regulatory mandates, to protect the common good. Consequently, it uses economics as the means to the end, not just as a factor that influences the calculation whether society can afford to use regulations to achieve a certain end. By using economic theory, it relies on an indirect means to achieve the end, not directly constraining freedom of decision as in the case of regulation. Similarly, its reliance on economics means that the environmental end – the

Among the existing ramifications, the theory of economist Arthur C. Pigou[4] stands out, emphasising that market agents tend to produce, in their contractual relationships, externalities that require regulatory treatment under the responsibility of the State, and that negative and positive externalities should be internalised in order to correct these distortions and promote a more efficient allocation of resources. On the other hand, in contrast to Pigou, some theories propose a neutral taxation whose incidence hypothesis is limited to consumption, without any effect on the behaviour of economic agents or causing any distortion in the market, with one of the emblematic theorists being the economist Ronald Coase.[5] What deserves to be highlighted in these two currents is the imposition, in the name of social and collective well-being, of the indispensable response of the State, capable of correcting market imperfections, conferring on tax law the function of inducing behaviours that collectively favour society.[6]

It can be stated, therefore, that the concept of a selective tax assumes Pigouvian premises in the Brazilian legal system. It demonstrates taxation on consumption with an inductive function, the purpose of which is to guide healthy and ecologically responsible behaviours, where there is a greater approximation between the price to be paid and the social cost of activities that are potentially harmful to health or the environment.

It is noted that the Brazilian Constitution provides that health and an ecologically balanced environment are fundamental rights protected by the State. State action in their defence is thus essential.

The doctrine of James Hines Jr. points to the existence of certain motivations for the implementation of the selective tax, such as: (i) generation of revenue; (ii) enforcement of the benefit of taxation; (iii) control of externalities; and (iv) use of special taxes on consumption to discourage the consumption of products that are harmful to health.[7] Analysing the Brazilian context, these

degree of environmental protection – may be less certain or absolute than the end achieved through regulatory mandates" (Milne, 2017, p. 31).

4 Pigou, A.C. (1920), *The Economics of Welfare*. London: Macmillan and Co.

5 Coase, R.H. (1960), "The problem of social cost". *The Journal of Law and Economics*, 3: 1–44. Available at: https://www.sfu.ca/~wainwrig/Econ400/coase-socialcost.pdf.

6 Cavalcante, Denise Lucena; Silva, Adriana Fonteles; Machado, Lara Ramos de Brito. (April./June 2024), "Coase, mercado de carbono e tributação ambiental: eficiência na sustentabilidade." *Revista de Direito Tributário Contemporâneo*, ano 9, v. 41, pp. 119–137.

7 "The first [motivation] is revenue generation: excise taxes can produce significant government revenues and may do so at lower political or economic cost than alternatives such as income taxation. The second motivation is application of

motivations were observed in the selective tax. However, they went beyond the regulation of goods and services that are harmful to health and included environmental protection.

It is true that, in this phase of regulating the selective tax, there are numerous uncertainties regarding its impacts on the behaviour of economic agents and the effects on the prices that will be incorporated into the goods or services. Therefore, it is clear that the configuration of the new selective tax has objectives that go beyond revenue collection and highlight the value of protecting health and the environment. This juncture requires critical attention so as not to distort the extra-fiscal nature of the selective tax, which has been frequently reaffirmed in the opinions of the legislative branch, as well as expressly mentioned in several passages in the Opinion of the Citizenship and Justice Committee of the Federal Senate,[8] when approving PEC No. 45/2019, on November 7, 2023. It is therefore confirmed that the targeting of the selective tax to extra-fiscal purposes, as provided for in the Brazilian Constitution, must be strictly observed by infra-constitutional legislation.

---

the benefit principle of taxation: excise taxes can be tailored to impose tax burdens on those who benefit from government services financed by excise taxes. Gasoline taxes are often justified as user fees for government-provided roads, and the tax on sonar devices is justified by government expenditures to maintain lakes and fisheries. The third motivation is control of externalities, which is the goal of a number of excise taxes on polluting substances, such as taxes on ozone-depleting chemicals. And the fourth motivation is that excise taxes may discourage consumption of potentially harmful substances (such as alcohol and tobacco) that individuals might overconsume in the absence of taxation" (Hines, 2007, p. 5).

8 "[...] the Selective Tax will play an important role in differentiating the consumption of products that are harmful to health and the environment. We believe that it will be a very useful instrument for the relevant policy of mitigating climate change. Looking further into the subject, we agree with Amendments No. 38 and 259, by Senator Mecias de Jesus and Senator Tereza Cristina, respectively, that improvements are needed in the text approved by the National Congress to make it clear that the tax will have an extra-fiscal nature. As a result, the tax will not be used for its primary revenue collection function but will have its rates determined by the National Congress to reduce the consumption of certain goods and the exercise of activities that are harmful to the environment (one of the guiding principles of the reform)." Available at: https://www25.senado.leg.br/web/atividade/materias/-/materia/158930?_gl=1*1qh0c8t*_ga*MTk2Nzc0ODAwMC4xNTg1MTY5OTg0*_ga_CW3ZH25XMK*MTcwNjEyMjg1MC43LjEuMTcwNjEyMzkwNC4wLjAuMA.#tramitacao_10611472. Accessed on June 23, 2024.

3. SELECTIVE TAX IN HEALTH PROTECTION

The initial text of Bill No. 68/2024, initiated by the federal executive power, when regulating the selective tax, identified alcoholic beverages, sugary drinks (soft drinks), and tobacco as goods that are harmful to health. Later, in the final text forwarded by the National Congress to the Federal Senate, the levy on gambling and fantasy games was included.

In relation to other products that are harmful to health, the literature has defined other examples, substantiated by empirical research. The World Bank released a study[9] in which robust evidence was presented about the potential of taxes on ultra-processed foods to improve life and health outcomes, particularly for the poorest segments of the population. Another analysis highlighted instances in relation to ultra-processed products, as in the case of the United States or Mexico, where, due to the lack of a replacement policy, such taxes were not able to impact obesity.[10] In Brazil, processed and ultra-processed foods were not included in the selective tax, mainly due to the strength of the sectoral lobby, including the questionable argument that it would be a regressive and unfair tax, as these foods form part of the diet of lower-income communities. Therefore, it is clear that selective tax is effective in reducing the consumption of the products on which it is levied, but its efficacy is limited if public policy does not comprehensively assess the products that are considered harmful to health.[11]

The selective tax is one of the fiscal instruments available for protecting health and the environment, but it is not the only one, nor the most relevant.

---

9 Shekar, Meera; Popkin, Barry. (Eds) (2020), *Obesity: Health and Economic Consequences of an Impending Global Challenge*. Washington, D.C.: World Bank Group. Available at: https://openknowledge.worldbank.org/server/api/core/bitstreams/cddcb99b-9d0b-5f08-9cf6-934974a308cf/content. Accessed on July 7, 2024.

10 Aguilar, A.; Gutierrez, E.; Seira, E. (May 2021), "The effectiveness of sin food taxes: evidence from Mexico." *Journal of Health Economics*, vol. 77. Available at: https://www.sciencedirect.com/science/article/abs/pii/S0167629621000400?via%3Dihub. Accessed on July 7, 2024.

11 Barry, Luke E.; Kee, Frank; Woodside, Jayne; Clarke, Mike; Cawley, John; Doherty, Edel; Crealey, Grainne E.; Duggan, Jim; O'Neill, Ciaran. (2023), "An umbrella review of the effectiveness of fiscal and pricing policies on food and non-alcoholic beverages to improve health." *Obesity Reviews*, Vol. 24, Issue 7, e13570. Available at: https://onlinelibrary.wiley.com/doi/full/10.1111/obr.13570. Accessed on July 7, 2024.

It must form part of a broad public policy, acting in conjunction with several other instruments that aim to regulate and modify behaviours.[12]

It is essential that the effects of the selective tax be monitored periodically. Changes should be made whenever inefficiency is demonstrated. The deadline for evaluating the selective tax in Brazil is still under discussion. The five-year assessment,[13] provided for in Bill No. 68/2024 is expected to be reduced, as five years is a very long time to wait, especially in relation to environmental protection measures.

As for the scope of the selective tax on health, while the parameters have been defined, they can still be changed, as PLP No. 68/2024 is still under discussion and, unfortunately, there is potential to expand its scope. This was also seen with the recent inclusion of the selective tax on gambling and fantasy sport,[14] under the argument that these activities would compromise the mental health of the population.

Each new inclusion, without due justification, has generated controversy around the selective tax. Each new item on the list, especially when it has a significant economic impact without a sufficient connection to harms to health, tends to distort the extra-fiscal nature of the selective tax.

In the case of tobacco products, a complementary bill recognises the importance and effectiveness of adopting tax policies to discourage smoking without disregarding the increase in revenue as it is part of an existing public health policy. It is true that tax instruments alone are not enough, considering that demand in this case is inelastic. However, when combined with several other

12 Andrade, José Maria Arruda de. (2024), Imposto seletivo e pecado: juízos críticossobre tributação saudável. São Paulo: IBDT.

13 "Art. 468. The Executive Branch of the Union will carry out a five-yearly assessment of the efficiency, effectiveness and effectiveness as a social, environmental and health policy, of the incidence of the Selective Tax, referred to in Book II." (PLP n. 68/2024).

14 "TechNavio's 'Fantasy Sports Market by Product, Platform and Geography – Forecast and Analysis 2023–2027' report analyses the market status and global and regional trends for electronic fantasy sports. The report points out that South America was the 4th largest region in the market in 2022 and will continue to be the 4th largest segment in 2027. The region is expected to have an average annual growth rate of 9.34% between 2022 and 2027, ranging from 8.27% to 10.51% annual growth. It will be the fastest-growing region in the overall market and will grow from USD 1.4 billion in 2022 to USD 2.2 billion in 2027, with an incremental growth of USD 8.6 billion and contributing 10.12% of the global market incremental growth between 2022 and 2027. South America contributed 6.57% to the global fantasy sports market in 2022 and its contribution will increase to 7.52% in 2027. The region will generate growth in every year of the forecast period between 2022 and 2027" (Games magazine, Brasil, 2023).

instruments, the efficacy of the measure has been demonstrated. Increasing taxation on tobacco products is not enough, as was seen in the example of the Philippines, which represents a case in which demand has remained high, despite several progressive increases in tobacco prices.[15]

As for alcoholic beverages, the complementary bill provides that the applicable rates should be established according to the alcoholic content of the products, relating the harmful effects of alcohol to its excessive consumption. This option of varying rates based on alcoholic content is also used in the Industrialised Products Tax (IPI), which is currently levied on alcoholic beverages. However, if the objective is to discourage consumption, there should be no difference in rates according to the percentage of alcohol since the harm to health is independent of the alcoholic content and depends on the amount consumed.

The complementary bill also provides for the tax levy on sugary drinks, initially levied on soft drinks,[16] with a selection of products remaining to be taxed to prevent the substitution effect. This taxation, despite being heavily criticised, is the result of intense debates on the public health costs resulting from the high consumption of sugar in the country,[17] as well as a new approach

[15] Cheng, K.; Estrada, M. (April 2021), "Cost-effectiveness analysis of the 2019 cigarette excise tax reform in the Philippines." *Preventive Medicine*, vol. 145. Available at: https://www.sciencedirect.com/science/article/pii/S0091743521000153. Accessed on July 7, 2024.

[16] PLP No. 68/2024 mentions the incidence of sugary drinks, but in its Annex XVII, it defines the type of sugary drink in accordance with NCM 2202.10.00, which refers to waters, including mineral waters and carbonated waters, with added sugar or other sweeteners or flavours.

[17] "According to the World Health Organization (WHO), high consumption of sugary beverages, associated with worsening global dietary patterns, is among the main causes of the increased prevalence of obesity and some chronic diseases worldwide. For this reason, since 2014, the WHO itself has recommended that countries study and apply taxes on the production chain of sugary beverages, since evidence points to such a proposal as a cost-effective policy for public health. This measure is often the main tool adopted to inhibit the increase in the consumption of sweetened beverages in various territories and, thus, reduce the potential health damage caused by excessive consumption of these beverages. Despite the importance of such taxation, the issue is very incipient and controversial in Brazil, and there is a need for further research on the subject" (Gigante et al., 2013, p. 13).

by tax law aimed at sustainable taxation. The national debate was based on data from the World Health Organization[18] and the Ministry of Health.[19]

The importance of developing comprehensive fiscal policies is evident. Fiscal policy cannot focus solely on tax collection but must also consider the public budget, taking into account the high amounts allocated to the treatment of chronic non-communicable diseases, including obesity, diabetes, and cardiovascular diseases, which are putting pressure on the Unified Health System (SUS).[20]

4. SELECTIVE TAX FOR ENVIRONMENTAL PROTECTION

The inclusion of environmental protection in the National Tax System is worthy of applause. It demonstrates the Brazilian State's notable stance of considering[21] issues of significance that extend beyond tax collection.

The expansion of the selective tax in relation to environmental protection, given its peculiarities, requires different parameters when compared to health protection. The global climate crisis, with its uncertainties and serious repercussions for the economy, accelerates the debate in Brazil. It is estimated that the global GDP will fall by 12% for each degree celsius of increase in the planet's temperature due to the emission of greenhouse gases. Environmental shifts that affect economic aspects are thus decisive even for classical economists who discounted the environment as an element to be considered in modelling and evaluation.

In environmental matters, great caution is needed when considering potential legislative gaps may allow for tax avoidance manoeuvres that limit environmental profit. An example of this situation occurred in Italy when it instituted the *Imposta Regionale sulle Emissioni Sonore degli Aeromobili*

---

18 WHO. (2015). *Fiscal Policies for Diet and Prevention of Noncommunicable Diseases*. Available at: https://www.who.int/publications/i/item/9789241511247. Accessed August 20, 2024.

19 Brasil. Ministério da Saúde. (2019), *Saúde Brasil 2018 – uma análise de situação de saúde e das doenças e agravos crônicos: desafios e perspectivas*. Brasília: Ministério da Saúde, p. 256.

20 On the subject, see: Piscitelli, Tathiane and Carvalho, Adriana (Coord.). (2023), *Tributos saudáveis: diálogo entre direito e economia*. São Paulo: Revista dos Tribunais.

21 On the role of taxes as vehicles for transmitting collective or public meanings, see: Carruthers, Bruce G. (2016), "The semantics of sin tax: politics, morality, and fiscal imposition." *Fordham L. Rev.* vol. 84, 2565. Available at: https://ir.lawnet.fordham.edu/flr/vol84/iss6/8. Accessed on August 23, 2024.

(IRESA), aimed at curbing noise pollution. It was converted into a regional tax on January 1, 2013.[22] As it is a regional tax on noise, charged on commercial and non-commercial flights that take off or land at airports located in specific Italian locations, some regions chose not to implement the tax. Many air network operators subsequently moved their air networks to these locations, thus avoiding taxation.

In the Brazilian context, the challenge with implementing a selective tax will be balancing the protection of the environment and combatting the harmfulness of products that threaten the health of human beings. Several examples in comparative literature should also be highlighted, whether as successful models or avoidable failures.

According to PLP No. 68/2024, at this first stage, the following goods are considered environmentally friendly for the purposes of levying the selective tax: vehicles, ships, aircraft, and mineral goods.

Regarding automobiles, it is important to note that road freight in Brazil generates significant emissions.[23] This part of the tax reform is still controversial as it excludes diesel trucks, the primary mode of cargo transportation in the country (Appendix XVII, of PLP No. 68/2024). On the other hand, it includes electric vehicles. The criticism is that the selective tax should be levied on fuel, not vehicles. To date, Bill No. 68/2024 provides that the rates of the selective tax on automobiles will be graduated in relation to each vehicle according to the following criteria: vehicle power; energy efficiency; structural performance; driving assistance technologies; recyclability of materials; carbon footprint; technology density; carbon dioxide emissions (energy-environmental efficiency); vehicle recyclability; completion of manufacturing stages in the country; and vehicle category (Art. 417, of Bill No. 68/2024).

Another point of great divergence has been the application of the selective tax on mining. Brazil has vast mineral reserves, and mining is one of the most important segments of the national economy. It is estimated that the taxation on mineral extraction, initially scheduled to be levied on iron ore, oil,

[22] Italia. Imposta Regionale sulle Emissioni Sonore degli Aeromobili Civili. Available at: https://ambiente.regione.emilia-romagna.it/it/aria-rumore-elettrosmog/temi/inquinamento-acustico/per-approfondire/iresa. Accessed on July 7, 2024.

[23] According to the National Energy Balance, in 2023, total anthropogenic emissions associated with the Brazilian energy matrix reached 428 million tons of carbon dioxide equivalent (Mt CO2-eq), with over half (217 Mt CO2-eq) generated in the transportation sector. In 2021, for each ton of oil equivalent (toe) made available, Brazil emitted the equivalent of 78% of the emissions of European OECD countries, 69% of the emissions of the United States, and 52% of the emissions of China (National Energy Balance – BEN, 2024).

and natural gas, including on exports, will raise the country's environmental tax standards, adapting to current international trade rules. However, despite Constitutional Amendment No. 132/2023 having stipulated that the maximum tax rate would be 1% (Art. 153, §6º, VII, FC), PLP No. 68/2024 reduced it to 0.25%, which could reduce the efficiency of the tax due to its low value. The tax rate is expected to be reduced to zero for natural gas intended for use as an input in industrial processes.

It is important to note that the Brazilian energy matrix is considered one of the most renewable in the world. The maintenance of the hydraulic supply and the significant increase in wind and solar sources in the generation of electrical energy (zero loss), as well as biomass, has contributed to the Brazilian energy matrix remaining at a renewable level of 49.1%, much higher than that observed in the rest of the world and OECD countries.[24]

It will only be possible to assess the effectiveness of the selective tax in terms of environmental protection after 2027, when it will begin to be charged. As seen in the in-scope hypotheses defined by the legislator, there is a lack of coherence in the goods selected. This is due to the strong pressure from the private sector in parliament, which is highly sensitive to lobbies, propaganda, and policy proposals based on undeclared interests, as well as the lack of prior public policies that consider the effects of fiscal instruments for environmental protection.

5. CONCLUSION

There is no doubt that one of the great benefits that tax reform provided in Brazil was to elevate the defence of the environment to the category of a principle of the National Tax System. Furthermore, the environmental agenda and sustainability, based on the tax reform project, were accepted and recognised as being of global and universal importance in political-legal debates.

For that reason, one of the striking characteristics of Constitutional Amendment No. 132/2023 is that it provided a greater number of tax provisions based on environmental sustainability in the Federal Constitution and granted complementary law the role of delimiting the scope of several legal provisions. Thus, it became a new milestone in environmental taxation, with the constitutional head office establishing a paradigmatic change in the Brazilian National Tax System.

---

24 Data from the National Energy Balance (BEN) for 2024. Available at: https://www.epe.gov.br/sites-pt/publicacoes-dados-abertos/publicacoes/PublicacoesArquivos/publicacao-819/topico-715/BEN_S%C3%ADntese_2024_PT.pdf. Accessed on August 24, 2024.

In this way, taxation is now understood not only from a merely revenue-raising perspective but also in terms of the emphasis and priority given to extra-fiscal taxation mechanisms. The State is able to guide the taxpayer towards healthy choices and activities that are considered sustainable.

Based on these premises, it is concluded that Constitutional Amendment No. 132/2023 introduces an observable element of moral judgment, which now coexists with other pre-existing constitutional norms. This translates into the introduction of new constitutional tax principles, whose fundamental scope is defined by simplicity, transparency, and environmental sustainability.

Thus, the final dimension of the selective tax is expected to conceive of an environmental taxation that links protective charging for natural assets and the indispensable observance of environmental sustainability. This ensures that legislators and economic agents do not diminish the effectiveness of the efforts to achieve this purpose.

To implement these new constitutional guidelines and ensure that the selective tax fulfils its purpose, there is still a lot of work to do, and the legislative procedures related to the complementary laws that will regulate the innovations introduced by Constitutional Amendment No. 132/2023 must be closely monitored.

The current innovation in the National Tax System, which provides for the use of tax instruments to protect the environment, must adapt to contemporary thinking regarding the necessity of a new State model focused on sustainable and inclusive development, acting in partnership with other nations. This major process will require effective global governance to combat the risks of climate change and ecosystem collapse.

REFERENCES

Aguilar, A.; Gutierrez, E.; Seira, E. (May 2021), "The effectiveness of sin food taxes: evidence from Mexico." *Journal of Health Economics*, vol. 77. Available at: https://www.sciencedirect.com/science/article/abs/pii/S0167629621000400?via%3Dihub. Accessed on 7 July 2024.

Andrade, José Maria Arruda de. (2024), *Imposto seletivo e pecado: juízos críticos sobre tributação saudável*. São Paulo: IBDT.

Barry, Luke E.; Kee, Frank; Woodside, Jayne; Clarke, Mike; Cawley, John; Doherty, Edel; Crealey, Grainne E.; Duggan, Jim; O'Neill, Ciaran. (2023), "An umbrella review of the effectiveness of fiscal and pricing policies on food and non-alcoholic beverages to improve health." *Obesity Reviews*, Vol. 24, Issue 7, e13570. Available at: https://onlinelibrary.wiley.com/doi/full/10.1111/obr.13570. Accessed on July 7, 2024.

Brasil. Ministério da Saúde. (2019), *Saúde Brasil 2018 – uma análise de situação de saúde e das doenças e agravos crônicos: desafios e perspectivas*. Brasília: Ministério da Saúde.

Brasil. Projeto de Lei Complementar 68/2024. Brasília, 2024. Available at: .https://www.camara.leg.br/proposicoesWeb/prop_mostrarintegra?codteor=2414157&filename=PLP%2068/2024. Accessed on July 7, 2024.

Carruthers, Bruce G. (2016), "The semantics of sin tax: politics, morality, and fiscal imposition." *Fordham L. Rev.* vol. 84, 2565. Available at: https://ir.lawnet.fordham.edu/flr/vol84/iss6/8. Accessed on 23 August 2024.

Cavalcante, Denise Lucena. (2024), "Inovações da Emenda Constitucional n. 132/2023: a proteção ambiental como princípio no sistema tributário nacional." In: Leonetti, Carlos Araújo (Coord.), *Direito Tributário Constitucional.* MG/Uberlândia: Marco Teórico, pp. 193–207.

Cavalcante, Denise Lucena; Silva, Adriana Fonteles, Machado, Lara Ramos de Brito. (April/June 2024), "Coase, mercado de carbono e tributação ambiental: eficiência na sustentabilidade." *Revista de Direito Tributário Contemporâneo*, ano 9, v. 41, pp. 119–137.

Cheng, K; Estrada, M. (April, 2021), "Cost-effectiveness analysis of the 2019 cigarette excise tax reform in the Philippines." *Preventive Medicine*, vol. 145. Available at: https://www.sciencedirect.com/science/article/pii/S0091743521000153. Accessed on July 7, 2024.

Coase, R.H. (1960), "The problem of social cost." *The Journal of Law and Economics*, 3: 1–44. https://www.sfu.ca/~wainwrig/Econ400/coase-socialcost.pdf.

Games magazine Brasil. (2023), Febre dos Fantasy Sports no Brasil impulsiona o crescimento do segmento na América Latina, Available at: https://www.gamesbras.com/esports/2023/5/3/febre-dos-fantasy-sports-no-brasil-impulsiona-crescimento-do-segmento-na-america-latina-37071.html. Accessed on August 24, 2024.

Gigante, Denise Petrucci; Cattafesta, Monica; Bielemann, Renata Moraes (Orgs). (2023), *Bebidas adoçadas: da economia à saúde pública.* Porto Alegre: Fundação Fênix.

Hines, James R. (May 31, 2007), "Excise taxes." Michigan: Office of Tax Policy Research. Product Number, WP 2007-2.

Itália. Imposta Regionale sulle Emissioni Sonore degli Aeromobili Civili. Available at: https://ambiente.regione.emilia-romagna.it/it/aria-rumore-elettrosmog/temi/inquinamento-acustico/per-approfondire/iresa. Accessed on July 7, 2024.

Milne, Janet E. (2017), "Environmental taxation: why theory matters." In: Milne, Janet E. (Ed.), *Environmental Taxation and the Law. Vol. I*, Cheltenham, UK and Northamption, MA, USA: Edward Elgar.

National Energy Balance – BEN (2024), *Summary Report 2024 (base year 2023).* Available at: https://www.epe.gov.br/sites-pt/publicacoes-dados-abertos/publicacoes/PublicacoesArquivos/publicacao-819/topico-715/BEN_S%C3%ADntese_2024_PT.pdf. Accessed on August 24, 2024.

Pigou, A.C. 1920, *The Economics of Welfare.* London: Macmillan and Co.

Piscitelli, Tathiane; Carvalho, Adriana (Coord.). (2023), *Tributos saudáveis: diálogo entre direito e economia.* São Paulo: Revista dos Tribunais.

Senado federal Projeto de Emenda Constitucional N° 45/2003. Available at: https://legis.senado.leg.br/sdleg-getter/documento?dm=9477037&ts=1696463578186&disposition=inline. Accessed on July 7, 2024.

Shekar, Meera; Popkin, Barry. (Eds) (2020), *Obesity: Health and Economic Consequences of an Impending Global Challenge.* World Bank Group. Washington, D.C. Available at: https://openknowledge.worldbank.org/server/api/core/bitstreams/cddcb99b-9d0b-5f08-9cf6-934974a308cf/content. Accessed on July 7, 2024.

World Health Organization (WHO). (2015), *Fiscal Policies for Diet and Prevention of Noncommunicable Diseases.* Available at: https://www.who.int/publications/i/item/9789241511247. Accessed on August 20, 2024.

14. The green hydrogen (H_2V) market in Brazil: the architecture of development in light of tax incentives

Roney Sandro Freire Corrêa

1. INTRODUCTION

Since the beginning of human civilisation, the evolution and expansion of certain regions have been closely linked to the energy development process, changes to which have permeated the structure of the global energy mix. The history of humanity has come a long way, with the discovery and use of the four natural elements, and the movement from coal, through natural gas, to oil. The economic indicators that have come to guide the progress of humanity have, however, neglected the importance of maintaining environmental balance.

The rise of *homo economicus* began with strenuous work and more sophisticated production techniques. During the Industrial Revolution, the steam engine and coal became instruments of economic and political power. With rapid growth underway, countries faced the prospect of unlimited economic growth in the face of limited natural resources. This translated into the increasing emission of fossil fuels, directly reflecting the increase in the planet's temperature. This fact, confirmed by the Intergovernmental Panel on Climate Change (IPCC) report, revealed that in the last 50 years (1970–2020), the rise in the Earth's temperature has been faster than in any other period in the last 2,000 years.

Given increasing temperatures, several countries have proposed moving the global economy away from fossil fuels to renewable energy sources, which would decrease carbon emission levels. Under the Kyoto Protocol in 1997 and the Paris Agreement in 2015, signed by 195 countries, the signatories agreed to reduce or even eliminate greenhouse gas emissions. Another important event was the United Nations Climate Conference in 2021 (COP 26), when the largest emitters of carbon dioxide into the atmosphere reached an agreement in which they promised to progressively eliminate the use of coal as an energy source, limit carbon emissions, and aim to maintain global temperatures at acceptable levels.

This led the US Department of Energy to announce the United States' goal of having 45% of its energy mix come from solar sources by 2050, while the European Union, through its corresponding body, announced that by means of tax incentives and other facilities, it intends to have its energy mix 100% clean by 2030, with 38% of the continent's energy already generated by solar panels and wind farms.[1] The international community appeared to have realised the importance of avoiding the looming catastrophe. However, several countries have not abandoned coal, oil, and natural gas, as pointed out in the *BP Statistical Review of World Energy – 2022*.[2]

In the case of Brazil, the situation has turned out to be somewhat different. Currently ranked as the fifth largest emitter in the world, its emissions pattern differs significantly from the global average. While some of Brazil's emissions are due to changes in land use, deforestation, and agriculture, 70% of the country's emissions are related to the energy sector. Another point of fundamental importance is that the Brazilian energy mix is more renewable than that of the world's largest economies, with over 80% of its generation coming from renewable sources, compared to the average of 29% for other G20 countries. This represents a comparative advantage in the energy transition context, positioning low-carbon hydrogen as a highly relevant asset in Brazil.[3]

However, for the energy transition from a high-yield economy to a low-carbon economy to happen, it is essential that immediate planning and deliberation take place, especially concerning government actions that encourage fledgling industries, new research into technologies and their viability, and more active participation from the private sector. The main challenge is the cost of making this transition effective. According to the Climate Policy Initiative, an investment of around 9 trillion US dollars is required by 2030. This would necessitate a model of greater participation and partnership between the public and private sectors.[4] In the case of low-carbon hydrogen, Brazil's energy mix guarantees it a privileged position, enabling competitive production from vari-

---

1 Evangelista, Eduardo; Magalhães, Gerusa; Mariani, Rômulo (Coord). 2023, *Hidrogênio Verde – Perspectiva Jurídica, Regulatória e Técnica*. 1ª ed. Rio de Janeiro: Synergia.

2 Ibid.

3 Ibid.

4 Mooney, Attracta. 2024, "Transição verde deve custar US$ 9 trilhões, mas como pagar continua incerto." Folha de São Paulo, 09 de maio de 2024. Seção Economia, Caderno Energia Limpa. Available at: https://www1.folha.uol.com.br/mercado/2024/05/transicao-verde-deve-custar-us-9-trilhoes-mas-como-pagar-conta-continua-incerto.shtml. Accessed on May 25, 2024.

ous low-carbon sources and giving the country a strategic advantage relative to other competitors.

2. THE DEFINITION AND CONSTRUCTION OF A LEGAL FRAMEWORK FOR THE H_2V MARKET IN BRAZIL

In 1671, Robert Boyle described the process of obtaining a flammable gas as a result of the dissolution of iron in dilute acids. Subsequently, in 1776, Henry Cavendish collected this gas and described the reaction in which two gases, which he called "inflammable air" and "life-sustaining air", combined with the aid of an electric spark and produced water. From 1820 onwards, hydrogen was used in various ways, such as for lighting in theatres or in airships. Considered the most common and abundant element on the planet, hydrogen is notable for its versatility, being obtained in the atmosphere through the breakdown of molecules, not necessarily water, or through the use of energy from other sources, which, depending on the type, will present taxonomic nuances.

Hydrogen has been touted as an energy source that will play an important role in decarbonisation. Hydrogen types are graded by colour, depending on the production energy source. For example, through electrolysis and the use of natural gas, grey hydrogen is produced; from the gasification of coal and the use of bituminous gas, black hydrogen is created; and when lignite is used, brown hydrogen is produced. Thus, as a result of their production process, not all types of hydrogen can be treated as low-carbon or desirable.

However, what is planned with the use of hydrogen are low-carbon production sources, which generate less impact on the environment. In this case, it is classified as blue if produced with the use of natural gas; as turquoise, if produced by pyrolysis of methane, without generating carbon; as pink, if produced by means of a nuclear source; as white, if coming from the extraction of natural or geological hydrogen; or as green, if resulting from the use of water electrolysis, using renewable electricity.

From the first studies dating back to 1970, Brazil has prioritised production around green hydrogen. In 2018, based on the document *The Future of Hydrogen: Seizing Today's Opportunities*, developed during the G20 meeting, the country became aware of the need to develop some low-carbon energy policies.[5] In 2021, the National Hydrogen Program emerged and established six thematic axes: strengthening technological bases; training and human

---

5 Evangelista, Eduardo; Magalhães, Gerusa; Mariani, Rômulo (Coord). 2023, *Hidrogênio Verde – Perspectiva Jurídica, Regulatória e Técnica*. 1ª ed. Rio de Janeiro: Synergia.

resources; strategic planning of the legal-regulatory framework; market growth; competitiveness; and international cooperation. In 2022, Bill No. 725 stated that only hydrogen produced from solar, wind, biomass, biogas and hydraulic sources, landfill gases, or geothermal, tidal and oceanic sources, via water electrolysis, would be considered low carbon. Subsequently, the Special Committee on Energy Transition and Hydrogen Production of the Chamber of Deputies defined low-carbon hydrogen as follows:

> hydrogen fuel or industrial input, collected or obtained from sources other than production processes, and which emits greenhouse gases (GHG), according to a life cycle analysis, with an initial value less than or equal to four kilograms of carbon dioxide equivalent per kilogram of hydrogen produced (4 $kgCO_2eq/kgH_2$).

Brazil has structured production around its energy mix, highlighting several comparative advantages. Hydropower is the largest energy source in the Brazilian energy mix, accounting for 61.9%; wind power is the second largest, accounting for 14.8%; solar power accounts for 4.4%; and sugarcane bagasse 4.7%.[6] This led the Senate and the Congress to establish special committees to foster economies of scale for clean energy generation technology. The Environment Committee proposed legislative measures to create a policy that regulates energy production and use. Proposals within the scope of the Senate included Bills No. 1.880/2022 and 1.872/2022, which deal with the creation of an incentive programme for the large-scale production of fuel cells, taking advantage of the entire existing ethanol and gas chain, as well as the role of the National Petroleum Agency to regulate, contract, and monitor economic activities aimed at the production of green hydrogen. Congress proposed Bill No. 1.093/2022, which deals with the activity of energy storage and the creation of the social biofuel seal. Legal initiatives that can support projects and attract new investments in the sector, especially by providing a regulatory framework that guarantees legal certainty and stability in business relations, are essential.

In the operational sphere, the challenges are centred on the costs of hydrogen production, notably the expenses incurred by the electrolyser equipment, with its production limitations, the renewable energy plant, and the storage system, which requires storage at a temperature of minus 454 degrees Fahrenheit. An average production cost of less than 1.360 US dollars per pound would be required to ensure competitiveness. This creates a challenge for taxation, especially in implementing and producing green hydrogen at scale as a fledgling sector.[7]

---

6 Ibid.

7 Ibid.

3. TAX IMPACTS FOR THE IMPLEMENTATION AND PRODUCTION OF GREEN HYDROGEN

The tax reform, approved and enacted in Brazil in 2023, introduced a new determining principle for environmental protection, highlighting the need to observe, whenever possible, environmental sustainability as a socio-environmental parameter to be respected. Furthermore, the reform accommodated low-carbon hydrogen in the constitutional text, emphasising the circular and low-carbon economy as a transition model to be implemented. Despite this, the tax reform did not encompass the necessary transformations to the current system, whose impacts, especially in terms of tax, are relevant in green hydrogen operations.

For example, consider the purchase of an electrolyser. In this case, if the product is purchased in the domestic market, according to Brazilian legislation, the buyer will be responsible for the Tax on Industrialized Products (IPI), the Tax on Circulation of Goods and Services (ICMS), the Social Contributions for Profit Participation Contribution (PIS), the Social Security Financing Contribution (COFINS), Corporate Income Tax (IRPJ), and Social Contribution on Net Income (CSLL). If the product is imported, according to Brazilian legislation, the purchaser will be responsible for the import tax (II) and the Tax on Industrialized Products (IPI), both levied by the Federal Government, the Tax on the Circulation of Goods and Services (ICMS-Import), the Social Contributions for PIS/COFINS-Import, and the Tax on Financial Operations (IOF) exchange rate.

It is worth noting that the current import tax rate on an electrolyser is 0%, thus dispensing, for now, with the need to apply for the ex-tariff regime, which also applies to IPI. In the case of PIS/COFINS–Import, the calculation basis is the customs value of the imported goods or services, and the applicable rates are 2.10% and 10.65%, respectively. Regarding ICMS–Import, which is the responsibility of the States and the Federal District, the average internal rate is 18% and is levied on transactions within the same State. The ICMS calculation basis is the customs value plus II, IPI, IOF, other taxes, and customs expenses. When importing the electrolyser, considering that there are financial remittances abroad, as payment for the product's price, the IOF Exchange rate is 0.38%, and the financial institution is responsible for withholding it.

Other tax costs incurred in implementing a green hydrogen project in Brazil include hiring specialised technical personnel for the implementation and structuring phase. In this case, the following are levied: Tax on Services of Any Nature (ISSQN), Contributions for PIS/COFINS–Import, Tax Withheld at Source (applicable to the remittance of amounts for the implementation of the green hydrogen manufacturing plant), Cide Royalties (10% on amounts paid, credited, delivered, used, or remitted, each month, to residents or domiciles abroad as remuneration), and IOF–Exchange. On the sale of the product, ICMS and IPI are levied, while the taxes and contributions levied on the income and revenue of a venture are IRPJ, CSLL, PIS, and COFINS. Finally, tax is also levied on the payroll of employees and collaborators involved in a green hydrogen venture, resulting from the employer's social security contributions and the contributions to workers' accident risk (RAT), Salary Education, and the 'S' system. In the case of the employer's social security contributions, the rate is 20% of the wages paid. An additional 1% to 3% is added, depending on the worker's accident risk (RAT), which depends on the level and degree of risk of the activity performed. In the case of green hydrogen, the risk is rated at 2%. Finally, the 'S' system, which is levied on the wages paid, can reach a rate of 5.8% of the total wages paid.

In other words, the Brazilian tax burden is onerous and restrictive to expanding investments in the green hydrogen sector, particularly in the implementation and production phase. The taxation model should be accompanied by a set of advantages in the domestic market, notably a tax incentive policy that fosters development.

4. TAXATION WITH NON-FISCAL PURPOSES AS A FACTOR IN INDUCING CERTAIN BEHAVIOUR IN THE SECTOR

Taxation for non-fiscal purposes can be of fundamental importance in encouraging economic behaviours that promote the transition to a low-carbon economy. The theoretical basis of taxation with non-fiscal purposes was outlined by Seligman and Wagner, who referenced the dual purpose of the concept, emphasising its bivalent character – political and social – which opposes the individualism and economic isolationism present in taxation, which until then had been defended by Adam Smith.[8] These thoughts consecrated the viability of the republican principle, whereby adequate State participation is a precursor for economic success. State intervention is justified by ensuring the reduction of social inequality and enabling greater compliance with environmental protection norms.

In the past, Wagner had already "defended the induction of tax law as a manifestation of state power", promoting the intersection of economic and

[8] Caliendo, Paulo; Campos, Carlos Alexandre de Azevedo; Cavalcante, Denise Lucena (Org.). 2018, *Leituras Clássicas de Direito Tributário*. In: Adamy, Pedro (Ed.), *Adolph Wagner*. Salvador: Jus Podium, p. 99, Available at: https://static1.squarespace.com/static/5a67928fdc2b4a9c1eb96ff4/t/5cb10811e79c702a81ca1306/1555105827513/Adamy_Adolph+Wagner.pdf.

legal thought, thus resulting in the so-called taxation with non-fiscal purposes.[9] This was corroborated by Caliendo, who understood it as an intersystemic phenomenon, a junction between law, economy, and politics.[10] This conception enables the State to use taxation to order, intervene, and induce behaviours or discourage improper conduct in society. This new conception of taxation has been subject to criticism from several scholars focused on the norms of pure and reductionist tax law. These scholars reject the purposes and extra-legal nature of the phenomenon that reached such inductive conclusions.

This theoretical basis was expanded upon in 1932 by Mario Pugliese in a work entitled: *Finance and its Extra-fiscal Tasks in Modern States* (*La Finanza e i suoi compiti extra-fiscali negli stati moderni*).[11] Further, Eros Grau understood it as an intervention in the economic domain through induction. In other words, the State acts through its constitutional prerogatives to influence the conduct of individuals in specific directions. This induction will be responsible for producing the desired effects and behaviours.[12]

In this sense, taxation with non-fiscal purposes came to be considered a State instrument to intervene in the economy for a specific purpose, whether environmental, social, political, economic, or even moral, but always in line with constitutional precepts, as Becker notes:

> None of the demands made today under the title of social rights can achieve their objective without state intervention in the economy. [...] Now, tax law is precisely the fundamental instrument of the state to be able to carry out its intervention in the economy. The use of tax legal instruments for this purpose has given rise, in recent years, to a new science: fiscal policy.[13]

This intervention of the State to encourage, plan, and monitor, was established in the Brazilian Federal Constitution of 1988. It established the State as the

---

9 Caliendo, Paulo; Campos, Carlos Alexandre de Azevedo; Cavalcante, Denise Lucena (Org.). 2018, *Leituras Clássicas de Direito Tributário*. In: Adamy, Pedro (Ed.), *Adolph Wagner*. Salvador: Jus Podium, p. 99, Available at: https://static1.squarespace.com/static/5a67928fdc2b4a9c1eb96ff4/t/5cb10811e79c702a81ca1306/1555105827513/Adamy_Adolph+Wagner.pdf.

10 Caliendo, Paulo. 2016, "Tributação e Ordem Econômica: Os tributos podem ser utilizados como instrumentos de indução econômica?" *Revista de Direitos Fundamentais e Democracia*, v. 20, n. 20.

11 Pugliesi, Mario. 1932, *La finanza e i suoi compiti extra-fiscali negli stati moderni*. Padova: CEDAM.

12 Grau, Eros Roberto. 2003, *A Ordem Econômica na Constituição de 1988*. 8ª ed. São Paulo: Malheiros Editores, p. 126.

13 Becker, Alfredo Augusto. 2007, *Teoria Geral do Direito Tributário*. 4ª ed. São Paulo: Noeses, p. 629.

normative and regulatory agent of economic activity. In accordance with the law, the State conducted the functions of monitoring, encouraging, and planning, as well as having the capacity to pursue economic development compatible with other pre-existing orders. The implementation of this instrument requires symmetry with other principles to ensure a balance between economic development and environmental preservation.

Having defined the theoretical basis, it is worth reiterating that taxation with non-fiscal purposes, when concerning environmental tax, is determined by the intrinsic relationship between the defence of a healthy environment, through interventionist policies, and the intersection of tax and financial rules, so that differentiated and favourable treatment can be allowed for taxpayers, without degrading nature.

This State interventionism is closely linked to tax guidelines with an environmental bias, as it is through policies coordinated by the State that the protection and planning of actions aimed at a healthy environment are aligned with the guidelines deliberated by the market, as Falcão explains:

> Extrafiscal taxation is a phenomenon that goes hand in hand with state interventionism, insofar as it is state action on the market and the once sacred free initiative. It also contributes to changing the concept of fiscal justice, which no longer persists only in reference to the taxpaying capacity. It presupposes an adequate structure of the public treasury, knowledge of the possibilities for intervention that can be considered and the desire to make use of these possibilities, including forcing their expansion, since immobility and extra-fiscality are mutually exclusive.[14]

Furthermore, in defence of the environment, the State constitutionally provides for a differentiation in treatment. The State must assess the minimum level of intervention necessary to guarantee environmental protection, implemented through the exercise of this function, thus supporting the economy and safeguarding socio-environmental values. It can be inferred from the 1988 Constitution, in the combination of Articles 3, I, 170, VI, 174, and 225, that the defence of an ecologically balanced environment, which cannot be observed autonomously, requires the integration of the economic and social orders.

In the environmental context, the extra-fiscal function implies a double dividend. In addition to raising foreign currency for the public coffers by allowing the State to promote a particular sector, it encourages environmentally sound behaviours. Taxation with non-fiscal purposes, therefore, must be driven by sustainable values, fulfilling a multidimensional function and integrated with other orders. Thus, environmental taxation is a legitimate path for formulating the parameters and incentives for societal regulation.

---

[14] Falcão, Raimundo Bezzera. 1981, Tributação e mudança social. Rio de Janeiro: Forense, pp. 47–48.

In the case of the green hydrogen sector, extra-fiscality must be present as a pre-condition to foster an energy transition to a future with low-carbon energy production. It differs from a traditional command-and-control regulation. As Janet Milne rightly points out, taxation with non-fiscal purposes is not a traditional command-and-control regulation, since environmental taxation, as an instrument of environmental policy, uses economic theory as a means to achieve the environmental goal.[15] In this case, the rule established by Constitutional Amendment No. 132 will only be effective if extra-fiscality is predominantly established and covers the green hydrogen sector.

5. THE NECESSARY TAX INCENTIVE POLICY AS A DEVELOPMENT POLICY

As already demonstrated, the regulatory structure of the hydrogen sector limits investments in technologies that rely on a standardised structure for use in all stages of the value chain and are reliant on incentives that the public sector must facilitate. Brazil has chosen to migrate demonstration projects to larger-scale projects to be implemented in hydrogen (H_2) hubs. Recently, the issue of green hydrogen has become more prominent. It is a highly competitive environment between different geographies, not yet differentiated by the Brazilian public sector.

By comparison, when implementing the Inflation Reduction Act, the United States established a hydrogen production credit with four emission level ratings for the production of green hydrogen.[16] For those who met the requirements, the amount of the credit varied between 0.27 US dollars per pound of hydrogen to 1.36 US dollars per pound of hydrogen, depending on the emissions of the production life cycle.

In the case of the European Union, there are several European auctions with equalisations that can reach figures of around 4 billion euros. These auctions aim to promote local investments in the production chain using mechanisms that promote competition and sustain demand for products derived from green hydrogen.

In Germany, the public sector launched a programme called H_2Global, designed by the sustainable development agency (GIZ) and the German H_2 and Fuel Cell Association (DWV). With a budget of 2 billion euros (2.4 billion

---

15 Milne, Janet E. 2017. "Environmental taxation: why theory matters." In: Milne, Janet E. (Ed.), *Environmental Taxation and the Law. Vol. I*, Cheltenham, UK and Northampton, MA, USA: Edward Elgar, p. 31.

16 Truby, J. et al. 19 June 2023. "Green hydrogen: energising the path to net zero." Deloitte. Available at: https://www.deloitte.com/global/en/issues/climate/green-hydrogen.html. Accessed on May 25, 2024.

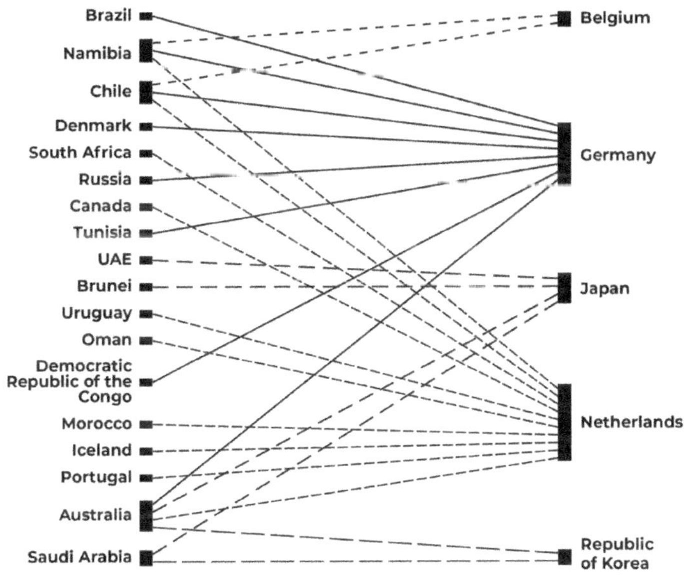

Source: Adapted from IRENA, 2022, https://www.irena.org/-/media/Files/IRENA/Agency/Publication/2022/Mar/IRENA_World_Energy_Transitions_Outlook_2022.pdf.

Figure 14.1 *International cooperation agreements are signed based on bilateral agreements and memoranda of understanding*

US dollars), this programme defined a strategy to support hydrogen projects until 2030.[17]

In Australia, the hydrogen sector is supported by investments in research and technology, the use of tax-exempt resources, and the expansion of tax incentives to attract investment.[18]

In short, regardless of the geographic region, nearly all countries have used cooperation agreements, which have the potential to create a new global model of synergistic collaboration, as shown in Figure 14.1.

---

[17] De Castro, Nivalde et al. 2023, "A economia do hidrogênio: transição, descarbonização e oportunidades para o Brasil." In: Elizário, Sayonara et al., *Experiência Internacional*, 1. ed. Rio de Janeiro: E-papers, pp. 93–159.

[18] Australian Government. 19 June 2023, "The Australian Government has a new economic plan called 'A Future Made in Australia.'" Available at: https://treasury.gov.au/policy-topics/future-made-australia. Accessed on May 25, 2024.

On the other hand, Brazil opted for a path to create tax incentives for sustainable H_2 by incentivising current hydrogen consumers. This will create a dynamic that makes the sector's growth compatible with the increasing need to strengthen demand.

This achievement was empirically demonstrated in the Brazilian wind sector, whose Alternative Sources Incentive Program (PROINFA) became an important pillar for its expansion. Notably, 85% of the Brazilian electricity matrix corresponds to renewable generation, with 13% coming from wind and solar sources. In other words, using tax incentives to develop nascent, low-carbon economic sectors has proven successful.[19]

In the case of green hydrogen, the Special Incentive Regime for Infrastructure Development (REIDI) was established by Law No. 11,488/2007 and regulated by Decree No. 6,144/2007, exempting the import of new machinery, devices, instruments, equipment, and construction materials from the payment of PIS or the Civil Servant Asset Formation Program (PASEP) and COFINS, valid for five years (from 2025 to 2029) and with values in the order of 18.3 billion reais (from 2028 to 2032).

The great challenge will undoubtedly be formulating public policies that leverage Brazil's numerous comparative advantages into positive competitive outcomes for developing the nascent green hydrogen industry. A key outcome is a policy of expanding tax incentives, with defined deadlines that are periodically assessed and capable of managing the energy transition process underway.

6. CONCLUSION

The low-carbon hydrogen market encompasses several production and implementation technologies, including combinations of economic and industrial processes, which require the development and maintenance of a clean energy mix.

In the case of Brazil, the country has an abundance of natural resources essential for the production of this energy vector, especially renewable sources that are growing rapidly. In addition, the country has an extensive strategic network of storage and transportation assets, which benefit from economies of scale. The challenge, however, is to formulate public policies that allow these comparative advantages to be used. When combined with other incentives, these competitive advantages have the potential to transform the development of the fledgling green hydrogen industry.

---

[19] Ibid, note 16.

The intersection of growing demand and market potential is establishing a new international dynamic, where natural resources are redefining the geopolitics of hydrogen and placing Latin America in a prominent export position. Brazil is one of the main countries capable of meeting international demand for green hydrogen.

In 2023, the Special Committee on Green Hydrogen was created in the Brazilian Senate. The committee is dedicated to discussing public policies on green hydrogen, promoting the scaling up of clean energy generation technology, and evaluating public policies that promote green hydrogen technology. A report presented by the committee states that Brazil has the potential to produce 1 million tons of hydrogen by 2025. Transporting thisproduction destined for export will require a significant investment in the Brazilian port sector, to establish the infrastructure necessary to consolidate the industry. Therefore, it is important to define a broader tax incentive policy that prioritises infrastructure development and the environment. Broader incentives will make it possible to relieve the burden on the productive chain of low-carbon economic sectors, facilitating investments for this fledgling industry.

The production cost of green hydrogen is still relatively high, especially when compared to other energy sources. The lack of tax incentives for the use of gas or for obtaining equipment will undoubtedly result in green hydrogen facing high barriers to entry, limiting other existing comparative advantages and negatively impacting less developed areas, where the so-called H_2 hubs are located. By using structured tax instruments directed at green hydrogen hubs, less economically developed regions will facilitate the energy transition process and aid in reducing economic and social inequality in Brazil.

According to Law No. 14.990, approved in 2024, the granting of tax incentives for the green hydrogen sector will only begin in 2028. Until then, there will not be sufficient data to assess whether the use of tax instruments is efficient or sufficient to nurture the development of the green hydrogen market.

REFERENCES

Australian Government. 19 June 2023, "The Australian Government has a new economic plan called 'A Future Made in Australia.'" Available at: https://treasury.gov.au/policy-topics/future-made-australia. Accessed on May 25th, 2024.

Becker, Alfredo Augusto. 2007, *Teoria Geral do Direito Tributário*. 4ª ed. São Paulo: Noeses.

Caliendo, Paulo. 2016, "Tributação e Ordem Econômica: Os tributos podem ser utilizados como Instrumentos, de indução econômica?" *Revista de Direitos Fundamentais e Democracia*, v. 20, n. 20.

Caliendo, Paulo; Campos, Carlos Alexandre de Azevedo; Cavalcante, Denise Lucena (Org.). 2018, *Leituras Clássicas de Direito Tributário*. In: Adamy, Pedro (Ed.), *Adolph Wagner*. Salvador: Jus Podium. https://static1.squarespace.com/static/5a6

7928fdc2b4a9c1eb96ff4/t/5cb10811e79c702a81ca1306/1555105827513/Adamy_Adolph+Wagner.pdf
De Castro, Nivalde et al. 2023, *A economia do hidrogênio: transição, descarbonização e oportunidades para o Brasil. 1. ed.* Rio de Janeiro: E-Papers.
Evangelista, Eduardo; Magalhães, Gerusa; Mariani, Rômulo (Coord). 2023, *Hidrogênio Verde – Perspectiva Jurídica, Regulatória e Técnica.* 1ª ed. Rio de Janeiro: Synergia.
Falcão, Raimundo Bezzera. 1981, *Tributação e mudança social.* Rio de Janeiro: Forense.
Grau, Eros Roberto. 2003, *A Ordem Econômica na Constituição de 1988.* 8ª ed. São Paulo: Malheiros Editores.
IEA. (2019). *The Future of Hydrogen: Seizing today's opportunities.* Paris: International Energy Agency.
Milne, Janet E. 2017, "Environmental taxation: why theory matters." In: Milne, Janet E. (Ed.), *Environmental Taxation and the Law.* Vol. I, Cheltenham, UK and Northampton, MA, USA: Edward Elgar.
Mooney, Attracta. 2024, "Transição verde deve custar US$ 9 trilhões, mas como pagar continua incerto." Folha de São Paulo, 09 de maio de 2024. *Seção Economia*, Caderno Energia Limpa. Available at: https://www1.folha.uol.com.br/mercado/2024/05/transicao-verde-deve-custar-us-9-trilhoes-mas-como-pagar-conta-continua-incerto.shtml. Accessed on May 25, 2024.
Pugliesi, Mario. 1932, *La finanza e i suoi compiti extra-fiscali negli stati moderni.* Padova: CEDAM.
Truby, J. et al. 19 June 2023, "Green hydrogen: energising the path to net zero." Deloitte. Available at: https://www.deloitte.com/global/en/issues/climate/green-hydrogen.html. Accessed on May 25, 2024.

15. Business Improvement Districts and the just energy transition: the compulsory contribution and environmental taxes

Roque Martínez Olmos

1. INTRODUCTION

The just energy transition is a complex concept that requires an interdisciplinary review, which is beyond the scope of this chapter. This paper aims to determine whether Business Improvement Districts (BIDs) can be used as an instrument to achieve a just energy transition. First, the concept of the just energy transition must be defined, and the characteristics of BIDs must be evaluated to determine whether they contribute to achieving a just energy transition.

A just energy transition fundamentally requires the development of an efficient and sustainable energy sector, not only in economic terms but also in environmental terms. The elements of a just energy transition are as follows:[1]

- Replacing fossil fuels with renewable energy. Achieving this requires the installation of solar panels, the construction of green hydrogen plants, and the development of self-consumption energy communities, among other measures.
- Improvements in energy efficiency and energy savings. This includes renovating the housing stock, one of the sectors with the highest energy consumption, as well as the automotive sector, which involves the highest greenhouse gas (GHG) emissions and use of fossil fuels.
- Compensation policies are required to ensure vulnerable sectors do not bear the brunt of the transition. Potential options include interventions such as social electricity vouchers, self-consumption energy communities, or the installation of photovoltaic panels for people with limited resources. The payment of these bills (through social electricity

vouchers or aid) by the town councils or social entities is a measure that potentially addresses a symptom but not the cause. Applicants may need subsidisation in subsequent months. Providing applicants with free energy through a photovoltaic energy installation can be a tool that helps reduce financial dependence and encourages active participation in the energy transition. It has the added benefit of reducing energy bills and carbon emissions. The use of collective self-consumption energy plants as an element of inclusion, which replaces emergency aid for the payment of energy bills, is already a reality in cities such as New York, where the state initiative SolarForAll provides solar energy to vulnerable households free of charge.[2]

- The energy transition will, as some authors have suggested,[3] have important implications for the labour market, including job losses as well as job creation. The transition will significantly affect the high-emitting regions and sectors. A just energy transition will require robust social dialogue and collective bargaining.
- Lastly, a just energy transition requires a change in habits and mindset. For instance, electricity consumption can be reduced through energy-saving habits such as adjusting daylight hours, replacing light bulbs with low-consumption LEDs, and installing double-glazed windows to regulate temperature, among other measures.

Having outlined the key themes of a just energy transition, an analysis of whether BIDs can contribute to achieving such a transition will be undertaken. To this end, BIDs will be examined from the perspective of public-private collaboration and its essential elements. In a later section, the actions carried out by two BIDs in the field of energy transition, the London Bridge BID in the United Kingdom and the Atalayas Ciudad Empresarial in Spain, will be analysed. The latter, although not expressly referred to as a BID in its legislation, can, in our opinion, be considered as such, since it presents the essential characteristics of this figure.

2. BIDs AND THE JUST ENERGY TRANSITION

BIDs originated in Toronto, Canada, in 1969,[4] subsequently spreading to the United States and Europe, and have also been developed in Cape Town, South Africa. A BID is a legal instrument by which most property owners or business owners within a defined municipal geographical area agree to make a self-imposed tax contribution to finance specific works and services. BID contributions are determined by the majority in the area. All property owners or business owners within the area must pay that contribution, even if not all have voted in favour of its establishment.

BIDs are characterised by their flexibility and adaptability. An interesting classification of the BID is that it is a modality encompassed within another broader concept: the City Improvement District (CID). Within the CID, there would be the BID, the Residential Improvement District (RID), and the Mixed-Use Improvement District (MID).[5] The difference between these entities relates to the subjects that make them up: BIDs are composed of businesses and entrepreneurs, RIDs are formed by owners of residential properties, and MIDs by entrepreneurs and owners of residential properties, jointly. The fundamental elements of BIDs are as follows:

(a) **Geographical area of the BID.** BIDs exist in a demarcated geographical area of a municipality. BIDs are authorised by the local municipality; membership is geographically determined and linked to fulfilling certain obligations. A entity manages the BID and implements the action plan to be carried out.
(b) **BID management entity.** This entity, usually of a private nature, is legally responsible for managing and implementing the action plan in the BID. The authority of the BID management entity is limited by the municipal council. The management entity comprises various bodies: a general assembly, presidency, secretariat, management, board of directors, vice-presidency, and treasury. The composition of the BID management entity will vary depending on its regulations; some of the bodies mentioned above are optional.
(c) **Action plan**. This instrument determines the functions and actions to be carried out in the BID. These actions cannot replace or reduce, under any circumstances, the municipal services provided by the council. However, they can enhance these actions by contributing to delivering greater value and excellence.
(d) **Agreement between the managing entity and the city council.** This agreement sets out the terms of reference for the managing entity and the city council regarding the action plan. The agreement specifies the form of participation of the city council in the managing entity, the term of validity, the modification regime, the causes for terminating the BID, the specific form of financing, and the rules for determining the amount of the levy or fee.
(e) **Compulsory quota, levy, or tax.** This is the contribution paid by all members included in the scope of the BID to finance its action plan, even if they did not vote in favour of its establishment. The distinguishing feature of the BID, relative to any other form of association, is the coercive and compulsory nature of the payment of this fee. The compulsory quota finances the work and services provided in the BID and avoids the existence of free riders.

2.1 The BID as a Form of Public-Private Partnership

Public-private collaboration is not a new concept. Throughout history, especially with the increasing influence of the public sector, collaboration between the public and private sectors has been used to combine efforts, realise common objectives, and achieve economic development.

Public-private collaborative forums have their roots in voluntary associations, in which a group of actors engaged in economic activity join together to represent common interests. These associations are significant and are present in many cities across the world. In these associations public-private partnership collaboration is based exclusively on the granting of aid, regarding which the association usually does not decide on its allocation. Aid is linked to objectives of the municipal entity and can be used towards projects that benefit not only those in the business association but all citizens. In addition to this source of financing, these private associations have been financed by voluntary contributions from their members.

These business associations have played and continue to play a vital role in representing specific interests, which cannot be overlooked. Nevertheless, for the sake of a just energy transition, the following considerations and problems should be addressed:

a) The main problem is the lack of funding[6] to carry out major long-term projects that would address the requirements of a just energy transition. Without a significant, stable source of funding that is constant, and not voluntary or dependent on the political party governing the city council, these traditional forms of partnership do not allow progress to be made towards an appropriate and just energy transition. It can certainly help to achieve certain targets, but with little funding, it will not be possible to propose more ambitious objectives, such as reaching zero emission targets.
b) Besides this main problem, the lack of actual funding can mean that other entrepreneurs are not interested in joining the project. In addition, there is the problem of free riders, since some entrepreneurs may perceive that even if they do not contribute, they could benefit from being in the field of action.
c) These associations typically only represent a particular group of employers or a specific sector of activity.
d) Public participation is minimal and sometimes non-existent. It is limited to granting aid or loans to carry out certain activities. Therefore, whether it is a genuine public-private collaboration could even be questioned. A real partnership between these two sectors requires a two-way collaboration.

The BID, however, is a public-private partnership whose characteristics can go some way towards addressing the considerations and problems outlined above:

a) Establishing a BID requires authentic participation of the public sector since it requires approval by law and municipal ordinance (as in the case of Spain) as a legal entity and the creation of a specific tax for its financing. In other words, without such public collaboration, the BID cannot exist. In addition, the public sector usually forms part of the governing bodies of the BID and regulates and controls its statutes and action plans.
b) This public-private collaboration is more evident and manifest in the number of agreements that are usually approved with the aim of the BID carrying out street-cleaning tasks in its geographical area, as well as recycling and waste management tasks, security tasks, and the development of standard and collaborative transport lines, which reduce the carbon footprint of the area, as well as collaborating in this task with municipal transport agencies.[7] In this way, this form of public-private collaboration becomes a true bi-directional partnership, which is not limited to granting aid.
c) The established tribute or mandatory contribution of BID financing is the key to this initiative's success, as it allows the BID to have an established structure and long-term, more ambitious projects.
d) Furthermore, it is a fairer and more democratic structure because, although a minority can take the initiative for its constitution, the final approval is usually twofold. On the one hand, it will require the approval of all the members involved (typically business people) and, on the other hand, the approval of the City Council (which has a significant democratic legitimacy placing it very close to the citizens). Therefore, BIDs are constructed on a more democratic and fairer basis.[8] In addition, BIDs are usually characterised by their inclusion of all the business people in that area in the general assemblies, giving them a voice and a vote and a chance to participate in the projects that will be developed. Also, sometimes, this public-private collaboration is constituted not only by business people (from all sectors) but also by owners of residential properties, making it fairer and more representative. In this way, BIDs constitute an essential example of public-private collaboration, particularly in the field of municipalism.

Consequently, BIDs, arguably, constitute a genuine public-private collaboration since the public sector does not have a mere financing function. Instead, it participates in the creation of projects, in provisioning these entities with financing from a tax – the key without which this entity would not work and would not be distinguished from a mere voluntary association.

Moreover, in the BID, the collaboration is bidirectional. The private sector collaborates in tasks that are usually the responsibility of the municipality and, as seen in the following sections, can contribute to achieving sustainable development objectives, especially in the move towards a fairer and more democratic energy transition. In this sense, many of the BIDs that have been developed incorporate, without supplanting, mandatory local services, including waste collection and street cleaning functions. Some BIDs[9, 10] have established complementary and consensual action plans with the city council to improve the street cleaning and waste collection system and facilitate waste recycling. Examples include the Heart of London Business Alliance BID or the Better Bankside BID.

For instance, in the case of BID regulation in Spain, the legislation of the Autonomous Community of Valencia includes the BID collaborating with the city council to fulfil the obligations of conservation, maintenance, surveillance, cleaning, and the provision of essential services among the managing entity's functions. The legislation also allows the BID to assume, if agreed by the owners and allocated by the competent city council, the management of municipal services limited to the scope of the industrial area. These characteristics make the BID a sustainable public-private partnership, both economically and environmentally.

2.2 The BID as an Instrument for the Just Energy Transition

The BID has been proposed as a measure against the dispersed city model. However, the environmental component is usually present in the actions and measures it carries out.[11] This chapter aims to analyse the BID not as an instrument for developing the compact city model or for municipal economic promotion, whose effectiveness is beyond doubt, but as an instrument that can contribute to achieving a just energy transition. The characteristics of the BID as a form of public-private partnership, make it a very suitable vehicle for developing a just energy transition. Specifically, the following characteristics should be highlighted to achieve the proposed objective:

a) The economic development that the BID has always sought must now clearly be accompanied by environmental development and progress towards a greener and fairer economy. No sustainable economic development can exist without a genuine change in the energy system to using alternative formulas and renewable resources that do not harm future generations.

b) Taxation, an instrument for financing its action plan and an essential element of this form of public-private collaboration, provides stable and sufficient income to implement the ambitious proposals for decarbonisation and the energy rehabilitation of buildings and properties, investment in clean energy sources, and the creation of local self-consumption energy communities.
c) The characteristic of its being a democratic and assembly-led organisation, based in a defined neighbourhood or area (including all types of economic activities), makes the BID a legal entity that can represent the interests of all the subjects included within that geographical area, regardless of their size, business volume, or sector, and even including residential properties. The participatory and democratic nature of its bodies makes it a dynamic and adaptable entity for the achievement of sustainable development objectives.
d) Finally, it should be noted that BIDs often aim to reduce costs by creating joint and synergistic systems (such as unified logistics centres that receive and transport the goods of all BID members), which leads to a reduction in costs. In this sense, reducing energy consumption through the rehabilitation of buildings or the greater use of self-consumption sources also represents a reduction of expenses that can be of great interest to BID members. The quantification of this cost reduction through the implementation of energy efficiency systems has also been elaborated on by the Las Atalayas BID, to which we will refer later. A later section will examine the actions carried out in this field by two specific BID examples, demonstrating the importance of this figure for a just transition.

3. THE COMPULSORY QUOTA AND ENVIRONMENTAL TAXES

The mandatory contribution is the essential element that differentiates the BID from other forms of voluntary associations. It is also the component that allows the development of the proposed ambitious plans and, therefore, the success, not only economic but also environmental, of this form of public-private partnership.

3.1 BID Regulation in United Kingdom

In the United Kingdom, BIDs are regulated by the Local Government Act 2003, Part 4, sections 41 to 59. This regulation refers to the compulsory quota as the BID levy, which is regulated solely in terms of its establishment; sections 45 and 46 refer to the agreements signed with the respective BIDs. According to this legislation, a fundamental role in the configuration of the BID levy is played by the specific agreements between the BID and the municipality, which will specify its amount, its form of quantification, and the subjects obliged to pay it.

"The BID arrangements must specify the description of non-domestic ratepayers" in the BID "who are to be liable for BID levy for a chargeable period" (Section 46(1) of the Local Government Act 2003). For instance, in the London Bridge BID, places of worship, schools, and communication stations, among others, are not obliged to pay the BID levy. Small businesses are generally not obliged to pay the BID levy. In the Marble Arch London BID, charities and schools must pay 10% of the BID levy. Establishing exemptions and deductions in the BID levy could encourage energy and environmental efficiency behaviours among BID members.

Section 45(3) of the Local Government Act 2003 states that: "The amount of BID levy for any chargeable period—(a) is to be calculated in such manner as may be provided in the BID arrangements, and (b) may be different for different cases."

The BID levy is based on the business rates system of rateable values set by the government's Valuation Office Agency. It is a surcharge on the municipal tax, the Non-Domestic Rate, which taxes the taxable value of properties where an economic activity is carried out. The BID levy is a small percentage (generally around 1%)[12] of a business's rateable value. For the London Bridge BID, it is 0.96% until 2025, and an increase of 3% has been proposed.

Finally, this tax or BID levy is not levied by the entity but is collected by the municipality. In the case of London Bridge BID, it is collected by Southwark Council. "The local authority in BIDs is the so-called billing authority, which corresponds to a basic local administration level." "The British local administration is quite complex and reaches several levels with different competencies and powers".[13]

Section 46(4) of the Local Government Act 2003 states, "Any amount of BID levy for which a person is liable is to be paid to the billing authority which made the arrangements."

3.2 BID Regulation in Spain

With similar characteristics, although the name has been adapted, BIDs have been regulated in Spain by some Autonomous Communities in so far as they have legislative powers to establish the compulsory financing quota. The quota's coerciveness and obligatory nature require it to be lawfully established.

At present, BIDs are regulated in Spain by Law 14/2018, of 5 June, on the organisation, modernisation, and promotion of industrial areas in the Valencian Community; Law 15/2020, of 22 December, on urban-economic promotion areas in Catalonia; Law 6/2023, of 16 March, on municipal commercial promotion areas in the Balearic Islands; and more recently, by the Foral Law 18/2024, of December 13, on economic promotion areas of the Foral Community of Navarra.

These regulations configured the compulsory fee or levy as a complex figure in Spain known as a non-tax public property benefits. According to Spanish tax legislation, the BID compulsory quota cannot be considered a tribute.[14] The reason for using this non-tax instrument is that the mandatory BID quota is challenging to fit into the traditional tax instruments of the Spanish legal system.

Regarding the quantification of the compulsory contribution, one aspect that is very interesting in terms of encouraging environmental behaviour and achieving the United Nations Sustainable Development Goals is the possibility of establishing reductions or rebates in the quota. Thus, the legislation of the Balearic Islands, for instance, establishes certain rebates for the compulsory contribution – specifically, in respect of activities that pursue charitable or general interest purposes (up to 80%) and unoccupied property suitable for economic activities (up to 20%), and in support of entrepreneurship (up to 50% for taxpayers starting a business, and down to 25% in their second year). Thus, it is up to the local authorities to establish, using their corresponding ordinance, the percentage of the rebate within the maximum rate determined in the law.

The concept of "activities pursuing aims of general interest", referring to the established rebate of up to 80%, in our opinion, could enable local councils to develop the following rebates:

- A rebate for those business owners whose primary purpose is to carry out economic activities for charitable purposes or in the general interest.
- A rebate for anyone carrying out a specific activity that pursues a general interest, which could be an environmental activity that benefits the rest of the BID and the municipality. Thus, in the same way that many companies make annual donations to specific charities as part of their corporate social responsibility, local councils could establish a rebate of up to 80% of the obligatory quota for those entities that carry out activities in favour of the environment.

Establishing environmental rebates and other environmental components in the compulsory quota could strengthen the ecological nature of this entity and promote more environmentally friendly behaviour.

These BID regulations establish the possibility that the compulsory contribution is collected by the BID entity itself rather than by the municipality. This is an essential difference from the BID regulation in the United Kingdom.

Table 15.1 Quantifying the mandatory quota of a BID in Catalonia

According to its regulations: Typology	According to its regulations: Cadastral built-up area[1]	According to its regulations: Payment obligation	Example calculation: Registered premises	Example calculation: Individual quota	Example calculation: Sum of quotas (individual quota * census premises)
I	$s \leq 300\ m^2$	X	93	787.4	73,228
II	$300\ m^2 < s \leq 800\ m^2$	1.5X	43	1.5*787.4 = 1,181.1	50,787
III	$800\ m^2 < s \leq 1{,}300\ m^2$	2X	10	2*787.4 = 1,574.8	15,748
IV	$1{,}300m^2 < s \leq 2{,}500\ m^2$	3X	3	3*787.4 = 2,362.2	7,087
V	$2{,}500\ m^2 < s \leq 10.000\ m^2$	4X	1	4*787.4 = 3,149.6	3,150
VI	$s > 10{,}000\ m^2$ (or collective establishment of 50 or more individual establishments)	5X	0	5*787.4 = 3,937.0	0
–	–	–	150	–	150,000

[1] The cadastral value is fixed administratively according to a property's characteristics (location, quality, age, land value, etc.).

Regarding quantifying the compulsory contribution, the following is an example[15] of quantifying the mandatory quota of a BID in Catalonia. Thus, in the case of a BID made up of 150 premises with a budget of 150,000 euros, the amount of the individual fee to be paid would be as shown in Table 15.1.

If a company owns three premises, two of 400 m2 and one of 1,100 m2, with an annual base fee of 787.4 euros, it must pay 787.4 * 1.5 + 787.4 * 1.5 + 787.4 * 2 = 3,937 euros.

4. BID ACTIONS FOR A JUST ENERGY TRANSITION

The previous sections have analysed the BID, its characteristics, and its configuration as an appropriate collaboration between the public and private sectors. This extends beyond granting aid for specific actions. A partnership is bidirectional insofar as mutual collaboration is manifested by both parties involved (the city council and the BID).

In addition, the chapter has analysed how the characteristics of this entity are very effective for the achievement of different sustainable development objectives, such as the construction of green areas, waste management, and street cleaning, as well as the just energy transition. "In achieving greater urban sustainability, the additional services provided by the BID play an essential role, many of which directly or indirectly impact the environmental footprint of commercial activities located in urban centres."[16] In this sense, the New West End Company BID in London has developed a Zero Sustainability Action Plan to minimise greenhouse gas (GHG) emissions.[17]

This section aims to show two examples of the actions of this figure in this specific environmental field. The first refers to the London Bridge BID (United Kingdom) and the second to the management entity Atalayas – Ciudad Empresarial in Alicante (Spain).

They have led to significant economic development in their respective geographical areas and have implemented numerous environmental measures.[18] Thus, BIDs are a public-private partnership with positive ecological implications. This section will focus specifically on the just energy transition.

4.1 The London Bridge BID (United Kingdom)

The London Bridge BID and other entities have developed a "Routemap[19] for decarbonisation and the transition to renewable energy. This is a unique plan that is aligned with Southwark Council's carbon reduction climate strategy. As stated in the "Routemap", businesses are crucial to the municipality's decarbonisation objective as the City Council is only responsible for 12% of emissions. Collaboration between the City Council and the BID is essential to achieve decarbonisation, thus demonstrating the necessity for public-private cooperation between these two entities.

For this reason, the proposal stipulated financial support and the use of urban planning among the different ways the City Council could collaborate with business. Specifically, reference was made to increasing pedestrian zones and reducing the use of vehicles powered by fossil fuels in some regions of the BID. The objectives proposed in the plan include enabling mechanisms, community projects, business-led interventions, and creating a sustainable transition fund.

The plan states: "This Routemap proposes five large-scale projects that require multistakeholder collaboration, particularly Southwark Borough Council and landlords, to be effectively delivered." The following two projects warrant a mention:

- Control of the carbon footprint of the BID buildings due to the use of heaters and refrigerators that generate 65% of the BID's carbon footprint and a third of the emissions. The objective of this project is to reduce these emissions. The project details that: "1. All buildings move away from fossil fuel-based heating systems and use technologies like heat pumps. This should be combined with purchasing renewable energy. 2. A heating and cooling network is built in the London Bridge area. This network would use low-carbon heat as its primary energy source (from a combination of sewer, ground, aquifer, the River Thames, etc.). An aquifer-type system operates close to the Tate Modern, and other small river-based systems exist, including on the River Thames."
- Investments in solar energy through implementing solar panels on any roof appropriate for this purpose. The project details that: "Individual asset owners can install solar panels and agree to a power purchase agreement with their tenants. An investor or community-owned company could be set up to install solar panels and sell renewable energy at an agreed price to occupiers or a significant energy user in a long-term Power Purchasing Agreement (PPA)".
- Regarding the creation of the sustainable transition fund, the plan states that there should be a community carbon fund. In this, "businesses offset and/or inset their emissions by contributing to the fund using the carbon price set by the GLA [Greater London Authority]. This money would be re-invested locally on sustainability projects that benefit local businesses and communities".

This fund is a very appropriate measure that could even be used to develop social bonds or electricity rates for vulnerable people, making the energy transition fairer.

4.2 The Atalayas Ciudad Empresarial (Spain)

The Atalayas Ciudad Empresarial is in an industrial park with an annual turnover of 1,700 million euros. It employs more than 6,000 people and contributes more than 8 million euros to Alicante (Spain) through taxes.[20] The Atalayas Ciudad Empresarial has prepared a document called "Energy and Sustainability as Factors of Competitiveness". This study analyses the different alternatives that can be used to move towards a more sustainable and decarbonised energy transition.

According to this study, installing photovoltaic panels in a self-consumption format covers 67% of the industrial estate's energy needs. This has implications for costs (it would mean a saving of 4.57 million euros) and stopping the use of non-renewable energy sources and fossil fuels, translating into 8,355 tons of CO2 emissions avoided.[21]

Achieving these objectives requires the creation of shared self-consumption networks, integrating the different companies that make up the network into a local energy community. Not only would the companies that make up the network participate in this, but so would the city council.

This project would also allow for integrated intelligent generation and distribution management with maximum energy optimisation.

In turn, to take advantage of its position as one of the municipality's most important industrial centres, it has drawn up an exhaustive mobility plan whose objectives include collaborating with the city council to promote the electrification of public transport, as well as conducting campaigns to encourage and promote public transport, and installing the corresponding infrastructure.

Economic development cannot be analysed in isolation or exclusively in monetary terms. Today, economic growth requires sustainable and environmental development. In this regard, as some authors point out: "those BIDs working in their second or third terms [are] increasingly confident in delivering urban greening as they have proven track records of successfully supporting local economic development".[22]

5. CONCLUSION

1. Environmental taxation can provide a significant impetus for moving towards a green economy and achieving sustainable development goals, specifically, a just energy transition. In this sense, different tax instruments

have been implemented, such as environmental tax rebates to improve the energy efficiency of buildings or taxes on the use of fossil fuels and carbon emissions.

2. After analysing the BID figure, its configuration, and its potential, as well as several concrete examples, it can be argued that it is a formula that enables the achievement of many of the objectives of sustainable development through public-private collaboration, most notably, achieving a just energy transition.

   On the one hand, financing the BID through special taxes is a very appropriate mechanism for providing the BID with adequate infrastructure to achieve ambitious targets in energy transition. These special taxes or mandatory quotas could be "greened" by including different incentives depending on how the carbon emissions have been addressed, thus encouraging more environmentally responsible behaviours.

   On the other hand, the BID's democratic nature means that the energy transition intended to be achieved through this public-private partnership formula is fairer and more democratic, fostering social dialogue and collective bargaining.
3. BIDs should establish environmental objectives in their statutes, and local councils should collaborate and consider these objectives when drawing up their environmental and decarbonisation strategies.

In the field of energy transition, BIDs can contribute to the just energy transition in the following ways:

- Improving the energy efficiency of the building stock within its area by using insulating materials and energy-saving light bulbs.
- Monitoring the carbon emissions and energy consumption of BID members and encouraging members to set short- and long-term reduction targets. This can be done in conjunction with the council's energy plans.
- Installing photovoltaic panels on the roofs of BID members to generate self-consumption grids and allocating possible surpluses to vulnerable households.
- Replacing, in collaboration with the city council, street lighting in its area of action with low-energy consumption street lights.
- Creating electric charging points and promoting the electrification of BID member vehicles. Collaborating with the city council to encourage the switch to electric buses and developing carpooling platforms.
- Establishing the BID as a local energy community to promote energy self-consumption.

Creating a sustainable energy transition fund is an exciting measure with the potential to reduce possible injustices in the energy transition. This fund could be established by collecting part of the mandatory quota or another quota based on the carbon footprint of the BID members. The fund's distribution could be targeted at vulnerable households within the BID to make the energy transition genuinely fair.

NOTES

1. Víctor Viñuales Edo, Cecilia Foronda Díez, Carlos Pesqué Castillo and Javier Tobías González. (2022), "La transición energética debe ser justa: tres grandes temas", 174 *Papeles de Economía* Española, p. 189.
2. Ibid., p. 189.
3. Azahara Merino Martos. (2023), "La incipiente transición energética justa en España", 2 *Noticias CIELO*, pp. 1–5.
4. Maria Luisa Esteve Pardo. (2017), "Una propuesta de adaptación del modelo BID (Business Improvement District) a nuestra realidad" in Maria Luisa Esteve Pardo, *Impulso a la actividad económica en los municipios: cuestiones tributarias de interés*, Huygens Editorial, p. 14.
5. See Section 1 of City Improvement District Bye-law, 2023.
6. Esteban Quintana Ferrer. (2017), "Aportaciones económicas obligatorias para financiar áreas comerciales urbanas: naturaleza y régimen jurídico", 133 *Tributos Locales*, pp. 16–17.
7. Agustín Rovira Lara. (2000), "Propuesta y modelos para la gestión estratégica de los centros urbanos desde la cooperación pública y privada", 19 *Gestión y análisis de políticas públicas*, p. 28.
8. Miguel Bratos Martín. (2013), "Business Improvement Districts: Una nueva forma de colaboración público – privada para la revitalización socioeconómica de áreas urbanas", 50 *Política y sociedad*, p. 282.
9. Irene Araguàs Galacerà. (2020), "Business Improvement Districts y sostenibilidad urbana. A propósito de la regulación de las áreas de promoción de la actividad económica urbana en Cataluña", XI 2 *Revista Catalana de Dret Ambiental*, p. 7.
10. Álvaro Costela Sánchez. (2019), "Caso de Éxito. Los BID de Liverpool y experiencias innovadoras en Reino Unido", BID Zaragoza. Available at: https://www.youtube.com/watch?v=c2MCT-VSlXg&t=159s, accessed on 12 August 2024.
11. Francisco Velasco Caballero. (2014), "Los 'Business Improvement Districts': un fenómeno municipal en expansion", Universidad Autónoma de Madrid, Instituto de Derechoy Gobierno Local. Available at: https://www.idluam.org/blog/los-business-improvement-districts-un-fenomeno-municipal-en-expansion/, accessed on 30 December 2024.
12. Albert Navarro García. (2018), "La financiación de las Áreas Comerciales Urbanas mediante un recargo en el Impuesto sobre Bienes Inmuebles" in Cristina García-Herrera Blanco, VI Encuentro de Derecho Financiero y

Tributario Tendencias y retos del Derecho Financiero y Tributario 3ª Parte, Documentos de Trabajo del Instituto de Estudios Fiscales 12, p. 194.
13. Maria Luisa Esteve Pardo. (2014), "Un recargo sobre el IBI como posible fórmula para financiar los planes público – privados de dinamización comercial local" in Francisco Adame Martínez and Jesús Ramos Prieto, *Estudios sobre el sistema tributario actual y la situación financiera del sector público.* Homenaje al Profesor Dr D. Javier Lasarte Álvarez, Instituto de Estudios Fiscales, p. 1383.
14. Helena Villarejo Galende. (2014), "Colaboración público – privada para la revitalización de espacios urbanos: la introducción de los Business Improvement Districts en el ordenamiento jurídico español", III, 2 *Revista de Gestión Pública*, p. 269.
15. Escola Universitària de Comerç i Distribució (ESCODI). (2021), "Guia Tècnica per inciar una área de promoció económica Urbana (APEU)", Direcció General de Comerç i Consorci de Comerç, Artesania i Moda. Available at: https://ccam.gencat.cat/web/.content/05_arees_actuacio/comerc/oficina_apeus/Guia-tecnica-APEUS-v2.pdf, accessed on 27 August 2024.
16. Irene Araguàs Galacerà. (2020), "Business Improvement Districts y sostenibilidad urbana. A propósito de la regulación de las áreas de promoción de la actividad económica urbana en Cataluña", XI 2 *Revista Catalana de Dret Ambiental*, p. 38.
17. New West End Company, "A sustainable district". Available at: https://www.newwestend.com/our-district/a-sustainable-district, accessed on 2 September 2024.
18. Helena Villarejo Galende, María Luisa Esteve Pardo and Clara Peiret García. (2019), "Smart cities: can business improvement districts reduce the environmental footprint of urban areas" in Marta Villar Ezcurra, Janet Milne, Hope Ashiabor and Mikael Skou Andersen (eds), *Environmental Fiscal Challenges for Cities and Transport*, Cheltenham, Edward Elgar, p. 56.
19. Team London Bridge. (2022), "London Bridge Business Improvement District's Carbon Neutral Routemap". Available at: https://static1.squarespace.com/static/58d15ded6a49638c26e0888c/t/62da9585a12b430376f11903/1658492301558/220706_London+Bridge+BID%27s+Carbon+Neutral+Routemap_FINAL.pdf, accessed on 30 December 2024.
20. Atalayas Ciudad Empresarial, "Área Empresarial". Available at: https://atalayas.com/area-empresarial/, accessed on 30 December 2024.
21. Juan Carlos Del Río García. (2022), "Energía y sostenibilidad como factores de competitividad", Las Atalayas Ciudad Empresarial. Available at: https://atalayas.com/wp-content/uploads/2022/06/INFORME-COMUNIDADES-ENERGETICAS.pdf, accessed on 30 December 2024.
22. Lucy Moore and Ian Mell. (2023), "Examining the role of Business Improvement Districts (BIDs) as contemporary alternatives for Green Infrastructure funding in London, UK", *Urban Forestry & Urban Greening*, p. 15.

Index